For the love of India

Henry Martyn

# For the love of India

## The story of Henry Martyn

### Jim Cromarty

**EP** EVANGELICAL PRESS

EVANGELICAL PRESS
Faverdale North, Darlington, DL3 0PH, England

e-mail: sales@evangelicalpress.org

Evangelical Press USA
P. O. Box 825, Webster, New York 14580, USA

e-mail: usa.sales@evangelicalpress.org

web: http://www.evangelicalpress.org

First published 2005

British Library Cataloguing in Publication Data available

ISBN-13 978-0-85234-598-6          ISBN 0-85234-598-4

All Scripture quotations, unless otherwise indicated or forming part of a longer quotation from another source (as in the appendix), are taken from the New King James Version. Copyright © 1988 by Thomas Nelson, Inc. Used by permission. All rights reserved.

Scripture quotations in the appendix are from the Authorized / King James Version

Printed and bound in Great Britain by Creative Print & Design Wales, Ebbw Vale

This writing is dedicated to the faithful, persecuted church
in the countries of the Middle East
and the Indian subcontinent.

# Contents

# Illustrations

# Maps

# Glossary

*Bastinado:* A beating with a stick or cudgel, usually on just one part of the body. The Chinese were known to whip the feet of the offender. After a period of time, even gentle whipping caused great distress.

*Brahmin:* A member of the highest Hindu caste.

*Buggala:* A two-masted Arabian boat used for trading in the Indian Ocean region. They were well known for their elevated sterns.

*Calean (or hookah):* A smoking arrangement where the tobacco smoke passed along a lengthy flexible pipe and through water, which cooled it. Smoking the calean was a social activity.

*Calvinist:* Calvinism rightly interprets the Scripture teaching that salvation is all of God. The Father chose a people to be saved; the Son lived and died on their behalf, paying the just penalty owed to God for their sins and gaining the perfect righteousness they need to enter heaven. The Holy Spirit applies Christ's saving work to God's people (the elect), giving them a saving faith in Christ. The elect often sin, but turn to God in true repentance. They cannot be eternally lost.

*Caravanserai:* An Oriental inn where caravans of travellers could find accommodation (usually a building with a square courtyard in the middle). Many of these 'inns' were unattended, making the quality of the accommodation very poor.

*Cherbuter:* A raised platform or dais in the open air. Henry used the one outside his house as a pulpit from which he addressed his congregation. He also used it for social gatherings with his friends. They sat on it talking and having supper together.

*Fakir:* A Muslim who had taken a vow of poverty and begged for his daily needs.

*Feringhee* (or *feringhi*): a derogatory name for a foreigner, especially one with a white skin

*Ghee:* This was a kind of butter made from the milk of a buffalo.

*Hegira* (or *Hejira, Hijra*): A time of separation linked to the flight of Mohammed from Mecca in A.D. 622. Muslims recognize their era as commencing on 16 July 622.

*Infidel:* The name given by the Muslims to all who were not of their faith, especially Christians. This title was given to the knights who fought to recapture Jerusalem from the Muslims.

*Juggernaut:* A popular name of the Hindu idol Jagannatha. When it was wheeled about on a 'car' many worshippers sacrificed themselves by throwing themselves under the wheels of the 'car'. Often they were killed.

*Lascars:* This is a term applied to sailors from India and the Far East, employed on European ships.

*Mihmander:* A guard.

*Mujtahid:* A professor of Muslim law.

*Mullah:* A Muslim learned in Islamic theology and sacred law.

*Moonshee (or munshi):* In India a Muslim professor, a teacher of languages, a secretary and interpreter.

*Nankeen:* A pair of Persian trousers or breeches (made from a yellowish-cotton cloth, from which they took their name).

*Pagoda:* A very ornamentally decorated Hindu temple or tower found in the Orient.

*Palanquin:* A covered, box-like carriage suspended on two poles and carried by bearers. The box had a seat, a door and sometimes a window with curtains.

*Paradise:* A Persian garden designed to give the owner and his friends a place of peace and tranquillity. Usually there would be a surrounding wall, intended to keep out evil, and a stream to water the plants and make a pleasant sound as the water washed over the stones in the creek.

*Philological mania:* The term Henry used to describe his own almost fanatical study of words and languages.

*Pinnace:* A small boat propelled by either oars or sails. It usually had two schooner-rigged masts.

*Pundit:* Pundits were men of the Brahmin class, having exceptional intellectual ability — scholars in the fields of Indian law, science, religion and languages.

*Punkah:* A large fan in Indian homes. It would be suspended from the ceiling and operated by a servant to make the air flow around the room.

*Raja(h):* The title of an Indian ruler — king, prince or chief.

*Ramayana:* One of the two great Indian epic poems. Its author was Valmiki, a Hindu from Bombay. It tells of the exploits of Rama, who, aided by Hanuman, the monkey-god, conquered Ceylon and brought back his queen, Sita, whom Rawana, the giant and tyrant of that island had carried away.

*Sanskrit:* The ancient language of the Hindus.

*Sais:* A horse's groom.

*Sepoy lines:* A sepoy was a native Indian soldier serving in the British army. The sepoy lines were the rows of houses where these men and their families lived.

*Senior Wrangler:* A title specific to Cambridge University, awarded to the candidate who gained first place in the Public Examination in Pure and Mixed Mathematics (Honours).

*Shaster* (or *shastra*): A Hindu law book. The Bible was described as a 'shaster' by many Indians.

*Sufi (or Soofi):* The Sufis were a sect of Muslim mystics who taught that there was no difference between good and evil, which meant there was no need of laws, and that finally everyone would be merged into the Deity.

*Suttee:* The evil practice in India where the widow threw herself upon the burning funeral pile of her husband. This self-immolation of the widow was abolished by the British.

*Tattie* (or *tatta*): A screen door made of fragrant, mosslike grass. It was constantly kept wet by the water carriers. This helped to reduce the temperature on hot days.

*Tavern:* An inn that could be used by travellers as a place to stay. The New London Tavern had a room which could be used for meetings, including Christian services.

*Yogi:* A Hindu who, like the fakir, lived the life of an ascetic. With others these men went to Henry begging for food and alms.

# Foreword

The Christian missionary is one of the most extraordinary persons in human history. Characteristically leaving comfort, career and popularity behind, the missionary ventures in the name of the invisible God into new, and sometimes alien, cultures. Through the work of missionaries the cause of Christ has prospered around the world, and today there are more Christians than ever worshipping the Lord.

In the list of missionaries, the name of Henry Martyn will always occupy a special place. He impressed his contemporaries with his intellectual stature, his godliness of life and the daring of his exploits. It is impossible to read the story without being deeply moved and, to this day, he provides an inspiration for other Christians to follow his example.

I am very glad that Jim Cromarty has written his story, and given a new generation of readers an opportunity to acquaint themselves with this remarkable man. I hope the reading of this book will inspire many more young people to follow the example of Henry Martyn, especially his desire to bring the Word of God to people in their own language.

**Peter F. Jensen**
Anglican Archbishop of Sydney

# Preface

The name 'Henry Martyn' meant very little to me when I commenced researching material for this biography. Indeed I would never have taken up the task if the suggestion had not been made that I write such a book.

Henry Martyn lived during the momentous events of the early nineteenth century. Great Britain was at war with France, which had suffered a violent revolution, and the spiritual life of the Anglican Church was at a low ebb. The Thirty-nine Articles of the Church of England were ignored by the church at large. However, the Martyn family lived in Truro, a town which had experienced revival under the preaching of the godly Samuel Walker.

It was a time when the gospel was almost unknown in Persia and the surrounding countries. The British were hated because they had used their military might to extend their empire into India and the surrounding region. Yet the godly young Henry Martyn ventured into the region, serving as a chaplain employed by the East India Company. Many chaplains had brought shame upon Christianity by using their position to make themselves wealthy at the expense of the local inhabitants. Then they had returned to their homeland to live a life of ease.

Henry faced almost instant sarcasm and mockery when he preached a Calvinistic understanding of the Scriptures to the sailors and soldiers on their way to India. Despite all the intolerance of those who were compelled to hear him preach, he remained faithful to his Lord and Saviour, Jesus Christ. The journal he kept for a decade is a record of the spiritual journey of the young chaplain. Henry knew that he was not an excellent orator, but his God-given brilliance with languages resulted in the translation of the New Testament and other Christian literature into the languages of India, Persia and Arabia.

Dying from tuberculosis, he travelled over sea and land to live in India and, later, Persia, where he faced the opposition of the Muslim mullahs, many of whom wished to see him dead.

Before leaving England he had fallen in love with Lydia Grenfell, the sister of his cousin by marriage. Despite her refusal to go to India and marry him, he bowed himself before the sovereignty of his God, who he was assured did only what was right.

Henry's time was spent serving his God and praying that his labours would result in the conversion of great numbers. He longed to hear many more voices joined in the joyful praise and solemn worship of Jehovah. The life of Henry Martyn should be compulsory reading for every believer.

In the Western world believers generally live lives of ease and pleasure, rarely taking up their God-given crosses. We live amidst crowds of unbelievers and do so little to present Christ to our spiritually lost relatives and neighbours. Why is it so? So many have lost their spiritual zeal.

My prayer is that God might use this biography, and similar works by other writers, to strengthen the faith of the saints and lead sinners to acknowledge Jesus Christ as their Saviour and Lord. In these troubled days let us pray that the church will grow and the forces of evil be driven back. Let us all pray that God will use us to bring sinners to the foot of the cross. May God use this biography of his faithful saint, Henry Martyn, to lead many to Christ.

**Jim Cromarty**

# 1.
# Dangerous times

When someone ... asked
the rector to remove
Samuel Walker from his
position, he was told, 'You go
and dismiss him, if you can; I
cannot. I feel in his presence
as if he were a being of
superior order, and I am so
abashed that I am uneasy till
I can retire.'

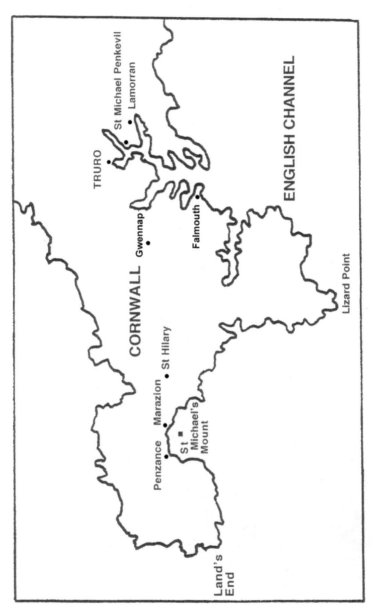

Map of Cornwall

# 1.

# *Dangerous times*

Henry Martyn was born on 18 February 1781 in Truro, a town in Cornwall. Times were difficult, the cost of living high, and many workers were unable to make ends meet.

In August 1789 the young Henry would have witnessed an event which could easily have resulted in the death of many workers. The local miners were holding a demonstration, demanding increased wages in order to provide for their families. Out of their small income they had to meet the cost of food, clothing, rent, schooling and taxes. The men marched along the street towards the town's public square, which could be clearly seen from the Martyns' home. No doubt there would have been a lot of noise as the men shouted out their demands for more money. At the other end of the street, also moving towards the square, was a troop of armed soldiers, who were there to make sure property was not damaged and to break up the demonstration. To all those who watched from the sidelines it seemed that when the two groups met, there was sure to be a violent confrontation, with the possible loss of life.

Before they came face to face, however, a silver-haired man, riding in a chaise (a two-wheeled carriage drawn along by a single horse) pulled up between the two groups of men. It was John Wesley, who had come to Cornwall to conduct some evangelistic meetings. At that time he would have been eighty-six years old, and no longer able to ride a horse as he had done in younger days. He knew that his days of open-air evangelism were drawing to a close, but he could still preach the old, old story of Jesus and his love of sinners. Standing up in his chaise, he once again called upon the miners and soldiers to repent of their sins and seek salvation through faith in the Lord Jesus Christ. This was enough to break up the demonstration!

Wesley then moved on to the 'Pit' at Gwennap to conduct worship with the local population. The 'Pit' was a natural amphitheatre formed by a collapsed mine, one of many in the area. Of that particular day Wesley recorded: 'I preached in the evening at the amphitheatre, I suppose for the last time, for my voice cannot now command the still-increasing multitude.'[1]

He had visited Truro and the surrounding region fifteen times previously, and over the years he recorded the great change in the spiritual well-being of the local citizens.

On 6 July 1745 Wesley made a visit to Truro and Gwennap and wrote in his diary, 'At Gwennap also we found the people in the utmost consternation. Word was brought that a great company of tinners, made drunk on purpose, were coming to do terrible things — so that [an] abundance of people went away. I preached to the rest on "Love your enemies." '[2]

In the years that followed, the Holy Spirit awakened people to their spiritual need, and when he visited the 'Pit' in 1775 he recorded in his diary: 'At five in the evening in the amphitheatre at Gwennap. I think this is the most magnificent spectacle which is to be seen on this side [of] heaven. And no music is to be heard upon earth comparable to the sound of many thousand voices when they are all harmoniously joined together singing "praises to God and the Lamb". Four-and-twenty thousand were present, frequently, at that spot. And yet all, I was in-formed, could hear distinctly in the fair, calm evening.'[3]

The Lord also used two local men to preach the gospel in Truro and Gwennap. One of them was the Rev. Samuel Walker,[4] who was held in the highest esteem by the Wesley brothers, Whitefield and the other evangelical ministers of that era. Henry Martyn's father was converted under the ministry of

Samuel Walker and came to be known as one of the 'serious' people. The second man of spiritual influence was George Conon, the principal of the Truro school.

Samuel Walker was born in Exeter in 1714 and died forty-seven years later. He gained his Bachelor of Arts degree at Oxford University and was ordained to the ministry of the Church of England in 1737. In 1746 he was appointed the minister of the Truro congregation. At first he lived an exciting social life. He carried out his pastoral duties but was a stranger to Christ. For some time he was the 'life and soul of the party', attending the dances, playing cards and generally having a good time.

While he was respected by the people, the Holy Spirit brought him under a deep conviction of his sin. When he heard some people discussing the way of salvation and the nature of justifying faith, he realized that he himself was a stranger to those fundamental truths.

George Conon was the person principally used by the Lord to lead Samuel Walker to a saving faith in Christ. Their friendship began in an unusual way. Some time in 1747 Mr Conon's doctor had prescribed French wine for a medical problem. Because of the tense political situation between France and Great Britain, he had bought some French wine from a merchant in Cornwall, but soon discovered that it had been smuggled into the country. To placate his guilty conscience he wrote to Rev. Samuel Walker, enclosing some money and asking him to pay on his behalf the excise duty he owed the government. George Conon knew the Scriptures: 'Render to Caesar the things that are Caesar's, and to God the things that are God's' (Mark 12:17).

It was not long before those who filled the pews became aware of big changes in their minister's preaching. He was proclaiming that the way into the kingdom of God was through the new birth. He was stressing repentance and a life of holiness. Consequently some of his parishioners despised the truths he preached. On one occasion one of the congregation

Samuel Walker's pulpit in St Mary's Church, part of the present-day
Truro Cathedral
*(Reproduced from* A Cornish Revival — The life and times of Samuel Walker
of Truro *by courtesy of Tim Shenton)*

interrupted the sermon with shouting, while others thought he
must be suffering a mental breakdown, especially as he no
longer took part in the social activities he once enjoyed. Some
of the congregation left and many, fearing a rebuke, avoided a
meeting with him, crossing to the other side of the street when
they saw him coming. His life was now one of prayer, sound
preaching and godly living.

As time passed, his church building came to be filled with
sinners hungry for the gospel and it was remarked that during
the time of worship, the streets of Truro were empty. Others,
however, approached the rector of the Truro church and the
bishop, pleading with them to remove Rev. Samuel Walker
from their town. This failed! When the rector tried to tackle
Samuel Walker he found himself lacking the courage to dismiss

his assistant. When someone in the congregation asked the rector to remove Samuel Walker from his position, he was told, 'You go and dismiss him, if you can; I cannot. I feel in his presence as if he were a being of superior order, and I am so abashed that I am uneasy till I can retire.'[5] Later, when the rector fell ill he asked Samuel to come to his bedside and pray for him.

When Samuel Walker fell in love with a wealthy young woman, he decided against marrying her in order that no one could accuse him of not practising what he preached. He could never preach self-denial while he himself lived in luxury.

In 1756 a regiment of soldiers was stationed at Truro and Walker undertook to care for their spiritual well-being. Each Lord's Day, he proclaimed the gospel to a large number of soldiers. During their time in Truro more than two hundred approached him, seeking teaching about the way of salvation.

Several months after their arrival in Truro the soldiers were ordered to move on. 'The parting scene was indescribably affecting. They assembled the last evening in the society room, to hear their beloved minister's farewell prayer and exhortation. "Had you," said Walker to a friend, "but seen their coun- tenances, what thankfulness, love, sorrow, and joy sat upon them! They hoped they might bring forth some fruit; they hoped to meet us again at the right hand of Jesus at the great day." It was an hour of mingled distress and comfort; the hearts of many were so full, that they clasped the hand of the beloved instrument of their conversion, and turned away without a word.'[6] As they marched out of the town many called out their thanks for the time spent with Samuel Walker.

During his time in Truro almost half the population pro- fessed a saving faith in Christ. This included Henry Martyn's father, John, who was a member of the 'society' led by Samuel Walker. When he visited Truro, John Wesley could see the great change in the townspeople which he attributed to the work of Samuel Walker. No longer did he face unruly mobs and when, in August 1755, he came to meet some of Mr Walker's congregation he wrote in his diary, 'As I was riding through Truro one stopped my horse and insisted on my alighting. Presently two or three more of Mr Walker's society came in, and we seemed to have been acquainted with one another many years.'[7]

Following the death of Samuel Walker and the appointment of Rev. Charles Pye in his place, the work lapsed. However, many of those who had loved the old doctrines preached by Mr Walker continued to meet and became known as the 'Walkerites' — men and women who remained faithful to the conservative, evangelical faith. But there were others who rejoiced to return to the pre-Walker days, many of whom were very critical of his formation of groups for Bible study and prayer.

About this time Christians began to look at the mission-field all around them — young people who needed an education. It was in 1780 that Robert Raikes opened Sunday schools for children and young adults who had never attended school and had very little understanding of Jesus Christ and the gospel. Originally these schools taught reading, writing and mathematics, with some teaching from the Scriptures. All learning was by rote and as people passed a Sunday school they would hear the class repeating what they were learning:

A is for angel who praises the Lord;
B is for Bible, his most holy Word.[8]

On the international scene, Great Britain was about to face an angry France. Soon the French Revolution would break out with the demand for the overthrow of the oppressive political power that resided in the nobility, especially the king. In January 1793 King Louis XVI and his wife Marie Antoinette would be beheaded and a few years later Napoleon would become the emperor of the nation. With the help of the Spanish, France would attempt the invasion of Great Britain, only to be defeated in the Battle of Trafalgar, fought during October 1805, by the British navy under the command of Lord Horatio Nelson.

In Great Britain many were calling for political and social reform, and for voting rights for the adult male population. A wise parliament slowly granted these rights, which prevented a bloody revolution such as had occurred in France. There was concern for public health, with the result that hospitals were opened to treat the sick, although by modern standards these were grim, unsanitary places where surgery was carried out without anaesthetic and the use of antiseptic. William Wilberforce and his political friends were working towards the abolition of the slave trade which forcibly transported Africans to the New World to work for their owners, especially to the United States of America, where they slaved away in the cotton fields.

Henry Martyn was the son of John Martyn and his second wife, Elizabeth (née Fleming). Their children who survived to reach adulthood were Laura, born in 1779, Henry, born in 1781, and Sally, born in 1782. John's eldest son, named after his father, had been born in 1766, the only child of John's first marriage. Both of the wives suffered from very poor health, and this trait was passed on to their children.

John Martyn was born in Gwennap, a centre for the mining of tin, copper and lead. Henry's great-uncle Thomas (1695–1751) undertook the mapping of Cornwall, a task which took fifteen years to complete, with all the surveying carried out on foot.

Henry's father had attended school, where he was taught reading and some mathematics. In an effort to obtain better work than mining, he commenced a study of mathematics, which resulted in his becoming the accountant for the Wheal Virgin Mine in Gwennap. This meant that the family moved to Truro, where their home backed onto the Coinage Hill Square, the scene of the confrontation between the striking miners and the soldiers. John's new job meant an increase in pay and with some of the money he purchased mining shares. This enabled him to move upwards in the social strata, mixing with well-to-do middle-class citizens of the town. Now the family lived a comfortable life, and the children could attend the local school.

It was into this setting that Henry Martyn was born.

# 2.
# School and university

At first he could not understand even the first proposition of Euclid and announced that the next day he would return to Truro. Mr Shepherd begged him to give Euclid another try and then, suddenly, everything fell into place... Very soon he had outdistanced all the other students in his year.

Map showing the principal places in England associated with Henry Martyn

# 2.
# *School and university*

When Henry turned seven, the decision was made by his father
that he should be enrolled in the Truro Grammar School, where
the principal was Rev. Dr Cornelius Cardew. Henry had an
enquiring mind and his father wanted him to gain academic
qualifications that would help him to obtain a good occupation.
Little is recorded of Henry's schooldays, but he proved to have
a pleasant personality although he was said to have been plain-
looking, with warts on his hands and very few eyelashes on his
unusually red eyelids.

The school had a good reputation for academic success,
both locally and in preparing scholars for Cambridge and
Oxford Universities, and Henry soon settled into his studies. He
did not study hard, but relied on his excellent memory to
succeed. He could answer questions that would have been too
difficult for many boys of his age, yet he was not known to
spend time studying. Like other students, he left his name in the
schoolroom, but while others scratched their names on a desk
or a chair, Henry etched his on the glass of the window. He was
also known to dip his finger in the ink and rub it on the sheet of
paper when he had made an error.

He was normally a happy child, but rather sensitive. The
bigger boys attending the school took advantage of this and
began tormenting him until he lost his temper. 'Little Harry
Martyn', as he was usually called,[1] was not one to submit

placidly to such teasing. Henry was not an athletic type and in the playground he rarely joined in the games with the other boys. Dr Cardew asked John Kempthorne, an older boy whose father was an admiral in the British navy, to take him under his wing. The friendship begun in this way continued for many years as later the two students both attended Cambridge University.

Henry loved his study of the classics and he excelled in both Latin and Greek. Mathematics was not his strong subject although in later years he was to excel in this study at Cambridge University. When Dr Cardew saw that Henry was progressing well, he put him in charge of his young cousin, Fortescue Hitchins.

Henry loved Cornwall and often roamed the countryside. Frequently he visited the homes of his relatives who lived in the Truro region. He particularly liked going to St Mary's vicarage, where his cousin Malachy was the vicar. There he enjoyed many happy times playing with his cousins Tom, Josepha and Fortescue.

In the autumn of 1795, when Henry was demonstrating sound ability in his classical studies, the decision was made by his father that he should go to Corpus Christi College in Oxford to sit for a scholarship examination. Henry was only fourteen years old when he made that journey, carrying a letter of introduction. While in Oxford he met with several examiners, but he was not awarded the scholarship, even though they recognized that he possessed a brilliance not found in many students.

A disappointed son returned home to tell his father that he had been unsuccessful. Henry was, at this stage in his life, unconcerned about spiritual matters. He lived for the praise of those who knew him, especially that of his father. He longed to make his father proud of his academic results, but after his failure at Oxford he returned to Dr Cardew's school to continue his study of the classics.

In the school holidays from June to October 1797 he spent a lot of time reading, especially travel books. Many hours were spent walking about the countryside with a gun over his shoulder, hoping to shoot game birds for meals. On many subsequent occasions during his short life, his thoughts would turn to Cornwall, with its many rivers, fields, hills and valleys, and its abundant wildlife. This was home to him!

Soon, however, the time came for Henry to commence his studies at Cambridge University as a financially independent student. In October 1797 he was given a place in St John's College, where he once more met John Kempthorne, his friend from Truro Grammar School days. Years later, after his conversion, Henry thanked God that he had not been accepted as a student at Oxford University two years earlier: 'Had I … become a member of the University at that time … the profligate acquaintances I had there would have introduced me to scenes of debauchery, in which I must, in all probability, from my extreme youth, have sunk for ever.'[2] The extra two years spent at Dr Cardew's grammar school gave him the maturity he needed to live a moral life in his new surroundings, as well as a greater appreciation of classical writings.

At the age of sixteen Henry settled into his new surroundings. To gain a place in St John's College he had passed an examination in the subjects he had studied at Truro. At Cambridge he would be studying mathematics, as that was the only way to obtain the degree of 'Bachelor of Arts'. He was largely ignorant of this field of study, but he was encouraged to work hard as his friend John Kempthorne, by now a fellow of St John's, had been awarded the title of 'Senior Wrangler' in 1796. This was the award given by Cambridge University to the person who gained first place in the public examination for honours in Pure and Mixed Mathematics. Henry's desire was to achieve the same title!

Henry found the university, and the city of Cambridge, very much to his liking — it was a new way of life. Nor was it all work and study. During his free time he enjoyed walking

St John's College, Cambridge, in 1797

along the many footpaths by the riverside or through the fields. The gardens surrounding the colleges were also a source of pleasure to the young scholar. Wealthier students would often drive a chaise or ride their horses.

The nation was then in a state of change and that also applied to fashions in clothing. Dr Glynn, a fellow at Kings College, was one of those who refused to change their ways. He took his daily walk with his cane in his hand, dressed in a scarlet cloak and with a three-cornered hat perched on his well-powdered wig. But for most people powdered wigs were on the way out, as Prime Minister Pitt had imposed a tax on hair-powder to help meet the cost of war with France. Some students had their hair curled regularly, instead of wearing a wig, while others refused to adopt the new fashion and had their wigs prepared by the barber each Saturday, ready to wear on Sunday. Frequently the more adventurous students would raid the barber shops while this was being done, seize the wigs and place them on the heads of statues around the university buildings. Then the students would enjoy watching their victims, forced to wear their second-best wigs, as they searched for the wigs and rescued them from the various places where they had come to rest.

Undergraduates wore gartered white stockings tucked into short knee breeches. Those who could afford it had silk stockings and a white waistcoat. Round hats, instead of cocked ones, were worn by MAs, while umbrellas were considered to be effeminate.

Student life was regulated by times set for lectures, church services and meals. Church attendance was expected of all students, but very few had any interest in attending worship or in the evangelical faith preached by the Rev. Charles Simeon. This godly man was to have a great influence on Henry's life. In his early days at university Henry enjoyed the singing in church, but he was not then a Christian.

He soon found mathematics — covering hydrostatics, astronomy, optics and mechanics — not to his liking. He could not grasp Euclid and even considered giving up university studies and returning home. His lecturer, Mr Catton, asked a second-year student, a Mr T. Shepherd, to take Henry aside for some private tutoring. At first he could not understand even the first proposition of Euclid and announced that the next day he would return to Truro. Mr Shepherd begged him to give Euclid another try and then, suddenly, everything fell into place. Henry threw his hat up into the air and shouted, 'Eureka!' Very soon he had outdistanced all the other students in his year.

In all his studies it was John Kempthorne who encouraged him to work hard. Henry agreed, but only in the hope of winning the praise of his friends and relatives. In 1797 he gained second place in the examinations, which boosted his ego. Two years later he returned home able to report that he had gained another second place, but had failed to win the college prize for 'themes'. This was a severe blow to his pride. He was by now determined to excel, as John Kempthorne had done when he was awarded the prize of 'Senior Wrangler'.

Like many students, Henry suffered mood swings and often displayed his temper. Once, when his good friend Cotterill upset him, he grabbed a knife that was lying on the table and threw it at Cotterill, narrowly missing his target. The point of the knife stuck in the wall, where the blade remained quivering for some time.

John Kempthorne began to urge Henry to seek the Saviour. He knew that his friend was unconverted, and pleaded with him to do everything to the glory of God, not to win the applause of onlookers. Of this Henry recorded in his journal: 'This seemed *strange* to me, but *reasonable*. I resolved, therefore, to *maintain this opinion* thenceforth; but never designed, that I remember, that it should *affect my conduct.*'[3]

A stranger to the grace of God, he was the subject of the prayers of many Christians who knew him, especially those of his father and his sister Sally. Sally was aware of the pride in her brother's heart and his desire that others should look up to him. Frequently she wrote to him, pleading with him to turn to

Christ, the Saviour, but her words grated on his ears. She was only sixteen at the time!

In December 1799 Henry was able to tell a very pleased father that he had gained first place in the examinations that term. He decided to remain in Cambridge for the vacation — a decision he would come to regret. In January he received word from his half-brother John that their father had died.

Later, after he had become a Christian, Henry looked back on the last holiday spent with his father. He wrote words of true repentance: 'I do not remember a time in which the wickedness of my heart rose to a greater height than during my stay at home. The ... selfishness and ... irritability of my mind were displayed in rage, malice, and envy; in pride, and vain glory, and contempt of all; in the harshest language to my sister, and even to my father, if he happened to differ from my mind and will. O what an example of patience and mildness was he! I love to think of his excellent qualities, and it is frequently the anguish of my heart, that I ever could be so base and wicked as to pain him by the slightest neglect. O my God and Father, why is not my heart *doubly* agonized at the remembrance of all my great transgressions against Thee...! I left my sister and father in October, and him I saw no more. I promised my sister that I would read the Bible for myself, but on being settled at college, Newton engaged all my thoughts.'[4]

# 3.
# A man of God

When, on one occasion, [Charles Simeon] concluded his sermon by urging all his listeners to repent of their sins and follow Christ, a small girl whispered in her mother's ear, 'Oh, Mamma, what is the gentleman in a passion about?'

# 3.
# A man of God

It was his father's death that the Holy Spirit used to convict Henry of his need of a Saviour. His friend John Kempthorne took the time to speak to him concerning death and judgement and his desperate need of a Redeemer. He loaned Henry a copy of Doddridge's *Rise and Progress of Religion in the Soul*. Henry didn't like this book as it spoke of the need of repentance and a life of humility. He was too proud to live such a life!

He commenced reading the Scriptures, starting at the Acts of the Apostles. This caused him to turn to the other books of the New Testament in order to learn something of the Christian doctrines they contained. However, as examinations approached, the Bible took second place to his studies.

In the summer of 1800, when the results were published, Henry was thrilled to discover that his name came first in the list of successful candidates. He wrote to his sister Sally, telling her the good news and thanking her for urging him to follow Christ. Still a stranger to God's grace, he attended church, prayed and read his Bible, but without any real sense of sin. Gradually, though, the Holy Spirit revealed to him his sins and showed him that Christ was the only way of salvation.

He began attending the services at Holy Trinity Church, where the much-ridiculed Rev. Charles Simeon was one of the few ministers in the Church of England who preached the great, but humbling, doctrines of the Reformation.

Charles Simeon came from a wealthy family and was privileged to attend Eton. In those early days he was known for his fashionable clothing — he wore fancy shoe buckles and silk waistcoats — and was very much involved in the social life of the community. He attended the dances, played cards, was seen at the horse races and mixed with others of the same social standing.

Charles Simeon

He came to King's College, Cambridge, to undertake further studies, and there found that he was obliged to take communion twice each year and, while at university, to attend matins in the morning and evensong at night. Like most students he took no part in spiritual activities. Hugh Hopkins quotes several lines of poetry that described the situation:

Each morn, unchill'd by frosts, he ran
With hose ungarter'd, o'er yon turfy bed,
To reach the chapel e'er the psalms began.[1]

In 1834, when the House of Lords debated the repeal of the law requiring the attendance at worship, Lord Palmerston spoke in support of the motion: 'Was it either essential or expedient that young men should be compelled to rush from their beds every morning to prayers, unwashed, unshaven and half-dressed; or in the evening from their wine to chapel and from chapel back again to their wine?'[2]

King's College, Cambridge

When Charles Simeon received a note requiring him to attend the services he decided to search out why he should take part in worship. Later he wrote concerning the requirement to attend communion services: 'Satan himself was as fit to attend as I.'[3] With the aid of his Bible and a booklet written by Thomas Wilson entitled *Instructions for the Lord's Supper*, he began a search for the truth. The Holy Spirit used both books to bring him to repentance. He now understood the truth of the doctrine of justification — that Christ had, on the cross, carried his sins, and at the same time placed his own righteousness to Simeon's account. Now worship was a delight to this once proud, well-to-do socialite.

On 29 January 1782 he gained his fellowship at King's and several months later, on 22 May, he was ordained as a deacon in the Church of England. At first he served a congregation at St Edward's Church and later, as a result of his father's friendship with the Bishop of Ely, he was appointed as the minister of Holy Trinity Church, Cambridge, where he was able to exert his influence preaching Christ in both town and university.

Holy Trinity Church in 1803

Charles Simeon arrived at Holy Trinity a converted man who loved his Lord and Saviour and served him with a great and courageous zeal. It was not long before he became the object of the scorn both of the university students and of many members of his congregation. When his brother heard of the stand he was taking he wrote to Charles, 'I trust that in the common course of things your zeal will slacken a little.'[4] This could never be. Simeon was determined that his preaching would bring glory to his Saviour, who was the Son of the living God and the Redeemer of his people. His sermons had a threefold aim: to humble the sinner, to exalt the Saviour and to promote holiness.[5]

He preached so that the congregation could understand what he said and with a zeal that caused men and women to listen. When, on one occasion, he concluded his sermon by urging all his listeners to repent of their sins and follow Christ, a small girl whispered in her mother's ear, 'Oh, Mamma, what is the gentleman in a passion about?'[6]

As far as the majority of students were concerned, Charles Simeon was fair game and they did all they could to make his life miserable! During his preaching, those outside the building would throw stones at the windows, while inside some would stand on pews shouting out comments about the sermon. Others impersonated him while he prayed, but a stare from his glaring eye would eventually bring about a degree of silence during the service. As they left the church, the congregation would become the object of the students' humour. Often Simeon would return home with his clothes covered in dust and rotten eggs.

However, that kind of behaviour was typical of many students of that era. In 1810, Isaac Milner, the university vice chancellor, deplored the 'breaking of lamps and windows, shouting and roaring, blowing of horns, galloping up and down the streets on horseback or in carriages, fighting and mobbing in the town and neighbouring villages; in the daytime breaking down fences and riding over cornfields, then eating, drinking and becoming intoxicated at taverns or ale-houses, and, lastly, in the night frequenting houses of ill-fame, resisting the lawful authorities, and often putting the peaceable inhabitants of the town into great alarm.'[7]

Charles Simeon continued to preach the gospel and many were converted. He then provided seating in the church building for the labourers and the poor who attended worship. He visited hospitals and stood beside those who were about to be executed for crimes against the state. He rejoiced that many people on the verge of eternity trusted a Saviour who would welcome them into paradise. He lived a humble life, and was involved with John Venn, Charles Grant and Josiah Pratt in founding the Church Missionary Society.

Many upper-class members of the congregation left the church as they could not tolerate such a minister or his doctrine; nor were they prepared to worship alongside working-class people, who often smelt quite strongly!

It was in 1799 that Henry Martyn commenced regular attendance at Holy Trinity Church, and he was to become a lifelong friend of Charles Simeon. During those early days of church attendance, as he walked to the examination room, the words of Scripture gave him comfort: 'And do you seek great things for yourself? Do not seek them...' (Jeremiah 45:5). He faced both oral and written examinations, but did so with peace of heart.

The result was that in January 1801, at the age of nineteen, he gained first place in his examinations and was awarded the most prestigious honour: Henry Martyn was the Senior Wrangler for that year. One of his contemporaries said of him, 'Martyn was perhaps superior in mental capacity to anyone of his day in the University.'[8] Two months later he was awarded the Smith's Mathematical Prize. Yet of those achievements he wrote, 'I obtained my highest wishes, but was surprised to find that I had grasped a shadow.'[9] Later, when introduced to some important visitors as the Senior Wrangler he recorded in his journal: 'How contemptible did these paltry honours appear to me! Ah, thought I, you know not how little I am flattered by these intended compliments.'[10]

On 15 September 1801 he wrote to his sister Sally, praising God and indicating that he was seeking to know more of God's purpose for his life: 'Oh may we be both thus minded! May we experience Christ to be our all in all, not only as our Redeemer, but also as the fountain of grace!'[11] Henry had found his Lord and in the months that followed he grew closer to his Saviour.

The year 1803 was momentous for the Cambridge Senior Wrangler. The saving work of Christ was now the driving force in his life. He had experienced the renewing work of the Holy Spirit and no longer did he look to his university studies with pride and joy, but basked in the sunshine of his Redeemer's love.

He also witnessed boldly for the Lord he loved. He was called to visit a dying man who had lived extravagantly, which meant that he would leave his family with nothing. The man was not a Christian and his wife urged Henry to pray for him. Some time afterwards, wanting to speak to the dying man's daughters, Henry found them at another home where they were listening to a student reading a play. He rebuked both the daughters and the student for their frivolity at such a time. The student was later to thank him for doing so, as that timely reprimand had made him aware of his own need to be prepared for death. As a result he was in time brought to saving faith, and subsequently to a work on the Indian mission-field.

Meanwhile, Henry was elected a fellow of St John's College and was given his own rooms free of charge. He became an examiner in the classics, which meant he had to make a detailed study of the writings of Butler, Locke, Xenophon, Juvenal and Euripides. He also gave assistance to those students who found their studies difficult. His life was so full that he became known as 'the man who had not lost an hour'.[12] He even found the time to enter a competition for the best essay in Latin. He won first prize, even though at university he had studied mathematics rather than the classics!

During the Easter vacation he returned home to receive the accolades of his family and friends, who were awed by the academic achievements of a local boy. On his return to Cambridge, his spiritual life went ahead in leaps and bounds. While his spiritual character was largely moulded by Charles Simeon, others made their mark upon him as well — his father, John Wesley, his sister Sally, his friend John Kempthorne, William Carey, the writings of David Brainerd and the Scriptures, which he began to devour like a spiritually starved man. He was also a member of Mr Simeon's prayer and Bible-study group, which gave him a greater appreciation of God's saving work through Christ.

There were now quiet times of sweet solitude when he withdrew from worldly affairs for a time of communion with God. In his own words, 'I walked in the fields and endeavoured to consider my ways, and to lift up my heart to God... I devoted myself to Him solemnly, and trust that when tempted to sin I shall remember this walk... Had a sweet, supporting sense of God's presence in the evening, when I walked by moonlight... My imagination takes to itself wings and flies to some wilderness where I may hold converse in solitude with God ... let me but walk alone in communion with God, and I shall surely be able to offer Him sacrifices more pure... From the church I walked to our garden, where I was alone an hour, I trust with Christ. The sudden appearance of evil thoughts made me very unhappy, but I found refuge in God... What is this world, what is religious company, what is anything to me without God? They become a bustle and a crowd when I lose sight of Him. The most dreary wilderness would appear paradise with a little of His presence.'[13]

During those quiet, pleasant days when God richly blessed his soul, Henry wrote, 'I enjoyed this summer, to my improvement; and not until then had I ever experienced any real pleasure in religion. I was more convinced of sin than ever, more earnest in fleeing to Jesus for refuge, and more desirous of the renewal of my nature.'[14]

He strolled along the footpaths and across the fields, meditating upon the character of God, learning by heart passages of Scripture — even whole books of the Bible — and praying for guidance concerning his future life. Henry had come to Cambridge to study law, but now he wanted to serve Christ in a different area.

In order to arrive at a wise decision he undertook a walking tour of Wales, away from the affairs of the world. He gave time to prayer and to the reading and meditation of the Scriptures. At one point he sailed down the Mersey in a small boat. This was very dangerous as the river was swollen and fast-running, because of storms in the region. While visiting a waterfall near Abergwyngregyn in North Wales, he was almost killed by falling rocks. With a guide, he climbed Mount Snowdon during a time of violent winds and rain. Despite all the dangers he encountered, he considered these experiences as good training for whatever the future held for him. Along the way he met a Welshman who carried an enormous bundle of hats which he was hoping to sell. The man looked very ill, but was remarkably cheerful. Henry asked himself if he could similarly be content in whatever state the Lord placed him.

After his trek he returned to Truro, where he spent time with his family, Sally, Laura and John, and those friends he had known for many years. It was during this time that he decided to offer his services as a missionary in the Far East. Before that move, however, he intended completing his university studies.

Soon it was back to Cambridge, where he was determined to serve his Lord and Saviour more fully. At first he had not been willing to become poor for the sake of his Redeemer and had planned to enter the legal profession, but now, after much prayer and guidance from Mr Simeon, he announced that he would seek ordination in the Church of England. This meant that many students referred to him as a 'Methodist'. 'Enthusiasm', or religious fervour, usually played no part in the spiritual life of the student body.

Henry was still involved in conducting examinations. After the required ten terms at Cambridge, many students had only a little knowledge of their subject and were unable to read Latin, the language of the academic world. The examinations usually included an oral section, which many students treated as a joke. Hopkins records that when 'Cock' Langford, who lived a busy social life, was undertaking his M.A. examination, he was asked in his oral testing 'whether the sun went around the earth or the earth around the sun. After some thought, he came out with the original comment, "Sometimes the one, sometimes the other." '[15] The answer was accepted and he was duly awarded his postgraduate degree!

Meanwhile Henry was preparing himself for missionary endeavours on the Indian or Chinese mission-fields. With other Christian students, he was invited by Charles Simeon to 'drink tea'. During those visits the Scriptures were discussed. Mr Simeon also reported on the work of overseas missionaries, stressing the work of William Carey, who had sailed for India in 1799, as an example of what even one missionary could accomplish.

When Henry told his family of his plans, it was Sally who raised objections. In a letter to his close friend and biographer

John Sargent, Henry wrote, 'My sister has also objected to it, on the score of my deficiency in that deep and solid experience necessary in a missionary.'[16] Attempts to dissuade him were also made by others living in Cambridge, but nothing was to change his mind.

At that time he was reading a biography of David Brainerd by Jonathan Edwards. He saw many parallels between Brainerd and himself. He wrote, 'I feel my heart knit to this dear man, and really rejoice to think of meeting him in heaven.' 'I long to be like him; let me forget the world, and be swallowed up in a desire to glorify God.'[17]

There were still times when Henry was embarrassed because of the weakness of his faith. On one occasion his conscience was troubled after he failed to say grace before his meal, because of the men who were seated at his table.

It was at this time that Charles Grant played a big part in Henry's move to India. Grant was the Chairman of the Board of Directors of the East India Company. As a friend of Charles Simeon, he had already been involved in the appointment of several chaplains whose names had been put forward by Simeon. Now Mr Grant received another suggestion proposing Henry Martyn as one who would faithfully serve the Lord and the East India Company.

In order to gain a greater understanding of what lay before him, Henry decided to become curate to Rev. Charles Simeon, which meant his ordination as a deacon. The dates set for his examination and ordination, which were to take place at Ely, were 22-23 October 1803.

# 4.
## A new curate

He prepared sermons, conducted worship, taught the catechism, visited the sick, almshouses and hospitals, and played an active part in the affairs of the congregation... He wanted to walk closely with his God at all times...

# 4.

# A new curate

Henry had now decided that he would sacrifice a life of relative ease in England for that of a missionary taking the gospel to the unevangelized peoples of the Orient. He knew that he could have remained in Cambridge, lecturing students and enjoying a very comfortable standard of living as a distinguished scholar, but the call to missionary service came loud and clear. Charles Simeon encouraged him, frequently speaking of the work of William Carey in India.

Most of his waking hours were spent in carrying out his pastoral duties. As well as studying the Scriptures he frequently visited the lonely, sick and dying. He also began to practise self-denial, turning his back on many quite legitimate comforts. He often ate his breakfast standing near an open window where he would feel the icy blast of the wind. He was very conscious of his own tendency to pride, and knew that, despite his academic brilliance, he needed to become a humble person. He wrote in his journal, 'Pride shows itself every hour of every day! ... What plans, and dreams, and visions of futurity fill my imagination every day in which self is the prominent object! O Lord ... humble my soul, let Thy Spirit secretly teach me what I am.'[1]

As the examination for the diaconate drew near, Henry took seriously the biblical command to search the Scriptures and pray without ceasing. On the day set for the examinations he and another student hired a gig, and set out for Ely. On the journey Henry had little to say, because he was feeling guilty that he had not set aside sufficient time for prayer and private devotions.

The examination proved not to impose any great burden on him. He had to analyse the text of Matthew chapter 11 and translate into Latin the first of the doctrinal statements of the Church of England known as the Thirty-nine Articles. He was called upon to outline the spiritual significance of the resurrection of Christ. He was also questioned about a number of topics, including some of the fundamental truths of Christianity, as well as the Pharisees, Sadducees and scribes and Jewish worship.

Henry left the examiner in a solemn frame of mind, with a consciousness of the importance of the work he was to undertake. That night he was disturbed by the levity which characterized the talk between the others who had just completed their examinations. Henry had a serious conversation with one man, urging him to spend time reading the Ordination Service. After spending some time in his room in prayer, he made his way into the common room determined to seize any opportunity of speaking to the other students about the solemn nature of the commitment they were about to undertake, but at the end of the evening he returned to his room feeling that he had failed in what he considered to be his duty. The next morning, after a time of prayer and going out for a walk, he joined the other students, only to find once more an atmosphere of joking and frivolity.

At Ely Cathedral he was well aware of the significance of ordination. Afterwards he pleaded with Christ to give him the necessary grace to carry out the promises he had made during the service: 'May I have grace to fulfil those promises I made before God and the people!'[2]

From now on Henry's time would be divided between fulfilling his obligations to the university as a fellow of the college and carrying out his work of assisting the Rev. Charles Simeon.

The most difficult duty that fell to the new deacon was sermon preparation. Henry spent a lot of time selecting a suitable subject and preparing the message so that the congregation would be able to understand all he said. As Charles Simeon's assistant he was given the oversight of Lolworth, a small village near Cambridge. After the service on 6 November 1803, he came away with a heart weighed down by the poor quality of the sermon. One member of the congregation had complained of a lack of solemnity in his conduct of the service. Another indicated that not everyone could hear what he said because he spoke in a low voice. Of the worship service that day Henry recorded: 'These things, with the difficulty I had found in making sermons, and the poorness of them, made me appear exceedingly contemptible to myself. I began to see ... for the first time, that I must be contented to take my place among men of second-rate abilities; that there were men who excelled me in everything.'[3]

On another occasion when a man pointed out some deficiencies in his sermon, Henry thanked him for his comments, and began to put more effort into sermon preparation and preaching. In his heart he was determined to preach in the spirit of the words:

I'd preach as though I ne'er should preach again;
I'd preach as dying unto dying men.[4]

Sometimes he spent the whole day preparing just one sermon.

He also found other duties thrust upon him — he now conducted funerals and marriage services. As a fellow of St John's he was appointed examiner in the classics, which meant the study of Mitford's *History of Greece,* Butler's *Analogy* and *Xenophon.* His life was very full!

When other people became aware of Henry's plans to serve his Lord on the mission-field, objections were raised. He wrote, 'Received a letter from my sister [Sally], in which she expressed her opinion of my unfitness for the work of a Missionary.'[5] A member of the congregation called him aside and spoke of his missionary plans: 'After church sat with —, two hours conversing about the missionary plan ... he told me that I had neither strength of body or mind for the work.' Those words dealt a blow to Henry's pride and he continued: 'This latter defect [strength of mind] I did not like at all; it was galling to the pride of my heart, and I went to bed hurt; yet thankful to God for sending me one who would tell me the truth.'[6] Others expressed their opposition to his plans on the ground that Great Britain was in need of evangelical ministers.

On 1 January 1804 Henry looked back over the past year, and recorded in his journal: 'I have learned, that neglect of much and fervent communion with God in meditation and prayers, is not the way to redeem time, nor to fit me for public ministrations. Nevertheless, I judge that I have grown in grace ... for the bent of my desire is towards God... In heavenly contemplation and abstraction from the world, my attainments have fallen far short of my expectations: in love to man, I perceive little or no increase. But in a sense of my own worthlessness and guilt ... I am inclined to think myself gaining ground. My ... only desire is to be entirely devoted to [God]. Oh may I live very near to him in the ensuing year, and follow the steps of Christ and his holy saints! It will be attended with much self-denial and warfare ...'[7]

Several days later Henry devoted a full day to fasting and prayer, yet he found himself downcast: 'I could not get near to God... I could feel no contrition; nevertheless, though the cloud hanging over the nation, and my own pride, cast a heavy gloom over my mind, with a sense of guilt, and of God's displeasure, I strove against an evil heart of unbelief, which tempted me to depart from the living God.'[8]

Two events followed which almost brought his missionary plans to a standstill. Early in 1804 he received news that his father's small bequest to his children had been lost.[9] Now his unmarried sister, Sally, was dependent upon him to meet her living expenses.

Then a mishap occurred when he opened the door to his rooms and in doing so hurt his landlady, who was the wife of a minister. Her face was severely injured as a result and Henry set aside an annual payment to her out of the income from a £1,000 investment. Now he saw little hope of leaving England because of his responsibilities at home. However, he became aware that chaplains serving the East India Company were paid very high stipends — approximately £1,200 at a time when ministers in Great Britain received approximately £50 annually.

Having to make a decision concerning his future, Henry set out, on 23 January 1804, to seek some advice from several good friends living in London. He was advised by his colleague that he should visit Mr Charles Grant, who was not only the Chairman of the Board of Directors of the East India Company, but also a Member of Parliament. While in London, Henry heard that many missionaries working overseas with the East India Company had a very bad reputation, but his one great desire was to walk closely with his God at all times.

Henry made his way to India House, the offices of the East India Company, where he met Charles Grant. The latter invited him to meet with William Wilberforce, who was also a member of the House of Commons and a member of the 'Clapham Sect'. This group of influential men were working to bring about

The old East India House

social reform, especially the abolition of the slave trade. As the two men were travelling to meet the others, Charles Grant spoke to Henry about India and its great need of Christian missionaries.

William Wilberforce

Upon their arrival Henry was introduced to William Wilberforce and asked to stay for dinner. Mr Wilberforce was 'a wiry, bright-eyed figure, with powdered hair, a diamond brooch in his linen, and an eyeglass which he fingered while he talked'.[10]

Some of the best-known members of the 'Clapham Sect' were Charles Grant, William Wilberforce, James Stephen, Henry Thornton, Lord Teignmouth, Hannah More, Henry Venn and his son John. Henry accepted a gracious invitation to stay overnight, where he heard much of the work of the chaplains of the East India Company. It was Charles Simeon whose recommendations carried weight when appointments were made.

Returning to London the following day, Henry had the privilege of meeting the aged John Newton, who because of his deafness had been unable to take part in the discussions. Before returning to Cambridge, he also attended a service at the New London Tavern in Cheapside, where he saw two young men set apart for missionary service. He wished that he was with them, as they were about to leave for India.

Back in Cambridge his workload was very heavy, even to the extent that on occasions he felt that he was neglecting his personal devotions. He prepared sermons, conducted worship, taught the catechism, visited the sick, almshouses and hospitals, and played an active part in the affairs of the congregation. He avoided wasting time in conversations about trivial matters. He wrote, 'I could live for ever in prayer, if I could always speak to God. I sought to pause, and to consider what I wanted, and to look up with fear and faith, and I found the benefit; for my soul was soon composed to that devout sobriety, which I knew, by its sweetness, to be its proper frame. I was engaged in prayer, in the manner I like — *deep seriousness*... I was led through the mists of unbelief, and spoke to God as one that was true; and rejoiced exceedingly that He was holy and faithful...'[11]

His preaching was sometimes criticized by members of the congregation, who urged him to speak in the common language, and not the educated, cultured language of graduates from Cambridge University. He commenced preaching extempore, but Charles Simeon urged him to keep closely to the words he had prepared in order to be understood more clearly. On one occasion he visited an elderly couple after the Lord's Day service and was distressed to find that they were unable to give an outline of his sermon.

Henry was aware of the enticements that this world has to offer and was determined not to be led astray. In a personal covenant, 'I solemnly renounced the world, and the comforts, even the lawful comforts of it, before God this night, that I might be entirely his servant. This was accompanied with some degree of melancholy, as if I were about to be a loser of it, but I was made to perceive the pride and ignorance of supposing I had made any sacrifice. The remembrance of what I had done to deserve destruction, and the view of the superlative excellency and glory of being the servant of God, and having him for my only portion, soon made me thankful at having made a happy exchange.'[12]

Frequently Henry was conscious of pride in his heart and earnestly sought forgiveness from an offended God. He also kneeled and pleaded with God for grace to live a more godly life.

When he and Charles Simeon went riding together, most of the time was spent discussing the need of chaplains in the East India Company. Mr Simeon pointed to the special need in India, where William Carey was already labouring, and said that it would be best to commence such a work as an unmarried man.

When Henry thought his time of departure for the mission-field was near, he decided to return to Truro and say farewell to his relatives and friends. He left Cambridge for London on 9 July 1804 and took the opportunity to visit Charles Grant, who told him that a chaplaincy would become available for him, but how soon he could not tell.

The following day he had a meal with his close friend John Sargent, who was about to be married. This made Henry's own thoughts turn to marriage, but he was concerned not to allow a desire for happiness or earthly comforts stand in the way of his sailing for India or make him less effective as a missionary.

Later in the day he dined with William Wilberforce, who, after some discussion about the evils of the slave trade, took him to the House of Commons. There he heard Mr Pitt, the prime minister, speak. He was delighted to hear Pitt's eloquence, but wished that he had been using this ability to preach the gospel.

On 11 July 1804 he boarded the coach for Bath, and was obliged to sit on top, where for fifty miles he was buffeted by the strong wind, which was biting cold. During the journey he suffered severe chest pains.

After passing through Bath and Exeter he spent some time with his cousin Tom Hitchins, who had married Emma Grenfell. This was a very happy time as Henry and Tom had grown up together and were good friends.

On 16 July he reached Truro and then went on to Lamorran. Everywhere he went he spoke to people of their need of a Saviour. At Lamorran he was pleased to meet his sister Sally.

Henry wanted to preach in the local churches, but his old teacher, Dr Cardew, refused to have a Calvinist in the pulpit of the Anglican church in Truro. For the same reason most pulpits were closed to him.

On 29 July, however, he conducted worship at the St Hilary church and was disappointed when he discovered that Emma Hitchins' sister, Lydia Grenfell, was missing from the congregation. However, he was pleased in one way, since he thought she might have upset his plans to leave for the mission-field unmarried.

Lydia, who was six years older than Henry, had been converted in 1800, the same year in which she had become engaged to Mr Samuel John, a solicitor at Penzance. Becoming aware of some dubious aspects of his character, she broke the engagement. Soon afterwards, out of a sense of responsibility for her actions, she privately vowed not to marry until Samuel had done so. Despite the broken engagement, it would appear that her love for him lingered on.

After tea, Henry called at the Grenfell home, where he found Lydia. A walk followed, in company with a third person, in the course of which the conversation was mainly about spiritual matters. His thoughts of this woman, whom he had known in his youth and now had met again after several years, so filled his mind that evening, and during the night, that he wrote in his diary, 'I felt too plainly that I loved her passionately.'[13] He began to wonder whether they should marry and then sail for India together. Often in his sleep he dreamed about himself being with the lovely Lydia. What should he do?

On 5 August he preached at St Michael's and was overjoyed to have, for the first time, his two sisters in the congregation. Sally was now married to Mr Pearson, the vicar of Lamorran and St Michael Penkevil. He departed rejoicing that the preaching had made a profound impression on both sisters and with good reason to hope that a true work of God had taken place in the lives of both. A visit to Tom and Emma Hitchins stirred up

View of Marazion (home of Lydia Grenfell) from St Michael's Mount

new hopes concerning Lydia, as Emma told him that 'My attachment to her sister [Lydia] was not altogether unreturned.'[14]

Two weeks later he preached at Kenwyn to an overflowing congregation, but when some spoke in praise of his sermon this distressed him on the grounds that it tended 'to fan the flame of vanity'.

Henry spent some very happy days wandering about the fields and along the coast that he had known in his youth. At one spot he discovered a cave overlooking the sea and used it as a quiet place to read the Scriptures, pray and meditate on what lay before him. And all the time he longed that Lydia might return the love that he felt for her.

At Marazion, on 27 August, he read to Lydia from a book written by Dr Watts. He wrote later of his thoughts when they read together a prayer that God might be given the first place, above any of his creatures: 'Now, thought I, here am I in the presence of God, and my idol. So I used the prayer for myself, and addressed it to God, who answered it, I think, for my love was kindled to God and divine things, and I felt cheerfully resigned to the will of God, to forego the earthly joy which I had just been desiring with my whole heart... Parted with Lydia, perhaps for ever in this life... Walked to St Hilary, determining, in great tumult and inward pain, to be the servant of God. All the rest of the evening, in company, or alone, I could think of nothing but her excellences.'[15]

After hearing Henry preach, Lydia wrote in her diary, 'Heard H. M. on "Now we are ambassadors for Christ, as though God did beseech you by us. We pray you, in Christ's stead, be ye reconciled unto God, for He hath made Him to be sin ... for us who knew no sin, that we might be made the righteousness of God in Him" [2 Corinthians 5:20-21]... In the text two things were implied — 1st — We were at enmity with God; 2nd. — We were unable to restore ourselves to his favour... A precious sermon. Lord, bless the preacher and those that heard him.'[16] Lydia did not, however, record any affectionate feelings towards the preacher!

Several members of the congregation strongly objected to Henry's Calvinistic teaching and refused to hear him any more. When he was asked to preach at a local Methodist church, he graciously declined, in order to prevent any more ill will towards him.

On one occasion he went riding with Lydia, in order to visit a brother and sister, both of whom were old and in poor health. Many times in the future Henry would reflect on that happy time spent with Lydia.

In London he again called on Charles Grant, who told him there was no chaplaincy available at that time. He visited St Paul's, where he heard a choir singing praises to God. The sacred music made him think of the wonders of heaven.

After a pleasant break from academic studies and the continual round of his pastoral duties, Henry returned to Cambridge.

# 5.
# Farewell, Cambridge

Charles Simeon told
Henry that ... [he] was
called to be a missionary, not
one who made an easy life
for himself... Henry agreed
with this and ... wrote,
'With my Bible in my hand
and Christ at my right
hand strengthening me, I can
do all things.'

# 5.
# *Farewell, Cambridge*

Back in Cambridge, Henry once again found his life very busy. He was responsible for worship services, which meant the preparation of sermons, and for visitation of the sick and dying, including those who were in hospital or in jail. When he visited the sick and dying, he reflected upon the day of his own death, a subject which at times caused him 'some dread'.[1] His pastoral responsibilities also included conducting baptisms and marriages, catechizing and a host of other duties. As a fellow at St John's he tutored, gave lectures, conducted examinations and assisted those students who needed special help. In the midst of all these activities he read the Scriptures, meditated upon them and committed many passages to memory. He continued to read the biography of David Brainerd, which lifted his spirits. And all the time he kept thinking of Lydia, whom he loved dearly.

However, more than ever Henry longed to be serving his Master in India, preaching the gospel to the native people of that far-distant land. Any spare time was devoted to a study of Bengali grammar. He also diligently searched for a copy of William Carey's translation of the New Testament in that language; this would be of great assistance in his language studies.

In October he received mail which included the advice: 'Let him marry, and come out at once!'[2] Henry's thoughts immediately turned to Lydia, but his intention was to travel to India as an unmarried man and then, if he found the area was safe, he would propose to her.

Before he could leave for India it was necessary for him to be ordained to the ministry, which was not possible until he was twenty-four years of age. Now it was time for him to prepare for the parting from his friends and relatives, and for departure from the land he loved.

On Sunday, 10 November 1804, he was told of a letter to Thomas Thomason, who was senior curate to Charles Simeon, stating that Mr Grant was sure that his application to the Board of Directors of the East India Company would be accepted, and he should receive further information towards the end of December. In his journal he wrote, 'I rejoiced greatly at the prospect of a speedy departure, feeling, I thought, joy and delight at the gathering in of the Gentile souls... The change of scene and sight of other countries, certainly are agreeable to me; but as far as I can see, they would not induce me to resign my ease and my life: no, I believe that I lay down these, in obedience and conformity to Christ, and from love to him and his elect; and had I ten thousand lives, my calm judgement, unruffled by dangers, testifies, that they ought all to be spent for Christ.'[3]

Several days later, Charles Simeon told a very disappointed Henry that it would be some time before he sailed. He longed to be in India, serving the Lord with all his God-given abilities.

Early in January 1805 he made his way to London and called on Charles Grant, who indicated that he would soon receive a chaplaincy in India, possibly at Fort William.

Meanwhile, Henry wanted Lydia's permission to correspond with her. He asked a friend to seek her agreement to this. (Elsewhere he refers to the 'Friend' who acted on his behalf by an 'E'. This is probably a reference to Lydia's sister Emma, who, as we have already seen, was married to Henry's cousin, Tom Hitchins, the minister at Plymouth.) When he received a favourable answer Henry considered himself 'to have engaged himself to Lydia'.[4]

In a discussion concerning his future, Charles Simeon told Henry that he was opposed to the idea of an appointment in Calcutta, as Henry was called to be a missionary, not one who made an easy life for himself in a large city. Henry agreed with this and, with joy in his heart, wrote, 'With my Bible in my hand and Christ at my right hand strengthening me, I can do all things.'[5]

On 22 January 1805 Henry received a letter from Mr Grant indicating that he would be sailing for St Helena in eight to ten days' time. Even though he was unable to meet this call, as he had not yet been ordained a presbyter, nor had he obtained his Bachelor of Divinity degree (which needed the approval of the university authorities and the king), he knew that his time in England was limited and there was much to do.

On the occasion of his twenty-fourth birthday, he offered thanks to God for preserving his life. In his journal he noted: 'May the world never have occasion to mourn at my birthday.'[6]

He made several trips to London and, while visiting St James's Chapel, he saw some of the nobility on their way to meetings. They were dressed in their best clothes, but Henry wrote of them that he 'was much affected with the melancholy, at seeing such a glare of finery on poor old shrivelled people, fit only to be shrouded in a coffin'.[7]

In London he met Dr Gilchrist, a missionary home on furlough who had worked with William Carey in Calcutta. Dr Gilchrist assisted Henry with the pronunciation of Hindustani words. Henry also visited Charles Grant, who told him that he would very soon receive an appointment and should be ready to leave with the next fleet.

On 10 March 1805 Henry was ordained a presbyter of the Church of England. The ordination service was a solemn occasion, with none of the frivolity which had marked the day when he was ordained to the diaconate. Now nothing stood in his way, preventing his departure for India. During the days that followed, he studied the Scriptures and prayed, asking that God would always be central in his life: 'I longed to forget the world, and to be swallowed up in entire devotion to God, to live always unto him.'[8]

While in London Henry was given opportunities to preach, but when he was criticized by the Rev. Richard Cecil, a leading evangelical clergyman, for lacking warmth and earnestness he found this another blow to his pride.

Henry was a kind person, ready to help those who were in need. When a penniless old man sat down beside him, he was happy to give the man some money.

A visit to Charles Grant's office resulted in his being told that if he returned the following day he should know what the future held for him. The next day he was told that he and another person had been accepted to work with the East India Company, but that objections had been raised about Henry's appointment because of 'his connection with Mr Wilberforce and *those people*'.[9] Mr Grant instructed Henry to present himself at his office at a set date to take the oath of loyalty to the company. He was told to wear his clerical robes in order to make a good impression.

On 4 April Henry returned to Cambridge to say his final farewells and to receive his Bachelor of Divinity degree. On 7 April, Palm Sunday, he conducted his last worship service there, preaching an appropriate sermon at Lolworth. There seemed little concern that Henry would not be seen by them again, except for an old farmer who broke down weeping.

Henry's last service at Holy Trinity Church concluded with Mr Simeon praying for God's blessing upon him. As Henry made his way down the aisle, the congregation rose to their feet as a mark of respect to the man they would see no more.

The following morning, accompanied by friends, he made his way through the mist to the coach which would take him to London. Soon the coach set out and as he looked back the university spires were quickly hidden from view by the thick fog. His days at Cambridge had come to an end.

# 6.
# *Never to return*

'It was a very painful moment to me when I awoke … and found the fleet actually sailing down the channel. Though it was what I had actually been looking forward to so long, yet the consideration of being parted for ever from my friends, almost overcame me'

(Henry Martyn in a letter to Charles Simeon).

# 6.
# $\mathcal{N}$ever to return

Despite there being another five months before he sailed, Henry used his time wisely. He was now in London, where he studied the Scriptures and gave time to reading material that would improve his knowledge of the languages he would find in India. Richard Cecil helped him prepare sermons and gave him wise advice on how to improve their delivery. Charles Grant informed him of the day that he was required to present himself at the offices of the East India Company to make his oath of allegiance.

He was somewhat disappointed that no letter from Lydia awaited him, but his disappointment drove him closer to his loving God, who loved him eternally. He was encouraged by a visit to John Newton, who told him that Satan would become his enemy for undertaking missionary work. There followed a time of prayer with the old man who had served the Lord faithfully for many years.

However, Henry differed from John Newton over the way they looked upon culture and the arts. John Newton saw these things as coming from sinful man and stimulating the 'depraved nature'.[1] He admitted that Paul admired such things, but said that the apostle was endowed with higher divine taste than others. On the other hand, Henry thoroughly enjoyed music, which, he said, 'brought heaven and eternal things and the presence of God very near to [him]'.[2] On another occasion

John Newton

he wrote, 'My heart adored the Lord as the author and source of all the intellectual beauty that delighted me; as the creator of all the fair scenes that employ the poet's pen; and as the former of the mind that can find pleasure in beauty... Since I have known God ... painting, poetry and music, have had charms unknown to me before. I have received what I suppose is a taste for them: for religion has ... made my mind susceptible of impressions from the sublime and beautiful.'[3]

Henry took time to go to Lambeth Palace to call on the Archbishop of Canterbury, Charles Manners-Sutton, who knew of his missionary plans and his high academic standing, including the fact that he was an MA. Before they parted the archbishop wished him God's blessing in his venture in the Lord's service.

This was followed by a visit to William Wilberforce, in the course of which he was informed that he was to attend the office of the East India Company, where he would swear the oath of allegiance. When information was received that the French and Spanish fleets were preparing for war, it became clear that the British fleet bound for India would not be able to set off until mid-June at the earliest.

Henry knew that his pride must be conquered. He attended a service where the subject of the sermon was missionary endeavour. He couldn't help seeing himself in the role of the one being commended by the preacher and proud thoughts flooded into his mind. One Lord's Day when he was complimented on his sermon, he was again filled with a sense of pride — until a member of the congregation at another service told him his sermon was 'very miserable'[4] and urged him to take more care with his delivery! He subsequently undertook some elocution lessons, which he believed would help him with sermon presentation.

It was on 22 May 1805 that Henry came before the Board of Directors of the East India Company and there swore the oath of fidelity. Following this, he realized that he had almost come to an end of his finances and for the first time in his life he had to borrow to survive until he received his pay from the East India Company. He felt great shame at having to ask for a loan.

As he went about the city he frequently saw beautiful women and feared that he might entertain lustful thoughts. Like Job he made a covenant with his eyes not to gaze in a sinful way upon any of the women he saw. The issue of marriage before leaving England was discussed with Richard Cecil, who told him it was utter foolishness to go abroad unmarried, as a wife would assist him in decision-making and help preserve his character. However, he was willing to follow in the footsteps of David Brainerd, who took the gospel to the North American Indians, and of the apostle Paul, both of whom were unmarried.

Early in June he received notice that the fleet was soon to sail, and his thoughts turned to Lydia. He feared that Satan was inducing him to make an idol of her. He recorded in his journal: 'How miserable did life appear, without the hope of Lydia! Oh, how has the discussion of the subject opened all my wounds afresh. I have not felt such heart-rending pain, since I parted with her in Cornwall... I could not help saying, "Go, Hindus, go on in your misery, let Satan still rule over you..." No, thought I, earth and hell shall never keep me back from my work. I am "cast down, but not destroyed"; I began to consider why I was so uneasy — "Cast thy care upon Him, for He careth for you." '[5] Later he wrote, 'Shed tears tonight at the thoughts of my departure. I thought of the roaring seas, which would soon be rolling between me and all that is dear to me on earth.'[6]

Again thoughts of Lydia stirred within him, and one day he wrote, 'My heart was sometimes ready to break with agony, at being torn from its dearest idol, and at other times I was visited by a few moments of sublime and enraptured joy.'[7]

On 20 June he received notice that the flotilla was expected to sail from Portsmouth some time during the following week. This meant a round of farewells with friends and relatives in preparation for sailing. He began purchasing books that he would need and sat for a portrait to leave with Charles Simeon. He considered himself to be in good health and ready to take the gospel to the 'thousands starving, thousands sick and forsaken, thousands groaning under the devil's bondage...'[8]

Then came the order to travel to Portsmouth and board the *Union*. On the way he visited John Sargent and other good friends. At one place where he stopped for the night he fainted and suffered a convulsion, which left him in severe pain, but the next morning he felt well enough to proceed with his journey.

On 10 July, after packing all his belongings into his cabin, he went ashore again to spend time with his many friends, who had come to bid him farewell. This was a precious time for Henry as they sang hymns of praise, meditated upon the Scriptures and gave time to prayer. Afterwards he spent his first night in his cabin, which he said was as comfortable as his room at Cambridge.

On Sunday morning, 14 July, he conducted worship for a congregation consisting of sailors, soldiers, passengers and friends. That evening Charles Simeon conducted worship, following which the group spent time singing praises to God. Before leaving, Mr Simeon presented Henry with a beautiful compass — a gift from himself and his congregation.

On 17 July the signal gun was fired and the fleet moved away from the harbour. Almost immediately Henry suffered his first attack of seasickness, which meant that he could neither walk about the ship nor read. The next day he spent some time

on deck, watching the coast of Devon and Cornwall fade away
into the distance. The following day a ship approached the
*Union* from the shore carrying, amongst other things, a personal
gift from Charles Simeon — a large folio Bible weighing 11lb.
11 oz. (5.3 kg). Also included in the delivery were packages of
Bibles and Christian reading material for distribution to the
passengers. On board the *Union* there were soldiers and their
families and some cadets who were employed by the East India
Company. The soldiers and sailors were a rough crowd, who
had little or no interest in spiritual matters.

Later, in a letter to Charles Simeon, Henry expressed his
feelings as the *Union* made her way out to sea: 'It was a very
painful moment to me when I awoke, on the morning after you
left us, and found the fleet actually sailing down the channel.
Though it was what I had actually been looking forward to so
long, yet the consideration of being parted for ever from my
friends, almost overcame me... It was only by prayer for them
that I could be comforted; and this was indeed a refreshment to
my soul, because by meeting them at the throne of grace, I
seemed to be again in their society.'[9]

A day later the fleet dropped anchor off the coast at Fal-
mouth as it was feared the combined French and Spanish
armada might attack. However, there was work to be done, as
several ships had run aground. Henry knew the coastline and in
the distance could see where Lydia lived. He longed to see her
again and was finding life on board difficult because of the
uncouth language of the sailors and soldiers. He was also
distressed to hear the swearing by members of the soldiers'
families.

As the fleet was unable to move, he spent time writing to his
many friends, but found it difficult to give time to prayer and
Bible reading because of the laughter, loud talk and foul
language. Some others on board had brought their drums and
fifes with them and the noise from these instruments added to
the din.

St Michael's Mount, showing the causeway that links it to the mainland at low tide. The mount, which overlooks Marazion, was one of the last familiar landmarks seen by Henry as he sailed.

When the commodore decided that the fleet was to remain where it was for the time being, the passengers were given shore leave. This suited Henry, as he saw it as an opportunity to visit Lydia once again. On 25 July he went ashore and caught the mail coach to Marazion, where he found her having her breakfast. Later, as they were walking together, he told her of his love and asked if she would be prepared to come to India and marry him. She replied that she could not give an immediate answer, but needed time to think. (It would seem that she made no effort to tell Henry the real reason for her apparent indecision.) In her diary she wrote, 'I was surprised this morning by a visit from H. M., and have passed the day chiefly with him... I felt as if bidding a final adieu to him in this world, and all he said was as the words of one on the borders of eternity. May ... the Lord moderate the sorrow I feel at parting with so valuable and excellent a friend... Oh, may we each pursue our different paths, and meet at last around our Father's throne; may we often meet now in spirit, praying and obtaining blessings for each other.'[10]

Several days later Henry wrote to her asking for another copy of a hymn she had transcribed for him, as a sudden gust of wind had blown it into the sea. As a result of that visit to Lydia he loved her even more.

On the last day of July, Henry was on board the *Union*, ready for departure, but the announcement was made that the fleet would remain where it was as Lord Nelson had not returned to take command, and there was a real danger of a French invasion. Henry was told that if war broke out he was to assist the surgeons with the injured.

Now he began to speak in Hindustani to several Lascars in the crew. (The name 'Lascar' was given to native sailors from the East Indies working on European ships.) He was overjoyed when he found that they understood him, but saddened when he realized that those on board had no interest in the gospel.

Believing that the fleet would remain where it was for some time, Henry decided to visit Lydia once again. When he called at her house on 8 August, she was not at home, but he set out to meet her and was encouraged by her reception of him. He visited her again on 10 August, but, just as he was conducting morning devotions with Lydia and her mother, reading Psalm 10 and a passage from a Bible commentary, he received an urgent message that the fleet was about to sail and that he must return immediately. He recorded that when Lydia came out to bid him farewell, he said 'that if it should appear to be God's will that I should be married, she must not be offended at receiving a letter from me,' adding that 'she made no objection whatever to coming out'.[11]

On the other hand, Lydia's own record of the event shows that marriage was not on her mind: 'I hope ... that it is clearly now understood between us that he is free to marry where he is going, and I have felt quite resigned to the will of God in this, and shall often pray the Lord to find him a suitable partner...'[12] Those words were hardly the words of one who was in love.

Henry in fact arrived back at the *Union* with plenty of time to spare as a tangled anchor line prevented departure until the following day.

At last he was on his way to India, to serve the Lord there. He prayed that the Holy Spirit would rescue many who were trapped in the kingdom of darkness, and transfer them to the kingdom of righteousness. As the *Union* made its way out to sea, he knew that soon a vast distance would separate him from those he loved — especially Lydia.

# 7.
# Hard times

Worship on the *Union* proved
very difficult to conduct...
'Some attended fixedly —
others are looking another
way — some women are
employed about their children
... some rising up and going
away ... and numbers ...
strewed all along upon the
deck fast asleep.'

# 7.
# Hard times

It was the start of a new life for Henry: he was responsible for the spiritual welfare of all on board the *Union*. Almost immediately, however, his plans came to nothing. When he asked permission to conduct daily worship, the captain informed him that once a week was all he could allow, as sailors on night duty needed to rest during the day. Worship services would interfere with the rest of those who slept on the deck. Henry had hoped to see many won to Christ through consistent preaching of the gospel, but now he knew that his chief hope of winning souls to Christ would be through personal contact.

For his first sermon on board he took the text: 'But now they desire a better, that is, a heavenly country. Therefore God is not ashamed to be called their God, for he has prepared a city for them' (Hebrews 11:16). His first words were to be: '… now the shores of England [are] receding fast from our view, and … we [have] taken a long, and to many of us, an everlasting farewell…'[1] Later there were tears in his eyes as he sat at his table. England, with all his friends, relatives and his beloved Lydia, had disappeared over the horizon and he felt so alone — at that time he believed he was the only Christian on board. There were times when he wondered whether he had done the right thing in leaving England as an unmarried man. He frequently meditated upon Christ's words to the seventy that they were to

take the gospel 'two by two' (Luke 10:1). He knew the wise
words of Ecclesiastes 4:9-11:

Two are better than one,
Because they have a good reward for their labour.
For if they fall, one will lift up his companion.
But woe to him who is alone when he falls,
For he has no one to help him up.

Frequently he spent time on his knees praying that the
gospel might win those on board to Christ. He continually
prayed for the blessing of God on the heathen in India and that
the missionaries already there would see many turn to Christ.
He was only a fair-weather sailor and during the many periods
of seasickness his thoughts turned to death and heaven.

Before too long Henry found that there were several other
Christians on board, including a cadet officer, Mr McKenzie,
who loved the Saviour and sought Henry's friendship many
times.

Following the second service that he held, Henry heard that
his sermon was offensive because of its Calvinistic doctrine.
Calvinism rightly interprets the scriptural revelation that salvation is all of God. Those on board heard that sinners were
unable to save themselves and that God had chosen a people
(the elect) to be his own. Christ, the Son of God, had come into
the world both to live a life of perfect obedience to God on their
behalf and to die upon that cursed Roman cross, accepting the
punishment due to all those whose names were written in the
Lamb's book of life. Even then sinners could not approach God
for salvation until the Holy Spirit brought about the new birth in
their hearts. This doctrine was not what the rough sailors and
soldiers wanted to hear. They wanted to be told that they could
earn their salvation by what they considered were good actions.

Of course, there were others who had no interest whatever
in an afterlife and just lived for their own pleasure. The doctrine

of hell was treated with contempt. The idea of eternal punishment for sin was considered vile.

There were complaints that his sermons were too hard to be understood by the uneducated, young cadets, soldiers and their families and the sailors on board. To overcome the problem, the ship's mate asked if the worship service could be conducted without a sermon.

On 14 August the flotilla was safely anchored in the Cove of Cork, Ireland, the first port of call. Henry devoted an afternoon to prayer and later wrote, 'My fervent prayer was that I might be more deeply and habitually convinced of [God's] unchanging, everlasting love, and that my whole soul might be altogether in Christ... I wanted to be all in Christ, and to have Christ for my "all in all" — to be encircled in his everlasting arms, and to be swallowed up altogether in his fulness ... to be one with Thee, and live for Thee, O God, my Saviour and Lord.'[2]

Going ashore, he asked if he could preach in the local Anglican churches, but the answer was 'No'. He received the same answer when he asked permission to conduct worship with the female convicts on board the *Pitt*, which was sailing to Botany Bay.

On one trip ashore, he saw what he described as the 'most horrid spectacle'[3] he had ever seen. The remains of two murderers were hanging in chains from supports. Bones were poking through their clothes, and one skull still had some hair and teeth hanging from it. As he moved away he meditated upon his God-given task and reflected that God had 'sent me as a sheep among wolves'.[4]

Worship on the *Union* proved very difficult to conduct. Henry started visiting the sick below decks, and commenced a reading of *Pilgrim's Progress* and other Christian books to any who cared to listen. 'Some attended fixedly — others are looking another way — some women are employed about their children, attending for a little while ... some rising up and going away — others taking their place; and numbers, especially of those who have been upon watch, strewed all along upon the

deck fast asleep — one or two from the upper decks looking
down and listening.'[5] He also organized a small group to sing
songs of praise to the passengers.

In the midst of all these activities he was plagued by his
besetting sin of pride — knowing as he did that he was intellec-
tually superior to most if not all of those on board — and
pleaded with God for forgiveness.

On 28 August the order was given for the ships to set sail,
but all too soon the strong westerly wind made headway
impossible and the ships returned to port. The strong wind
whipped up the seas again, making Henry seasick. He wrote in
his journal, 'Nothing but death and heaven appeared as a
pleasant end in view.'[6] He spent time in prayer and in reading
the Acts of the Apostles and the biography of David Brainerd.
He also gave time to the study of Hindustani.

On 31 August he awoke, once again feeling sick and with a
severe headache, but it was time for the fleet of 150 ships,
commanded by Sir John Baird, to set sail. The next port of call
was to be Madeira. Only the senior officers had any idea of the
route being sailed to avoid the French fleet; nor were the sailors
and soldiers aware of their destination.

The fleet was accompanied by two men-of-war, the *Diadem*
and the *Belliquese*, each carrying sixty-four guns. They were
small by comparison with Nelson's *Victory*, which carried 100
guns. There were also two frigates, the *Leda* and the *Narcissus*.
This was all that could be spared as all other war ships were
needed to repel the French and Spanish fleets.

Henry spent time daily in private worship, especially reading
and meditating upon the book of Isaiah. Chapters 60 and 66 of
that prophecy were his constant companions. And day after
day, with little break, he suffered from seasickness. Sometimes
he was so ill that he believed he would not live to see India, let
alone be fit enough to go below deck to minister to the sick.
Nevertheless, he took comfort in the words of the apostle Paul,
who said, 'I have learned in whatever state I am, to be content,'

and 'I can do all things through Christ who strengthens me' (Philippians 4:11,13).

As the winds increased in strength, the *Union* fell behind the rest, as she was one of the heaviest vessels in the fleet. On 7 September, Henry was again very ill when he awoke. After some time on deck he returned to his cabin, which was awash with salt water that was coming in through a broken porthole. The following day he woke up feeling 'sick in body and wounded in spirit'.[7]

As the seas calmed, Henry could see the rest of the fleet and made the attempt to read to the passengers between decks, but this was made impossible as the sailors were cleaning up after the stormy weather. A week later he preached on the subject of hell and this was not well received. One person told him he had heard someone comment: 'Mr Martyn sends us to hell every Sunday.'[8] Another man told him that many of those on board 'had become more hostile than ever, saying, they should come up to prayers because they believed I was sincere, but not to the sermon, as I did nothing but preach about hell'.[9]

A high-ranking officer warned him that if he preached again on the subject of 'hell' he would lose his congregation. Henry refused to be daunted and took for his text Psalm 9:17: 'The wicked shall be turned into hell, and all the nations that forget God.' As soon as he announced his text one of the officers got up and walked away to feed the geese, which added to the noise disrupting the service.

He fought a continual battle with pride. Many times he recorded this besetting sin, and his efforts to overcome it: 'Prayed at length for my sister, my brother R— Dr J. E. and Lydia. After praying nearly two hours, my heart seemed to be at last really poor and broken... I pictured myself strutting about the streets and walks of Cambridge, wrapped in content, thinking myself very amiable and admired, as much by others as by myself. Yes, it is pride which surpasses all my other sins, hiding from me the extreme guilt of laziness and lukewarmness.'[10]

Henry Martyn preaching to the ship's company

Henry gave himself to prayer, the study of the Scriptures, sermon preparation, the study of Hindustani, which he practised with the Lascars, and to reading many of the books he had brought with him. In an effort to gain the friendship of those on board, he offered to hold classes in mathematics, French and the classical writings that he loved, but few showed any interest.

Often he gazed out across the ocean as the sun sank below the horizon, thinking that the day would soon come when he would be in that land where the sun would never set. He thought a lot about his friends in England, especially Lydia, but despite his loneliness he longed to be about the Saviour's business in India.

On 28 September, Madeira appeared on the horizon and, as he watched, he thought of the land the saints would one day occupy. In his journal he wrote a few lines from a hymn:

> By faith I see the land,
> With peace and plenty blest;
> A land of sacred liberty
> And endless rest.[11]

The fleet dropped anchor near Funchal. It was the Lord's Day, but worship was not permitted as the sailors had work to do. Henry went ashore and made his way into a Roman Catholic church. He was shocked to see the members of the congregation talking to one another during the service, while others were laughing loudly. When he saw the incense burning and a priest crossing himself he asked himself, 'Is it possible … that this should be a Christian church?'[12]

That night he dined with about twenty people including officers and their wives. He was unhappy because of all the worldly talk at the table and was surprised at the amount of food served, especially the wide variety of fruit — apples, bananas, pears and grapes, with raisins, walnuts and almonds.

Several days later, the senior officer called a meeting of officers (including Henry) aboard the *Diadem*, at which they were told the reason for the large number of soldiers on board the ships. The British government had decided to take the Cape of Good Hope from the Dutch, as it was of strategic importance for the large number of British ships that sailed via the Cape to the Middle and Far East. Now more than ever, Henry saw the urgency of preaching the gospel. He feared that some soldiers on board the *Union* might be killed in the ensuing battle.

While the sailors were making preparations for the next leg of their journey, he seized every opportunity to defend the cause of Christ, speaking out to those who mocked the gospel with their oaths and blasphemies. He also took time to write to his friends in England.

Soon all the ships were ready to weigh anchor. Fresh water and supplies, including two dozen bottles of good Madeira wine for the sick, were carefully stowed away on the *Union*.

On 3 October the huge fleet set sail into the Atlantic Ocean, making the distance between Henry and those whom he loved much greater than before. On board each soldier was given sixty rounds of ammunition in preparation for war. On the Lord's Day the men were paraded, which again meant that Henry could not preach the gospel to the ship's company. Of the soldiers he wrote in his journal, 'Poor souls, now that they are to take the field while I am with them, how anxiously should I watch over them. I said to Captain — "... what godly men your soldiers ought to be, who may be so suddenly called upon to give up [their] account!" '[13] To this the captain replied that he was not afraid of what lay before him. He had no interest in turning to Christ!

Following the parade on deck, many soldiers asked Henry concerning the ship's destination — was it the Cape, Tenerife, the West Indies, or Mexico? He had been sworn to secrecy, so he revealed nothing, but began thinking of a much 'better country, where there would be no more war or bloodshed'.[14]

# 8.
# San Salvador:
# a pleasant stopover

He afterwards wrote,
'A slave in my bedroom
washed my feet. I was
struck with the degree of
abasement expressed in the
act, and ... I remembered
the condescension of the
blessed Lord. May I have
grace to follow such
humility!'

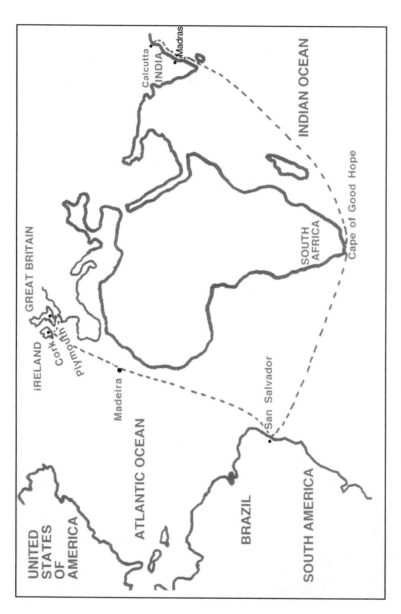

Map showing the route of Henry Martyn's voyage to India

# 8.
# San Salvador: a pleasant stopover

On Sunday, 6 October 1805, Henry preached on the text: 'Jesus answered and said to her, "If you knew the gift of God, and who it is who says to you, 'Give me a drink,' you would have asked him, and he would have given you living water"' (John 4:10). Once again the congregation was inattentive and when Mr McKenzie pointed out defects in his preaching, Henry was discouraged, convinced that he was 'only fit to be a book-worm'.[1] When further criticisms were directed at him, he was even more discouraged, but rejoiced that he could spend time in prayer with his God, who listened.

On 10 October, the *Union*, with other ships, crossed the Tropic of Cancer, heading for San Salvador, in order to avoid a confrontation with the French fleet. Henry spent hours gazing in amazement at the flying fish. He recorded: 'The poor little things are emblems of my soul. They rise to a little height, but in a minute or two their fins are dry, and then they drop into the waves.'[2]

Meanwhile, Henry's small choir was an encouragement, as they were often below deck, singing well-known hymns and psalms to those who had their sleeping quarters there. Yet he was disappointed at his own lack of courage. On one occasion when he wanted to give a bundle of tracts to the captain of the ship bound for Botany Bay, he walked silently away. He didn't have the courage to interrupt the captain, who was discussing plans with other high-ranking men. And frequently during those day-to-day activities, he found his thoughts turning to Lydia and wondered whether he had been right in deciding to sail for India alone.

Without warning, on 21 October, the fleet, all unaware of the decisive battle that was being fought that same day off Trafalgar under the leadership of Lord Nelson, sailed into a severe squall. The planking and ropes began to moan as the wind howled through the rigging. Henry feared that the ship might sink with all lives lost, but the Lord quietened the wind and waves, which made sailing a pleasure.

On 30 October the *Union* crossed the equator, almost coming to grief. The ship's alert night watch spotted a rocky reef with big waves breaking about it. Only the quick action of the captain saved the vessel from disaster. Later it was learned that two other ships had run aground with some loss of life.

1 November was a day for Henry to remember — it was on that day that Mr McKenzie first prayed with him for missionary endeavour worldwide, especially in India, and gave thanks for God's protective care. Meanwhile the weekly worship services were still disrupted by those who came and left partway through, many of them making rude comments for all to hear. One day he met a soldier who had been particularly offensive during the service. He decided that he would not let that rudeness pass and wrote in his journal, 'B. broached the most blasphemous and abominable sentiments; said he was deter-mined he would never pray, for if he did, he should not be able to fight; that he was a soldier, and robbery was his business; that he would rob his father for grog; that he had often robbed, and would continue to do so.' Henry continued: 'I shuddered at this wretched bravado, but persisted in showing the folly and madness of all these thoughts, till the ringleader, B. rose up and went his way, and then the rest listened to me in silence.'[3]

On the Lord's Day, 10 November, a strange sail could be seen some miles away and, as the *Union,* the heaviest ship, had fallen some miles behind the rest of the fleet, the soldiers were given ten rounds of ball cartridges in case they were attacked. It was feared that the ship they had sighted might be a pirate vessel looking for treasure. When Henry spoke to the captain and was told that they would fight, if necessary until the ship went down, he felt much easier. However, there was a general sigh of relief when the ship turned away.

The next day a pilot came aboard, to guide the ship through the numerous reefs to the San Salvador harbour. The fleet had sailed across the Atlantic, to avoid meeting the French fleet. After five weeks at sea everyone longed to be put ashore, and this included Henry! The first thing he noticed were the Negro slaves going about their business. To him they appeared to be a healthy, happy people. He also observed with pleasure the many varieties of fruit that were for sale — water melons, pawpaws, limes, bananas, oranges and tamarinds.

Soon he was surrounded by people who began asking questions. 'Are the English baptized?' asked one. Henry replied that he was English and had been baptized. Standing there, he thought, 'I am one of those supposed heretics who has a precious gospel entrusted to him which he would preach to you if he could.'[4]

Feeling weary, he began to search out a quiet place where he could rest. Spotting an orchard with an open gate and a pathway leading to a house, he walked in and, seeing some of the slaves watching him, made his way to the house. The slaves directed him to a spot in the garden where an old man was sitting under a tree. Unfortunately, the lack of a common language was a barrier to communication. However, a young man and woman soon appeared on the scene and Henry found he was able to converse with them in French. They invited him to sit down at a small table, where he was served some fruit, while the young man began a discussion about Cambridge

University. Antonio Corrè was a graduate of a Portuguese university and he thought very highly of Cambridge.

Henry was invited to visit the house whenever he wished, and after eating the fruit he was shown around the property, where he saw coffee plants growing. Later, as he left for the *Union*, he was once more invited to come again. Unfortunately this proved impossible the following day owing to a violent storm, but the day after Antonio welcomed him to his home, where he dined with his host. He was interested to observe the local customs, although he found much of the food not to his taste.

On another occasion Antonio took him to visit a Carmelite monastery, where he was introduced as a man who knew everything! Henry tried to speak to one of the priests in Latin, but the man had no knowledge of the language. Henry was sorry to have caused him embarrassment.

Later, as they returned to the house, Antonio told Henry that he wanted his son to study at a British university. In the house Henry was shown to his bedroom, where a slave came to wash his feet. He afterwards wrote, 'A slave in my bedroom washed my feet. I was struck with the degree of abasement expressed in the act, and as he held the foot in the towel, with his head bowed down towards it, I remembered the condescension of the blessed Lord. May I have grace to follow such humility!'[5]

During his stay he took every opportunity to speak of Christ and to point people to the teaching of the Scriptures, but was embarrassed when a retired major from the Portuguese army asked if the British army had pastors to give spiritual aid to dying soldiers. When Henry had to admit that this was not the case, the major shrugged his shoulders in horror. Later he spent time talking to some Franciscan friars, discussing various points of doctrine and showing that the teachings of their church were contrary to Scripture.

While in San Salvador Henry saw pepper and tapioca being grown and was shown how the tapioca was prepared for eating. He was particularly interested to see the natural beauty of the area. He also made time to write to his relatives and friends in England.

On his return to the *Union,* he found the Lascars dressed in white and singing hymns to Mohammed in commemoration of the *Hegira* (Mohammed's flight from Mecca in AD 622. Muslims calculate their calendar beginning on 16 July 622). When he pointed out some of the errors in their religion to the man sitting next to him and began to explain the gospel, he received the reply that all that was necessary was for a person to live a good, sober and honest life. At this Henry 'turned away, and, with a deep sigh, cried to God to interfere in behalf of his Gospel'. He went on to write, 'In the course of one hour I had seen three shocking examples of the reign and power of the devil, in the form of Popish and Mohammedan delusion, and that of the natural man... All my clear arguments are good for nothing: unless the Lord stretch out his hand I speak to stones. I felt, however, no way discouraged; but only saw the necessity of dependence on God.'[6]

In addition to the time on shore, he was also called upon to carry out his duties as chaplain to the fleet. On the *Pitt* he baptized a baby. While he was on board he also took the opportunity to distribute tracts and twenty New Testaments to the women convicts. Before he left, the captain invited him to visit the ship whenever he could in order to give spiritual guidance and counsel.

Before they left San Salvador he was called upon to bury a man who had been killed in a brawl. Another man was seriously injured and three others made good their escape from the *Glory.* Henry's comment on the events was: 'Oh, in what a state are they hurried to judgement!'[7]

Despite all these calls upon his time, Henry continued to study the Scriptures and pray, which proved a real blessing to his soul.

On 28 November the fleet set sail on its long journey to the Cape of Good Hope. Henry's fortnight in San Salvador had been a time of spiritual and physical refreshment.

## 9.
# The Cape of Good Hope at last!

Before they parted company, Henry asked Dr Vanderkemp if he ever regretted becoming a missionary. The old man smiled. 'No,' he said, 'and I would not exchange my work for a kingdom.'

# 9
# The Cape of Good Hope at last!

The journey to South Africa was marked by bouts of seasickness, again proving that Henry was only a fair-weather sailor. Strangely, however, when a gale struck the fleet in late November he didn't succumb to this 'enemy', as he called it. As the storm raged, the sailors battened down the hatches and anything that was likely to be washed overboard. The usual Lord's Day services could not be held, but he spoke to three men who had been rescued from the *Britannia*, which had sunk. The men showed no interest in his words about the Day of Judgement, and changed the subject whenever he spoke of Christ and the gospel.

Many times during the long evenings he thought of his friends back in England, but he was willing to turn his back on the world, his friends and relatives in order to bring glory to his God and Redeemer. Of Lydia he wrote, 'Still the glory of God, and the salvation of immortal souls, is an object for which I can part with thee.'[1] Many times his thoughts turned to her and on one occasion, he wrote in his journal, 'My mind has been running on Lydia, and the happy scenes in England, very much; particularly on that day when I walked with her on the seashore, and with a wistful eye looked over the blue waves that were to bear me from her.'[2]

On board the *Union*, he visited the sick and on one occasion when he stood at the bedside of the ship's steward, who was seriously ill, the lamp which he used for reading flickered, and almost went out, because the air was so foul. Services were held when possible, but he faced a continual barrage of snide comments and other disruptive activities aimed to interrupt him in what he was saying. Frequently he called the troublemakers aside and warned them of the judgement to come, but usually they replied with crude comments. The services held soon after lunch proved a failure, as the members of the small congregation kept falling asleep.

Once Mr McKenzie brought a corporal with him to Henry's cabin. When it was suggested that both men come regularly for a time of prayer, objections were raised. They claimed they were not afraid of following Christ, but feared the trials and tribulations the cross would bring.

When dysentery broke out on board, Henry felt so ill that his thoughts turned to death and the glory of heaven. He went on to write, 'I had so much delight and joy in the consideration of heaven, and my assured title to it, that I felt far more desirous of dying than living.'[3]

His health improved sufficiently for him to conduct worship on Sunday, 22 December 1805. His congregation was larger than usual, but once again he heard critical comments about his preaching from those who had been present. While disappointed, he was thankful that he had preached the pure gospel. In the afternoon he spoke to more than fifty men and women, taking as his text Matthew 12:42, concerning the Queen of Sheba, who travelled a great distance to visit Solomon. He was saddened by the fact that others were unwilling to walk the few yards to hear about the King of kings.

On Christmas Day he was permitted to hold public prayers, but not to preach a sermon. The ship's captain was ill and close to death, so after prayers, Henry made his way to the captain's cabin. When the captain saw him, he ordered him away. The following day Henry again entered the cabin, but this time the man was too ill to speak. Henry read Isaiah 55 and John 6 to the dying captain. The man died with a short prayer upon his lips: 'I am going; I shall not be long here; Lord help me, Lord help me.'[4] It was then Henry's task to read the burial service for the dead captain at sea.

That same day he meditated upon God's punishment of sinners in eternal hell: 'The passages of God's holy word that proved the certainty of hell torments, were brought to me in such a way as I never before felt; I flew trembling to Jesus Christ, as if the flame were taking hold of me. Oh, Christ will indeed save me, or else I perish.'[5]

29 December was the last Lord's Day of 1805, and he recorded some thoughts in his journal: 'Ah! why cannot I rise and go forth and meet my Lord? Every hindrance is removed; the wrath of God, the guilt of sin, and severity of affliction: there is nothing now in the world that has any strong hold of my affections... I have nothing to distract me from hearing the voice of my beloved, and coming away from this world and walking with him in love, amidst the flowers that perfume the air of Paradise, and the harmony of the happy spirits who are singing his praise.'[6]

The new year, 1806, meant that he had been travelling for about six months. Everyone on board, including Henry, longed to set foot on land once again. On 3 January, after prayers and the evening service, the Cape of Good Hope could be seen in the distance.

The following day, as the sun was setting, the fleet dropped anchor between Robber's Island and the mainland. The soldiers were given thirty-six rounds of ball cartridges and commanded to prepare to land. Soon boatloads of well-armed men were heading for the beach, but the rough seas forced them to return to the safety of the ships. Several men asked Henry to draw up new wills for them in case they were killed in action.

On 6 January, a landing was made while the two British men-of-war sailed back and forth giving whatever protection they could to the soldiers who were moving inland. During the landing, one boatload of sixty-three men struck a rocky outcrop. Only eleven reached the shore in safety. Henry sought permission to accompany the soldiers in order to give spiritual comfort to the injured and dying, but this was refused. All he could do was pray for all the men involved in the fighting. On board he felt the cabin window and door shake every time rounds were fired from each of the two gun-brigs on the commodore's ship.

The next day the spectators on the ships witnessed a fearful demonstration of firepower. Henry wrote, 'Soon after seven, a most tremendous fire of Artillery began behind a mountain abreast of the ship; it seemed as if the mountain itself were torn by intestine convulsions. The smoke rose from a lesser eminence on the right of the hill, and on the top of it, troops were seen rushing down the farther declivity; then came such a long-drawn fire of musketry, that I could not have conceived anything like it. We all shuddered at considering what a multitude of souls must be passing into eternity.'[7] As it turned out, none of the soldiers travelling on the *Union* were killed.

At last Henry was able to make his way ashore, and after attaching himself to a group of cadets, trekked almost six miles through hot, soft sand. Finding a Highlander who had hip injuries, the cadets rendered first aid and then carried him back to a field hospital. As the rest moved on they came across some bodies. Most of the soldiers were dead, but, finding one person still alive, Henry urged him to turn to Christ and be saved. He received nothing but curses by way of reply.

Making his way to one field hospital, Henry asked an injured Dutch captain where he could find the well-known missionary Dr Vanderkemp. As no one knew the doctor's whereabouts, he moved on to other hospitals, where he learned that the Dutch had suffered casualties of 200 injured men, all of whom were being treated by the British doctors at the field hospitals.

On his way back to the scene of the battle, Henry was assisting an injured Hottentot when he was approached by a drunken Highlander, who accused him of being French. Taking out his gun, the man was about to kill Henry, who told him he was a British clergyman. He added that, if the man didn't believe what he said, he should be taken to the British camp as a prisoner. Everything changed when a doctor arrived on the scene and recognized Henry. Then, after examining the badly injured man whom Henry had been trying to help, the doctor said nothing could be done for him. He was simply left there to die!

Later, Henry sat down and, while looking over the battle-field, prayed to the God of peace. He thanked the Lord that he had witnessed such a terrible sight, because once again he had seen the reality of fallen human nature, and he longed for the day when God's love would permeate the hearts of all, when 'Nation shall not lift up sword against nation, neither shall they learn war any more' (Isaiah 2:4).

On 10 January 1806, the British flag flew over the Dutch fort, the Dutch commander having ordered his men to retreat, as he could see that the British forces greatly outnumbered his own. Despite efforts to bring about peace between the warring factions, the battle resulted in a sickening toll — 600 Dutch nationals had been injured or killed, with British casualties numbering fifteen dead, 189 wounded and eight missing. As the soldiers returned to their ships, Henry was distressed to hear them boasting of their victory and their personal acts of gal-lantry. He longed to see Britain not just as a military power but as a people distinguished for godliness, whose missionaries took the gospel worldwide.

On 13 January he found some accommodation, and in the evening he finally met Dr Vanderkemp, an elderly man who was surrounded by native Africans. Henry introduced himself to the missionary and another man, a Mr Read. Henry spent several happy days in fellowship with the missionaries. Before they parted company, Henry asked Dr Vanderkemp if he ever regretted becoming a missionary. The old man smiled. 'No,' he said, 'and I would not exchange my work for a kingdom.'[8]

On 23 January, Henry returned to the *Union*, expecting that the fleet would soon be leaving the Cape. The small boat being used to ferry him to the ship was hit by an unusually large wave. Of that incident Henry recorded: 'Oh! may I love and serve him with all my soul, till I "reach that blissful shore, where storms and danger shall be known no more".'[9]

When the departure date was delayed, Henry again went ashore to mix with the friends he had made, and see more of the Cape. He conducted worship at Dr Vanderkemp's home, and later climbed to the top of Table Mountain. There he was able to gaze out upon the spot where the great Indian and Atlantic Oceans met.

There were times when he felt very lonely despite being often in company. He missed his friends back at home and sometimes felt that all that was happening was strange: 'It seemed like a dream — that I had actually undergone banishment from them for life... But at this time I solemnly renewed my self-dedication to God; praying that I might receive grace to spend my days in his service, in continued suffering, and separation from all I held most dear in this life.'[10]

Before the fleet departed for their various destinations, Henry sought permission to hold a service on the convict ship, *Pitt*, but this was refused on the grounds that they were too busy.

After farewells with his new friends at the Cape, he returned to the *Union* and tidied his cabin in preparation for the long trip to India. On Sunday, 9 February, the ships bound for India and the Far East sailed from South Africa.

# 10.
# India ahoy!

19 April 1806 was a day
... to remember — after
ten weeks at sea, he saw in
the distance the island of
Ceylon... Standing on
deck, Henry caught the
scent of some of the plants
and longed to stand once
again on land...

# 10.
# *India ahoy!*

After sunset on the first night back at sea, Henry and Mr McKenzie spent time praying for everyone on board, and for the mission work being undertaken throughout the world, especially in India. During the night the wind picked up and the next morning Henry was seasick once more. So sick was he that he could do little more than sit in his chair, unable even to change his clothes. When a sail appeared on the horizon and the *Union* turned to give chase, he felt much better with the wind and waves coming astern. However, when the distant ship turned out to be one owned by the East India Company, the *Union* turned back and continued on her course for India.

Henry was very disappointed that he could see no fruit for his labours on board. He was often mocked, while others simply ignored him. He was distressed that the people treated Christ, and the gospel he loved, with contempt. 'I go down,' he wrote, 'and stand in the midst of a few, without their taking the slightest notice of me: Lord, it is for thy sake I suffer such slights — let me persevere notwithstanding.'[1] All he could do was leave the outcome of his labours in the hands of the Lord.

Dysentery broke out again, and Henry fell ill and for a time was confined to his cabin. Realizing that those below deck suffered far more than he did, he sent them much of his food, water and wine, in the hope that they would improve in health as a result of the better-quality food. In early April he sought the captain's permission to send all his food below deck to the sick, offering to eat 'junk' (the tough, very salty meat eaten by the sailors) instead. Several other passengers agreed to do the same, but the captain refused. The cook had used the last of the wine and tea, and the captain feared trouble if the best of the remaining food was sent to the sick.

Henry found that each day he was growing closer to God. His prayers were a time of joy: 'I do not know that anything would be a heaven to me, but the service of Christ and the enjoyment of his presence. Oh how sweet is life, when spent in his service!'[2]

On 18 February 1806 it was Henry's twenty-fifth birthday. He spent the day in prayer, meditation, the preparation of a sermon, the study of Hindustani, and in visiting a sick person. His life was very busy!

Despite all his efforts to assist those on board, he was the subject of cruel remarks. Many clergymen had used their time in India to accumulate riches for themselves, and the sailors and soldiers believed Henry to be no different. He was criticized because of his large salary and the opportunity he would have to amass a fortune when in India. Mr McKenzie told him what others were saying: 'Martyn, as well as the rest, can share the plunder of the natives of India; whether it is just or not he does not care.'[3]

Life on board the *Union* was very tense at times. Living below deck, especially with families, proved stressful, with the result that one soldier committed suicide by jumping overboard. Arguments broke out frequently and sickness was common. When deaths occurred it fell to Henry to conduct the funeral services. On several occasions men died without his having been aware that they were ill.

The weather varied greatly as the *Union* made its way across the Indian Ocean. There were times of strong winds and rough seas, which caused seasickness, pleasant times when the ship travelled along smoothly and also periods when the ship was becalmed. One of these occurred when they were in the vicinity of the equator. The weather was both hot and humid, which was not to Henry's liking. He recorded in his journal: 'I have nothing to attract me to this life, and therefore why should I not be refreshed at the thought of death?' The atmosphere below decks was so foul that he could only spend a couple of minutes at a time down there helping the sick. So unhealthy were the conditions that the captain made everyone whose quarters were below the deck come up while the fresh air was allowed to penetrate right down to the lowest deck, the orlop.

Once again Henry heard critical remarks about his sermons — few could understand what he was talking about. This caused him much stress. However, he was called to the side of a young man who was expected to die, and there spoke to him of sin and a Saviour. At the time the man's response was a great encouragement to Henry, but, sadly, when he recovered, he turned his back upon both the gospel and Henry himself.

19 April 1806 was a day for all on board to remember — after ten weeks at sea, he saw in the distance the island of Ceylon (now Sri Lanka). Standing on deck, Henry caught the scent of some of the plants and longed to stand once again on land, but the wind dropped and the ship was again becalmed. The hot, humid weather caused breathing difficulties and he began once more to think of death. He wrote, 'Come what will, it shall be best for me; if I die, I die to be happy — if I live, I shall live to glorify God. Sweet necessity!

'All must come, and last, and end,
As shall please my heavenly Friend.'[4]

On Sunday, 20 April, he preached using as his text Revelation 22:17: 'And the Spirit and the bride say, "Come!" And let him who hears say, "Come!" And let him who thirsts come. Whoever desires, let him take the water of life freely.' Believing that this would be his last opportunity to preach to many of the passengers on the *Union*, he preached a solemn farewell message, yet the men and women who had mocked and ridiculed him during the course of the journey continued to do so to the very end: 'It pained me that they should give a ridiculous turn to anything on so affecting an occasion as that of parting for ever in this life... Yet I desire to take the ridicule of men with all meekness and charity, looking forward to another world for approbation and reward.'[5]

The following day, Monday, 21 April, was a day for Henry to remember. When he walked onto the deck he was overjoyed to see the coast of India. The Union was off Tranquebar, and during the course of the day sailed past Cuddalore and Pondicherry.

Tuesday was a further milestone in his life — at sunrise the Union dropped anchor off Madras. He was about to begin his service for the Lord in India, where the name of Christ was unknown, except to a small number who had some contact with the few missionaries who had already come to their land. He recorded in his journal how he felt concerning the work that lay before him: 'Oh the awfulness of the ministry! How shall I ever be pure from the blood of all men? I do nothing all the day but in reference to my ministry... O my God, there is nought upon earth that I care for, but thee, and thine...'[6]

Then it was into the small boat with his belongings, and so to the shore, where he was quickly surrounded by a crowd of coolies (as the local unskilled labourers were called) all eager to carry his possessions — at a price! Suddenly he found that various articles of his property were going off in all directions, until he managed to restore order and made his way to the customs' house, accompanied by several porters, who had attached themselves to him of their own accord, without consulting his wishes on the matter!

He carried with him a letter of recommendation from Charles Simeon to the Rev. Dr Kerr, a minister at Madras, which included the words: 'Our excellent friend, Mr Martyn, lived five months with me, and a more heavenly-minded young man I never saw.'[7]

Boats in the surf off Madras

That night, at dinner, the Europeans were waited on by at least a dozen Indians. Later Dr Kerr took Henry to visit some of the schools that had been established. He also saw a publishing house where about 300 Indians were at work, printing, engraving and carrying out a multitude of tasks.

Wanting to see something of the local countryside, Henry walked with his new servant, Samees, to the latter's native village, which had been untouched by European ways. Henry later recorded his thoughts on seeing it: 'Here all was Indian — no vestige of anything European. It consisted of about two hundred houses — those in the main street connected, and those on either side of the street separated from one another by little winding paths. Everything presented the appearance of wretchedness... The sight of men, women, and children, all idolaters, makes me shudder, as if in the dominions of the Prince of Darkness. I fancy the frown of God to be visible; there is something peculiarly awful in the stillness that prevails.'[8]

The following day was the Lord's Day, Henry's first in India. He was invited to preach at the Fort St George church, and took as his text Luke 10:41: 'And Jesus answered and said to her, "Martha, Martha, you are worried and troubled about many things. But one thing is needed, and Mary has chosen that good part, which will not be taken away from her."' Henry was encouraged to see that the congregation paid close attention to all he said, and after the service, Lord William, the Governor of Madras, paid him the compliment of asking for a copy of his sermon. The next day Sir E. Pellow, the Port Admiral at Madras, greeted him with the words: 'Upon my word, Mr Martyn, you gave us a good trimming yesterday.'[9]

After lunch on the Sunday Henry was taken to a chapel where the service was conducted in the Malabar language. It was so very hot that he sat in the doorway, where there was a slight breeze. He recorded his joy at hearing the gospel preached in India and joining in the singing of praise to God.

On the Monday, 28 April, he walked to Dr Kerr's home. On the way, across fields which reminded him of the countryside

around Cambridge, he stopped to watch some people plough-
ing and others who were collecting a juice called 'toddy' from a
palm tree. (This would be used to make a highly alcoholic
liquor.)

In the course of their conversation, Dr Kerr gave him a good
deal of information about India and her people, as well as the
work of missionaries there. Later he heard some Portuguese
children singing the hymn, 'Before Jehovah's awful throne'.
The words reminded Henry of the majesty and greatness of the
God he served, especially the line: 'Wide as the world is thy
command.'[10] In the darkness of the night Henry's thoughts
turned to the spiritual darkness of India.

The next day he walked inland to visit a Mr Torriano. The
temperature was well over 100° F (over 36° C), but he was kept
cool by two servants who sprinkled him with cool water. He
also spent time studying the language and praying that God
would bless his labours in India. He knew success depended
upon the gracious work of the Holy Spirit, and for this he
prayed continually.

All too soon it was time for the *Union* and the remaining
ships to set sail once more. On Saturday, 3 May, Henry was
safe in his cabin, having packed his belongings, ready for the
last part of his journey. The fleet was sailing for the Hooghly
River, and then to Calcutta, accompanied by the *Victor*, a war
sloop. Again he found the hot weather very debilitating.
Feeling as he did, he lost all incentive to work and became
depressed. He wrote in his journal, 'I looked forward to an idle,
worthless life spent in India to no purpose — exertion seemed
like death ... but it pleased God afterwards in prayer to afford
me some deliverance, by enabling me to exercise faith, that
though it went so badly with me now, it should by and by be
otherwise...'[11]

# 11.
# Starting work

When he saw other missionaries hard at their work ... he ... recorded in his journal: 'I feel pressed in spirit to do something for God. Everybody is diligent, but I am idle... I have hitherto lived to little purpose ... now let me burn out for God.'

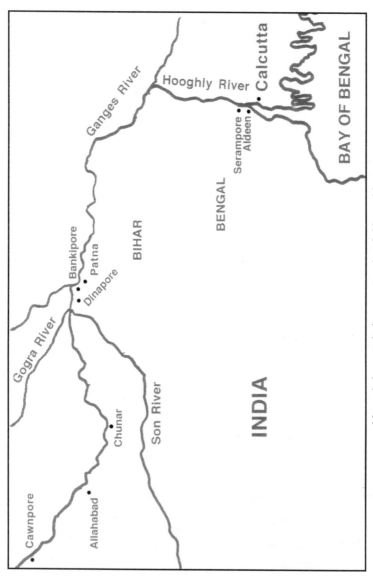

Map of places in India associated with Henry Martyn

# 11.
# Starting work

As the fleet, now reduced in size, made its way along the coast of India, Henry spent time on deck catching sight of places of interest. It wasn't long before everyone on board could see the famous pagoda of the Hindu god Juggernaut (or Jagannatha). (His name means 'the lord of the world'. A pagoda was a tall temple, in the shape of a tower, devoted to the worship of a god and often covered in carvings depicting the god.) Often as the 'car', or chariot, bearing the image of Juggernaut was pulled through the streets in a procession, worshippers were known to throw themselves under the wheels, an action which frequently resulted in death or serious injury. Henry was horrified to see this evidence that the spirits of darkness were so widely worshipped by a spiritually blind people.

When the *Union* arrived at the entrance to the Hooghly River, pilots came aboard to direct the ship through the treacherous waters. With little warning, a hurricane struck, bringing boisterous winds, lightning and the roar of thunder. The ship's sails were torn to shreds and huge waves smashed over the deck. Every effort was made to allow the ship to be driven before the gale-force winds, but everyone on board knew there was a risk of its capsizing, or being driven onto sandbars.

Henry knew that, whatever happened, the Lord was watching over him, yet he experienced a natural fear of drowning. Later he wrote in his journal, 'When nature began to shrink at

The temple of Juggernaut

approaching [death], I was much reconciled to it, by considering, What have I here? Why should I wish to live? Is it not better to go and be with Jesus, and be free from my body of sin and death? But for the sake of the poor unconverted souls in the ship, I prayed earnestly for [the ship's] preservation.'[1] During the stormy weather Henry suffered from sunstroke and severe headaches.

When the wind finally eased, the *Union* dropped anchor and repairs were made. The navigation through the entrance to the river was carried out under the guidance of the pilot, but on 13 May the ship ran aground on a sandbank known as James and Mary. Many ships had come to grief on that shallow sandbar. Henry and two Christian friends went to his cabin, where they prayed for the safety of the ship and those on board. Several hours later, the *Union* floated off the shoal and into deep water, which was cause for praise to God.

The following day they made their way up to Hooghly, about twenty-five miles from Calcutta, where they were met by the *Charlotte*, onto which were loaded valuables from the *Union*. Henry too was transferred to the smaller ship and was able to get a good view of the Indian coastline when the *Charlotte* sailed closer to the shore.

Very soon he arrived at Calcutta and began writing letters to friends back in England. In one letter he wrote, 'My long and wearisome voyage is concluded, and I am at last arrived in the country in which I am to spend my days in the work of the Lord. Scarcely can I believe myself to be so happy as to be actually in India; yet this hath God wrought. Through changing climates, and tempestuous seas, he has brought on his feeble worm to the field of action; and will, I trust, speedily equip me for my work... I sigh to think of the distance that separates us... Day and night I do not cease to pray for you, and I am willing to hope that you also remember me daily at the throne of grace. Let us not, by any means, forget one another...'[2]

Now Henry could only wait to be appointed to a specific post by the officers of the East India Company. He had arrived

in the hottest month of the year, which made life uncomfortable. To make matters worse, there was discontent, and even
some outright opposition, in government circles with regard to
mission work, which was believed to be creating tension
amongst the Indian population.

For some years the leaders of the Christian community in
Calcutta had met weekly to pray for missionaries to be sent to
India, but when Henry stepped ashore, after a journey of
15,000 miles, there was no one to welcome him. David Brown
was at his home in Aldeen, about fifteen miles up the Hooghly
River. Dr Claudius Buchanan had just left to make a tour of the
Syrian Christian churches; in fact the ship in which he was
travelling would have passed the *Union* at the mouth of the
Hooghly River.

Henry decided to visit William Carey, the well-known Baptist
missionary whom he greatly admired. Arriving early, he was
invited to share breakfast with Carey and to join him in family
devotions. These were held in Bengali for the sake of the
servants, but they showed little interest in what was being said.
Then William Carey and his pundit (a learned Brahmin, especially in the Sanskrit language) commenced their translation
work.

Henry made arrangements to travel by boat to Aldeen,
where he hoped to meet David Brown, but before these had
been finalized he received word from David directing him to
stay at the latter's rooms next to the old Calcutta Cathedral.
These rooms had been used as an orphanage for children born
out of wedlock to soldiers. (Interestingly, it was Charles Grant
who had, in younger days, been responsible for the construc-
tion of this building.)

Mary Sherwood (a godly woman who was the wife of the
paymaster of the King's 53rd Regiment of Foot and a well-
known writer, especially of children's books), has left us the
following description of David Brown: 'One day ... that most
excellent of men, the Rev. David Brown, came over to see us
from his country house at Aldeen, near Serampore. Mr Brown

was a fine, tall, handsome, dark man, with a countenance beaming with Christian charity.' She added, 'This was the only time I ever saw him.'[3]

Henry found the rooms comfortable and, while awaiting David Brown's arrival, he devoted time to prayer and reading God's Word. He also began writing to Charles Simeon, but was interrupted when Mr Brown's moonshee arrived. The two men then spent a couple of hours discussing the teachings of Christianity and contrasting them with those of Hinduism. Henry was surprised at the moonshee's knowledge of the Scriptures, which made him believe that India was ripe for the gospel.

Some of the missionaries and chaplains already working in the area urged him to remain in Calcutta, where his translation skills could be put to good use. But Henry was concerned to take the gospel to those living inland, where there were as yet no missionaries. His friends also failed to understand that, as an employee of the East India Company, he had to go wherever he was sent by the company. At least Dr Buchanan understood his desire to take the good news of Christ to Indians living outside the large cities.

When he saw other missionaries hard at their work, while he was still waiting for his appointment, he felt lazy and recorded in his journal: 'I feel pressed in spirit to do something for God. Everybody is diligent, but I am idle; all employed in their proper work, but I tossed in uncertainty; I want nothing but grace; I want to be perfectly holy, and to save myself and those that hear me. I have hitherto lived to little purpose, more like a clod than a servant of God; now let me burn out for God.'[4]

19 May was an important and interesting day for Henry, as he was formally introduced to Sir George Barlow, the acting governor general, and then shown around Fort William College. This school had been built to educate future generations of civil servants. Law and languages were of great importance. Beside the school was a building where 700 guests had sat down to breakfast at the opening ceremony for the college.

Serampore College

Soon Henry was taken by boat to the Browns' home in
Aldeen, sixteen miles (twenty-five kilometres) up river from
Calcutta. On his arrival he was escorted to the mission house
where, after he had been introduced to all the missionaries, 150
guests sat down to tea. Those present gave much time to prayer
and mutual encouragement. They longed for the day when the
name of Christ would be held dear by the peoples of the Far
East.

Henry was to form a close friendship with one of those
whom he met at this time, Joshua Marshman, who was preparing a Chinese dictionary as well as a translation of the Scriptures
into Sanskrit and Gujarati. He was one of three brilliant trans-
lators, William Carey, William Ward and Joshua Marshman, of

whom Henry wrote, 'Three such men, so suited to one another and to their work, are not to be found in the whole world.'[5]

David Brown and his wife had prepared accommodation for Henry at Aldeen — a pagoda that had once been devoted to the worship of the Hindu god Bulhub. The building was near the river and beside the Browns' house. Henry recorded his feelings about living in such a place: 'Thither I retired at night, and really felt something like superstitious dread, at being in a place once inhabited as it were by devils, but yet felt disposed to be triumphantly joyful, that the temple where they were worshipped, was now Christ's oratory. I prayed out aloud to my God, and the echoes returned from the vaulted roof... I like my dwelling much ... it has so many recesses and cells that I can hardly find my way in and out.'[6] He claimed that several years earlier he could never have imagined himself living in such a building. The ceilings were very high and on the brickwork he found carvings representing Hindu gods. David Brown had prepared one room as Henry's study, and in the garden there were many shrubs. Near the entrance was a huge Indian Fig Tree, or banyan tree, under which Henry played with the Brown children and where he rested in the cool shade on the very hot days.

It wasn't long before he fell sick. He was so ill that his mind turned to the reality of death, yet he prayed that he would be given time to preach the gospel to the local inhabitants, especially the Soodars — the lowest of the four Hindu castes.

When he recovered, David Brown took him to a local pagoda, where he watched the worship of the god to whom the pagoda which he had now made his home had formerly been consecrated. Henry was distressed by what he saw and heard. To the accompaniment of the continual beat of drums and the clashing of cymbals, the worshippers were gathered around a wooden idol in the centre of the building, which Henry described as 'a little ugly black image, about two feet high, with a few lights burning round him'. He continued: 'At intervals they prostrated themselves, with their foreheads to the earth. I

Henry Martyn's home at Aldeen

shivered at being in the neighbourhood of hell; my heart was ready to burst at the dreadful state to which the Devil had brought my poor fellow-creatures.'[7] He wished he could speak the local language in order to preach the gospel to the deluded Indians. Joshua Marshman appeared on the scene and began addressing the worshippers, but soon his words were drowned out by loud music.

David Brown later took him to see an idol of Juggernaut paraded through the streets in a 'car', a vehicle decorated with flags and flowers and pulled along by the priests. In the car the Brahmins walked from room to room catching the offerings that were being made to the idol. In return the Brahmins threw garlands of flowers to the worshippers to be worn about their necks. Often the car stopped and the idol was lowered to the ground. Most of the onlookers then bowed to the ground and tapped the earth with their foreheads.

Before long Henry came into contact with one of the cruellest rites of Indian heathenism — 'suttee' (or 'sati') — in which the widow of a dead husband jumped into the cremation flames that were consuming his body. This took place against a background of the most fearful noises being made by the onlookers and their musical instruments. Henry was horrified by this cruel, ungodly practice and the first time he heard the sounds made by a suttee, he ran to the funeral pyre in an attempt to rescue the woman, but arrived too late. All he could do was to watch as the two bodies were reduced to ash.

While he awaited instructions from the East India Company concerning his future, Joshua Marshman urged him to remain in Calcutta until he had a good grasp of Hindustani, and then when he was ready to move inland to take with him several Indian Christians who could preach the gospel and open schools for the children. This was impossible, however, as Henry had no say in the selection of an area in which he would serve the East India Company.

When he preached in the New Church in Calcutta for the first time, on Sunday, 8 June, he took as his text 1 Corinthians

1:23-24: '... but we preach Christ crucified, to the Jews a stumbling block and to the Greeks foolishness, but to those who are called, both Jews and Greeks, Christ the power of God and the wisdom of God.' As he explained his text, he became aware of some whispering between members of the congregation. Others, he noticed, 'became attentive and serious'.[8] The reason for this was that many in the congregation were hearing the gospel for the first time. When Henry told them to look away from themselves and to the Lord Jesus, opposition mounted. Many hated the biblical teaching that salvation was all of God. They believed that salvation was God's reward for living a 'good' life. Yet Henry faithfully preached that salvation was all of God.

In that sermon he told his hearers, 'There is, in every congregation, a large proportion of Jews and Greeks. There are persons who resemble the Jews in self-righteousness; who, after hearing the doctrines of grace insisted on for years, yet see no occasion at all for changing the ground of their hopes. They seek righteousness "not by faith, but as it were by the works of the law; for they stumble at that stumbling-stone" (Romans 9:32); or, perhaps, after going a little way in the profession of the Gospel, they take offence at the rigour of the practice which we require, as if the Gospel did not enjoin it. "This is a hard saying," they complain; "who can hear it?" (John 6:60).'[9]

Henry did not fear opposition to the gospel; he had remained unshakable while travelling to India with a boatload of godless individuals. In Cambridge he had stood firm with Charles Simeon for the Lord and his salvation. What he now suffered was nothing new!

While Henry was ill, a Dr Ward preached a sermon in which he made a personal attack upon Henry and the gospel he preached. He even criticized the evangelical wing of the Church of England and preached against the great Reformation doctrine of justification by faith alone. Henry refused to be drawn into a dispute as he knew what damage would be done to the Christian witness in the area.

A Mr Limerick, who was one of those who preached a gospel of works, also attacked Henry and the Reformation doctrines which he preached, claiming that to say that repentance was the gift of God encouraged men to sit still and wait for God, and that to teach the doctrine of total depravity resulted in sinners throwing up their hands in despair. He ridiculed the doctrine of the imputed righteousness of Christ, arguing that this encouraged people to sin. He attacked Henry personally, saying that his sermons came from a proud heart that lacked Christian love. Another minister openly condemned Henry's sermon that taught 'justification by faith alone'. Others suggested that the congregation didn't want doctrinal sermons but ones on Christian morality.

While awaiting his appointment Henry also conducted worship at St John's Church, which was attended by many of the highly educated British residents. Some stayed away and others mocked him, suggesting he was now trying to exercise authority. He was given the nickname 'a son of thunder'.[10]

However, not everyone was critical of him and what he preached. One chaplain regularly read the Homilies to the congregation. These were some of the official doctrinal statements of the Church of England and they confirmed the doctrines which Henry preached. He wrote, 'Mr —, to the great satisfaction of all serious people, after stating the diversity of opinion which had lately occurred in the pulpit, began to read a homily by way of sermon'; and, on another occasion, 'at the New Church, I read, and Mr — preached the second and third parts of the "Homily on Salvation".'[11] Henry rejoiced at the presentation of biblical truth in this way.

While living at Aldeen, he preached at the old Mission Church for David Brown on twenty-one occasions — thirteen of them on very hot Sundays and in eight weekday services. Much of his time was given to the study of the Indian languages, as he wanted to both speak and write the local languages in order to preach the glorious gospel. He studied Bengali and Hindustani, and soon mastered the Nagree alphabet. Before long, helped by a moonshee who was a Kashmiri Brahmin, he was able to write in Hindustani.

He never wasted time. Even when travelling between Calcutta and Aldeen, he continued his studies. He was also eagerly awaiting the arrival of two new ministers, Daniel Corrie and John Parsons, both of whom were recommended by Charles Simeon.

Prayer was vital to Henry's plans and on Sunday, 24 May, he recorded in his journal: 'In the morning my heart was tolerably spiritual; I felt withdrawn from the world, and found pleasure in being alone with the blessed God. Oh what heavenly-mindedness might I enjoy by more communion with God!'[12] Prayer was the secret of his devotion to the God he loved. There were times in his devotions when he felt he was walking the golden streets of paradise, in sweet communion with Christ. On one occasion he wrote, 'At night had much nearness to God in prayer. I found it sweet to my spirit, to reflect on my being a pilgrim on earth, with Christ for my near and dear friend, and found myself unwilling to leave off my prayer.'[13]

As the days passed, he knew that his time of loving fellowship with the godly Brown family at Aldeen was drawing to a conclusion. He was prepared to move on, but again and again there was a longing in his heart for Lydia, the woman he loved so dearly.

# 12.
# 'My dearest Lydia'

'Dearest Lydia, in the sweet
and fond expectation of your
being given to me by God,
and of the happiness which I
humbly hope you yourself
might enjoy here, I find a
pleasure in breathing out my
assurance of ardent love'
(Henry Martyn, in a letter
to Lydia Grenfell).

# 12.
# 'My dearest Lydia'

Lydia was never far from Henry's thoughts. Nine months had passed since he had said goodbye to her. It was his understanding that she would one day come out to India and marry him, but she did not believe that she had said anything to give him that impression. In her diary she wrote, 'It is clearly now understood between us that [Henry] is free to marry where he is going, and I ... shall often pray the Lord to find him a suitable partner.'[1] Yet while Henry was travelling to India she referred to him as 'my dear absent friend'[2] and kept a close watch for ships that could bring mail from him.

On 12 July, on a visit to Calcutta with David Brown, Henry found letters waiting for him from Charles Simeon, his good friend John Sargent, Tom Hitchins and his wife Emma, and from Lydia. This was Lydia's second letter, her first having been lost in transit. Henry was greatly encouraged by the contents of her letter. Charles Simeon had written some words in praise of her, and that night Henry found sleep difficult. He longed to have Lydia as his wife, assisting him in the Lord's work. He decided to discuss the matter with David Brown and, after reading him her letter, asked for help in coming to a decision concerning his next step. David suggested that he write to her at once, proposing marriage and asking her to come to India.

Henry was convinced that her presence would greatly assist him in his work, although he knew that there were advantages in a celibate life for someone engaged in mission work. There were times when he was alarmed by thoughts of the responsibilities that marriage and children would bring. How could children be educated, and what would their spiritual state be, growing up surrounded by so many heathen influences?

During all this turmoil of mind, he continued with his language studies, the preparation of sermons, personal devotions and housekeeping. He was conscious that he was wasting precious time thinking about Lydia and the possibility of marriage — time that would be better spent in leading Indians to a saving faith in Christ.

On 30 July 1806, he took up his pen and began a letter to Lydia:

> My Dearest Lydia,
>
> On a subject so intimately connected with my happiness and future ministry, as that on which I am now about to address you, I wish to assure you that I am not acting with precipitancy, or without much consideration and prayer, while I at last sit down to request you to come out to me to India...
>
> You are acquainted with much of the conflict I have undergone on your account. It has been greater than you or Emma have imagined, and yet not so painful as I deserve to have found it for having suffered my affections to fasten so inordinately on an earthly object.

After describing his situation in the Calcutta area he requested that she sail with the next fleet leaving for India. He concluded:

> Dearest Lydia, in the sweet and fond expectation of your being given to me by God, and of the happiness which I humbly hope you yourself might enjoy here, I find a pleasure in breathing out my assurance of ardent love. I have now long loved you most affectionately, and

my attachment is more strong, more pure, more heavenly, because I see in you the image of Jesus Christ.

I unwillingly conclude, by bidding my beloved Lydia adieu.

H. Martyn.[3]


Henry began making arrangements for her arrival by tidying the pagoda and sending an order to Josiah Wedgwood, potter to Queen Charlotte, asking for his latest 'Queensware cups and saucers' which were made in Staffordshire.

On 1 September, he again wrote to Lydia proposing that she come to India and marry him in the not-too-distant future. He concluded his letter with words that expressed his abiding love:

> Now, my dearest Lydia, I cannot say what I feel — I cannot pour out my soul — I could not if you were here; but I pray that you may love me, if it be the will of God; and I pray that God may make you more and more His child, and give me more and more love for all that is Godlike and holy.
>
> I remain, with fervent affection,
> Yours, in eternal bonds,
>
> H. Martyn.[4]


Now all he could do was wait for her arrival. He expected his proposal to reach her early in 1807, which would mean that she could sail with the fleet which was due to leave England in February 1807, but in fact his letter was not delivered until after the fleet had already sailed.

At last, on 14 September, the East India Company appointed Henry as chaplain of Dinapore, near Patna. Before setting out he received news that Daniel Corrie had been accepted as a chaplain of the East India Company, to serve in India. This thrilled him as Daniel was a friend, and had been a member of Charles Simeon's congregation. Later Daniel was appointed Bishop of Madras.

Daniel was to become a good friend of the Sherwoods and Mary has left a description of him: 'He was a tall man, nearly six foot high; his features were not good, from the length of his face, but the expression of his countenance was as full of love as that of my father's … with a simplicity wholly his own. He never departed from the most perfect rules of politeness; he never said a rude or unkind thing, and never seemed to have any consciousness of the rank of the person with whom he was conversing. He was equally courteous to all, and attentive to every individual… I had been greatly pleased with Mr Martyn; I could not be less so with Mr Corrie.'[5] Daniel was accompanied by John Parsons, who was also a chaplain of the company.

For Henry, October was a very busy month. He had to pack all his belongings in readiness for his trip by boat to Dinapore. There were the farewells to be said, as well as all the normal day-to-day activities that occupied his time. He also purchased goods and materials for use in his new work.

Several days before his departure, his friends gathered at his pagoda for a time of prayer and devotions. He recorded in his journal: 'My soul never yet had such divine enjoyment. I felt a desire to break from the body, and join the high praises of the saints above. May I go, "in the strength of this, many days". Amen. "My soul doth magnify the Lord, and my spirit hath rejoiced in God my Saviour." How sweet to walk with Jesus — to love Him, and to die for Him.'[6]

With his houseboat, or budgerow as it was called, packed with all of his belongings, Henry stepped aboard with the boatmen and his friends David Brown, Daniel Corrie and John Parsons, who were to accompany him for part of the way. As they passed the Baptist mission compound, his dear friend Joshua Marshman rowed out to meet them and together they had a time of sweet fellowship.

On 17 October the river became rough because of the very strong winds. Henry's friends were forced to leave him and he found himself in a new situation: 'I was left alone for the first time, with none but natives.'[7] He now faced the work he had

Henry and his moonshee translating the Scriptures on the journey to Dinapore

come to India to do — to preach the gospel to both Europeans and Indians alike. He had sacrificed a life of comparative ease in England to serve his Lord and Saviour, Jesus Christ. He was willing to sacrifice everything for his Master, even life itself. His willing service to God can again be summed up in his words soon after reaching India: 'Now let me burn out for God.'[8]

The six-week trip to Dinapore was a learning experience for Henry. First, he made sure he didn't neglect his devotional time, during which he sensed the very presence of God. He continued studying the local languages and, with the help of his moonshee, resumed the translation of portions of the Scriptures, especially Bible stories which would be useful when he established a school.

He carried a gun and this was put to good use in providing fresh meat. He particularly enjoyed a colourful bird called a culean and a large one known as a minca, both of which he cooked without the usual accompaniment of curry. One afternoon he saw a large boar and regretted that he had left his gun on the boat.

The boatmen, who were responsible for moving the boat upstream, using manpower, tide and the wind, were Hindus. Each night the houseboat was moored and Henry went ashore to make contact with the local Indians and seek to bring the gospel to them. In the course of the journey, he discovered that the Hindus considered him to be 'unclean'. One night when the boat was moored, he went ashore and returned to find the Hindus cooking their evening meal. His walking cane accidentally touched the cooking pot in which rice was being prepared. At once one of the men grabbed the container and threw the rice into the river. Henry was told that defilement passed from him through his walking stick into the cooking pot, and then into the rice, making it unfit to eat.

Early in his journey, Henry witnessed the worship of the idol Cali. With the houseboat securely moored for the night, he walked in the direction in which he heard the sound of cymbals and drums. Soon he found himself face to face with a Brahmin and a hundred or more devotees of Cali. He asked questions of the Brahmin and took the opportunity to tell them about his own beliefs as a Christian. He rejoiced that he had been able to present the gospel to people in the very presence of Satan.

On another occasion, he saw boats drifting down the river carrying brightly decorated images of the goddess Cali. The worshippers, standing on the river bank, threw effigies of the goddess into the water. When Henry's boat came alongside, they turned the images to face him and blew a trumpet. He showed his disgust by turning his back on the idols.

Henry was well aware of the hatred the Indians felt towards the British; after all, the latter had by force of arms become the rulers of their nation. Many Indians abused this power, making demands upon their own countrymen in the name of their British employers. One of Henry's boatmen had approached an old fisherman, demanding that he hand over his fish without any payment, claiming that his British master had ordered him to do so. When Henry discovered what was happening, the fisherman was overjoyed to find that Henry had given no such order but intended to pay him for the fish. Turning to the boatman responsible for the theft, Henry then told him plainly that if he was caught a second time stealing in the missionary's name, he would go to jail.

Often when he visited a village in the cool of the evening, everyone ran away, especially the women and children. On one occasion he was able to speak to some of the men, but found that there was no one in the village who spoke Hindustani. This saddened Henry and made him realize that he needed to devote more time to learning the various languages spoken by the people.

When, on 27 October 1806, he arrived at Berhampore, another outpost of the British Empire, he called in at the hospital and, seeing a surgeon approaching, he began to apologize for being there without having asked for permission. The surgeon looked into his face and exclaimed, 'Bless me, it is Martyn!' Henry recognized that it was John Marshall, a school-friend who had attended the grammar school at Truro.

The next day he returned to the hospital, hoping to preach the gospel to the patients, but of the 150 soldiers in the hospital, not one showed any interest in coming to hear him or in reading the books he brought with him. Finally he gave up. As he left the building, he did so to the vulgar sneers and laughter of the common soldiers. This was no different from what he had experienced on the *Union*.

That evening when he went on shore he forgot to take any tracts with him and was afterwards ashamed that he had lost an opportunity of distributing them. He was always conscious that on the Day of Judgement he would be called to account for the use he had made of the gospel. He could not afford to be lazy in any way. He had no desire to have anyone stand up on that day and point an accusing finger at him.

On Sunday, 2 November, the houseboat entered the Ganges River. The following day, at Chandny, he met some missionaries, Mr Grant and Mr Ellerton, who took him to see a school where he saw the boys sitting cross-legged on mats on the floor, reading, while proud parents looked in through the windows and door.

At Rajemahl, Henry handed a Hindustani tract to a Muslim whom he met. When the man realized what it was, he became embarrassed and handed it back with the comment: 'A person, who had his legs in two different boats, went on his way uncomfortably.'[9]

That night Henry spoke to a chief from the nearby hills, explaining that when Christians died their souls went upwards to heaven to be with God, but those who had no love of God and his Son Jesus Christ went downwards to the place of fire — the place of everlasting punishment. His statement that the wicked went downwards into the place of fire made a great impression on the chieftain, who kept coming back to this topic.

On 12 November Henry passed from the state of Bengal into Bihar. He became more conscious that he was moving further away from his friends in England and at Calcutta.

On the evening of 14 November, when he visited the village of Nuckanpore, everyone ran away, except a sick old woman, who was begging. Henry found difficulty in understanding what she said, but when he gave her half a rupee she was surprised and said one word he did understand: 'Chula' ('Good!').

The following day he stopped at another village, where he met an old soldier who spoke about the campaigns in which he had fought. He believed there was only one God, claiming that everyone was equal before him. When Henry spoke to him of Christ he replied dismissively, 'Ah! that is your shaster.'[10] (A 'shaster', or 'shastra', was a Hindu term for a book of law.)

Each Lord's Day Henry devoted time to prayer and to reading and meditating on the Scriptures. He spent much time praying for his sisters, Sally and Laura, especially Laura, as he feared she might still be unconverted. His dear Lydia was never far from his mind. He loved her dearly and longed to know that she was coming to India to be his wife.

On 17 November, he arrived at Monghir, which was about eight days' travel from Patna, Dinapore and Bankipore. From there he travelled to Jangheera, where he again distributed tracts, and sometimes New Testaments, to those who could read. Many believed he was giving away copies of the *Ramayana*, one of the two great Indian epic poems.[11] The next day he was confronted by a man who prostrated himself on the ground, his head in the dust, to beg for a copy of the book, which he was firmly convinced was the *Ramayana*, despite all that Henry said to the contrary. The man accepted a copy of the New Testament and went away clutching it to his breast.

On another occasion Henry met an aged Brahmin working in the fields. When he was asked why he was working at his age, the man answered that the British had stolen his country, so he had to work. Henry was becoming aware that often the Indians only paid him attention and called him 'Sahib' ('Sir,' or 'Master') because he was British. Henry realized that very soon he would suffer many trials and tribulations as a British missionary in a foreign land where the British presence was resented. In his journal he wrote, 'The disaffection of the people gave rise … to many reflections in my mind on what may be my future sufferings in this country… Come what will — let me only be found in the path of duty, and nothing shall be wrong. Be my sufferings what they may, they cannot equal those of my Lord, nor, probably, even those of the apostles and early martyrs. They, "through faith, subdued kingdoms, wrought righteousness, out of weakness were made strong, etc.," and why shall not I hope that I, too, who am indeed "like one born out of due time", shall receive strength according to my day.'[12]

His six-week journey was an eye-opener to Henry. Constance Padwick describes the many scenes that he observed en route: 'Muddy children splashing at the waterside; sesame or towering hemp plants standing tall against the sky; cotton pods bursting milky white; rustling winds swaying water-rice sown on the river silt; [colourful] groups where women stood in the water bathing and washing clothes; bamboo stakes hung with fishing nets spread out to dry; "sweet fields dressed in living green" where new-sown wheat was springing; clusters of thatched roofs among shivering bamboos or plantains; each village of those days guarded by its own absurd mud fort; paddy birds standing in line where mud and water meet; and over all the wheeling kites watching the river life with the keen eye of hunger.'[13]

On 25 November 1806, Henry's budgerow approached Patna, the fifth largest city of India at that time. The following day he arrived at Dinapore, a town that would be his home for some time. He was to be chaplain to the 400 British troops and their forty-five officers under the command of General Clarke. This was Henry's parish, where he expected to be a lone voice proclaiming the majesty of God and the Lord Jesus Christ.

After meeting some of the officers and discovering the difficulties he would face, he recorded in his journal: 'Let men do their worst, let me be torn to pieces, and my dear Lydia torn from me; or let me labour for fifty years amidst scorn, and never seeing one soul converted, still it shall not be worse for my soul, in eternity, nor worse for it in time. Though the heathen rage and the English people imagine a vain thing, the Lord Jesus who controls all events is my friend, my master, my God, my all. On the Rock of Ages when I feel my foot rest, my head is lifted up above all mine enemies round about, and I sing, yea I will sing praises unto the Lord. If I am not much mistaken, sore trials are awaiting me from without. Yet the time will come, when they will be over. Oh what sweet refuge to the weary soul does the grave appear! There the wicked cease from troubling, and there the weary are at rest. Here every man I meet is an enemy…! Oh what a place must heaven be, where there are none but friends. England appears almost a heaven upon earth, because there one is not viewed as an unjust intruder; but, oh! the heaven of my God! the general assembly of the first-born, the spirits of the just made perfect, and Jesus!'[14]

# 13.
## Henry's first Indian parish

'The sight of the multitudes
... filled me with astonishment and dread... What
shall be done for them all? I
feel constrained to pray and
to beg your prayers, for a
double, yea, for a tenfold
portion of the Spirit to
make me equal to my work'
(Henry Martyn, in a
letter to David Brown).

# 13.
# Henry's first Indian parish

Henry quickly discovered that his workload was much heavier than anything he had experienced before. In the first place, he needed to be able to speak fluently and write correctly in Hindustani, in order to be understood by the majority of the Indian population. His plan was to translate the Scriptures before taking the gospel to the people. This translation work was well underway, and he was even suggesting that he would replace sections of the Authorized, King James Version of the Scriptures with his own translation of those parts into English. He aimed to open schools where the young people were taught reading and writing, since he realized that it was pointless presenting a people with the Bible if they could not read. However, as he travelled to Dinapore, he discovered that a variety of dialects were spoken, which made translation work more difficult.

Henry was the first Christian chaplain appointed to the area and he was to work amongst Europeans, who were largely unconcerned about spiritual matters. The Europeans were also of the opinion that Henry would be wasting his time evangelizing the Indians, and if he did win a convert they were certain the person's character would be even worse than before.

As a matter of protocol, he presented himself to General Clarke. That night they dined together and the following day Henry moved all his belongings to the barracks, where he would live until he found better living quarters. He knew the difficulties he would face and prayed: 'Oh, henceforth let me live with Christ alone!'[1]

On 29 November, he wrote to his friend David Brown expressing his feelings: 'General Clarke has been exceedingly civil ... and so has invited me continually to his house... Even my own Hindustani I speak with greater hesitation than ever, insomuch that I feel reluctant in uttering a single sentence! ... The sight of the multitudes at Patna, and on the banks toward this place, filled me with astonishment and dread... What shall be done for them all? I feel constrained to pray and to beg your prayers, for a double, yea, for a tenfold portion of the Spirit to make me equal to my work. There are four hundred European troops here, and forty-five officers ... they are "impudent children and stiff-hearted", and will receive, I fear, my ministrations, as all the others have done, with scorn.'[2]

He very quickly found out that the Indian population hated him, not just because he taught another religion, but because he was one of the despised British overlords. He saw it in their faces as he went about carried in a palanquin. When he compared England with India, his homeland seemed like a heaven on earth.

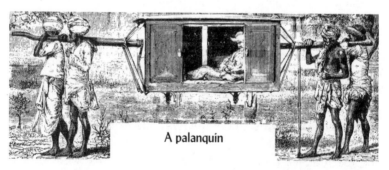

A palanquin

30 November was his first Lord's Day in Dinapore and the worship service was to be held before sunrise as the weather was very hot. He had no church building and had to use a long drum as his pulpit. Since no seats were provided and the

congregation had to remain standing, he was requested not to preach a sermon.

Following a time of private devotions, he visited the hospital before the midday meal. Life was to be no different from what he had experienced on the *Union* — he suffered scorn and sarcasm. After lunch he returned to the hospital, where he read a portion of Doddridge's *Rise and Progress of Religion* to the patients. He also left some tracts for the men who could read.

In the midst of all his work his thoughts often turned to Lydia. He longed to receive her response to his proposal of marriage. One night he had a most vivid dream about her: 'A dream last night was so like reality ... that I must record the date of it [10 December 1806]. It was about Lydia. I dreamt that she had arrived, but that after some conversation I said to her, "I know this is a dream, it is too soon after my letter for you to have come." Alas! it is only a dream... Perhaps all my hope about her is but a dream! Yet, be it so; whatever God shall appoint must be good for us both, and with that I will endeavour to be tranquil and happy ... whether with or without a companion.'[3]

Henry set to work, aware of his responsibility for the spiritual well-being of the European soldiers and civil servants and all those associated with the East India Company. He also looked upon the Indian population as part of his responsibility, which was to last for the next two and a half years.

On 9 December a pundit arrived to assist him and commenced work, together with his moonshee, translating portions of the Scriptures into the Bihar dialect and Sanskrit. (Pundits were men of intellectual ability — scholars in the fields of Indian law, science, religion and languages.) The two men found some aspects of Christian teaching beyond their ability to believe. When his moonshee read the words of Christ recorded in John 3:13 that 'No one has ascended to heaven but he who came down from heaven, that is, the Son of Man who is in heaven,' he stated that such a teaching was *'nickal'* (impossible), arguing that even God could not make anything be in two places at the same time! Henry explained that this was possible for Jesus Christ because he was both God and man in the same person. He then turned the discussion to show how Christ needed to be both man and God in order for his death on the cross in the place of sinners to satisfy the requirements of a holy God.

The moonshee was surprised to read that on the last day all unrepentant sinners would be separated from the elect. He said that such a teaching was not to be found in his *shaster*! He believed that 'At the end of the world, the sun would come so near, as first to burn all the men, then the mountains, then the *debtas* [inferior gods], then the waters: then, God, reducing Himself to the size of a thumb-nail, would swim on the leaf of a peepul [also known as the 'pipal' or 'bo'] tree.'[4]

Henry's days were very full — he had so much to do that he didn't want to waste even a minute! He had no taste for social gatherings where there was little opportunity for serious conversation and sought to be excused from them. Once he complained that he had better use for his time than calling on the general or conducting marriages.

Many soldiers disliked Henry because he rebuked their sinful ways. On one occasion, after speaking to some men who were playing a game of 'fives' on a Sunday, he turned to the general for support in preserving the sanctity of the Lord's Day.

He always longed for mail from Calcutta and England, and towards the end of December a parcel of letters arrived which took him four hours to read. He was very disappointed that Lydia's letter made no mention of his marriage proposal.

Because he had heard that some Catholic priests were translating parts of the Scriptures, he wrote to them in Latin, hoping for mutual encouragement in that work, even though he was never afraid to speak out against the doctrines of the Roman church.

His next move was to obtain accommodation away from the barracks, where he had rented rooms on a temporary basis. Soon he was settled in a suitable house. It was sparsely furnished, but had everything that he needed. As was expected for a European in India at the time, he found himself employing a number of servants. He had a cook, a washerwoman, a sweeping-woman, six palanquin bearers, a groom and a 'factotum' who oversaw everything, in addition to the moon-shees and pundit who assisted him in his translation work.

The times he set apart for his devotions were periods of close communion with his Lord. As well as praying and reading the Scriptures, he often sang a hymn or psalm of praise to the Lord. The day before the year's end, he experienced a very real sense of the presence of God, both in his time of prayer and when he sang the hymn, 'Day of judgement, day of wonders'. His journal records: 'I was drawn in prayer, especially to worship and adore the great Messiah, and to feel assured that he shall reign. If his blood was shed for his people, what a very small and trifling thing it is, for mine to be shed in the same cause.'[5]

On 31 December he received a letter from a Mr G—, who indicated that the congregation at Dinapore was 'very well satisfied with his written sermons, but did not like extempore preaching'.[6] Henry resented the interference of the congregation in matters which he considered were for him to decide, but he would gladly have written out a whole book of sermons for them, if by this means they might be brought to repent of their sins and turn in faith to Christ, the Saviour.

On the first day of 1807 he summed up the seven years since his conversion to the Lord Jesus: 'Seven years have passed away since I was first called of God. Before the conclusion of another seven years, how probable is it that these hands will have mouldered into dust! But be it so: my soul through grace hath received the assurance of eternal life, and I see the days of my pilgrimage shortening, without a wish to add to their number. But oh, may I be stirred up to a faithful discharge of my high and awful work; and ... may I give myself to this "one thing". The last has been a year to be remembered by me, because the Lord has brought me safely to India, and permitted me to begin, in one sense, my missionary work. My trials in it have been very few; everything has turned out better than I expected; loving kindness and tender mercies have attended me at every step: therefore here will I sing his praise... May He continue his patience, his grace, his direction, his spiritual influences, and I shall at last surely come off conqueror! May He speedily open my mouth, to make known the mysteries of the Gospel, and in great mercy grant that the heathen may receive it and live!'[7]

# 14.
## Satan's kingdom under attack

After twelve months of Christian witness he wrote, 'Precious souls! Millions perishing in the neighbourhood of one who can preach the gospel to them! How dreadful! I trust the Lord will open a great and effectual door; but oh for faith, zeal, courage, love!'

# 14.
# Satan's kingdom under attack

In his new surroundings Henry had two basic aims. Firstly, he wanted to live his own life in such a way that he was prepared for death. It was his earnest desire to be ready to pass into the presence of God at any time. Secondly, he wanted to see people converted and living Christian lives.

He mixed freely with the Indians despite the fact that most Europeans treated the locals with contempt. He wanted to know if the East India Company acknowledged any spiritual responsibility for the Indian population, and on 1 January 1807 he received a letter containing an extract from the charter of the company which specifically authorized and required its chaplains to teach the native population.

Henry began reading out his sermons from a prepared script as requested, but was very frustrated that there was no church building. The first people to show any real appreciation of his sermons were Major Young and his wife, although Mrs Young complained that there was too much gloom in what he said. [1] In mid-February the Youngs told him that the members of his congregation were very pleased with his preaching and its contents, but what Henry really wanted was to have the hearts of every member of the congregation pricked by what he said and for them to turn to Christ in saving faith. [2]

There were times when his hearers paid close attention to his words, but he was distressed to learn that, after he had preached on Hebrews 9:22, the soldiers, and others, spent much of their time ridiculing his sermon. This stirred him to even greater efforts to preach the gospel and pray for the powerful work of the Holy Spirit to change hearts. He also saw the need of the Indian population to turn to Christ. He was well aware of the situation he faced and after twelve months of Christian witness he wrote, 'Precious souls! Millions perishing in the neighbourhood of one who can preach the gospel to them! How dreadful! I trust the Lord will open a great and effectual door; but oh for faith, zeal, courage, love!'[3]

Early in 1807 Henry started translating the Anglican liturgy and prayer book into Hindustani. He also translated forty parables and the Sermon on the Mount, which he believed could be used in the schools he planned to open. Helped by his moonshee, he translated the New Testament into Hindustani while supervising its translation into both Persian and Arabic.

Henry was also expected to baptize infants and marry couples, although the marriage of soldiers to Indian women was prohibited and he had to refuse the baptism of children born to those couples who lived together in irregular, *de facto* relationships. One woman living in such a relationship said that she would save up the money so that they could be married, but when Henry questioned her, he found out that she only wanted membership in the church because it meant that her body would be treated with respect when she died. Occasionally Indian couples would come seeking to have their babies baptized, but again Henry refused as the parents knew nothing about the Christian faith.

He was often called on to baptize children of European couples, which he did, but this sometimes necessitated travel of hundreds of miles. When he was called upon to conduct the marriage of a Portuguese couple, he translated the ceremony into their language, so that they would understand what was being said. Weddings, of course, were always a reminder of the woman he loved — his dear Lydia. He could love no other woman and eagerly awaited her reply to his proposal of marriage.

Fighting between Indian tribes and the soldiers often resulted in deaths. One day he was called upon to conduct the funeral of fifteen men. He also visited the hospital to speak with injured soldiers and encourage them. He read *Pilgrim's Progress* and other Christian writings to the sick and injured, but met with little interest by way of response.

Visitors came to speak to him and five in particular stood out — a Jew from Babylon, a learned Muslim from Patna, a Roman Catholic father from the Propaganda (a committee of Roman Catholic cardinals responsible for foreign missions), an Armenian from Jerusalem and a Prussian soldier who was concerned about his soul.

Henry also corresponded with many people, and always rejoiced when he met Daniel Corrie, who would stop over at Dinapore when travelling by boat.

Yet, in spite of being surrounded by so many people, Henry was lonely. This would soon be made even worse when he received a letter from Lydia telling him that she would not be coming out to India to join him. Although Lydia's letter has not been preserved, it appears from Henry's reply and from his letters to his friends that she cited her mother's refusal to consent as the principal objection to her doing so.

Another sad blow was the news of the death of his sister Laura. It was a great comfort to Henry to know that before her death she had truly come to trust Christ as her Saviour, but he still felt her loss very keenly. He wrote to David Brown, 'Her departure has left this world a frightful blank to me; and I feel not the smallest wish to live, except there be some work assigned for me to do in the church of God.'[4]

Around that time a group of local Anglican ministers joined together to form a club which they called 'The Associated Clergy'. The members were David Brown, John Parsons, Daniel Corrie, Marmaduke Thompson (the chaplain at Madras), Claudius Buchanan and Henry himself. This group had no formal structure, but in addition to the normal parish work they proposed to aid the work of the British and Foreign Bible Society, to make translations of the Bible into Oriental languages and to meet the cost of providing Sanskrit and Greek New Testaments. David Brown also undertook to circulate monthly reports to all the members.

Henry was the most active member of the group and he found this helped him cope with the loneliness. He raised questions of practical value to everyone, such as whether it was sinful to prepare sermons, or devote time to the translation of the Scriptures, on the Lord's Day. He faced several dilemmas with regard to Sabbath observance. Was it right for Christians to insist that their servants work on the Lord's Day? Then there was the question of soldiers being required for parade on a Sunday. While Henry found this practice highly objectionable, most of the soldiers were glad to have an excuse for missing worship, which they considered to be a waste of their time. On Sunday, 21 July 1808, the 67th Regiment was absent from worship as the men were obliged to attend a field day. The commander-in-chief was expected to visit the barracks and it was necessary for the soldiers to prepare for his visit. Henry sadly noted in his journal: 'Thus the Sabbaths of the supreme God are made to give way. Why do they not prepare for the coming of the Lord Jesus Christ?'[5]

On 5 August 1808 the commander-in-chief arrived in Dinapore and Henry was invited to dine with the senior officers. This was his opportunity to raise the matter of a church building. In December 1807 he had applied for funds to construct a church and had received the reply that he would have to find the cost of such a building. Now that the general was actually present, Henry pleaded with him to use his influence in having money released, saying it was a 'duty we owed to God as a Christian nation'.[6] The general promised him he would do what he could to have funds not only allocated for a building in Dinapore, but also in Serampore. Henry enjoyed the evening as he had the opportunity to speak on religious matters. So pleased was he that he concluded that those present were all 'truly well-bred people'.[7]

His parish was extensive, covering fourteen miles on both sides of the Ganges River. The military garrisons were stationed at Dinapore, the civil government officers at Bankipore, and in Patna millions of Indians lived. The Ganges at that point was about two miles in width, giving him a very extensive work-load. Because he and Daniel Corrie freely mixed with the local Indian population, they were given the nickname of 'the Black Chaplains'.

Henry wanted to establish schools in Patna, Bankipore and Dinapore, despite the opposition that came from the Europeans, who believed that an educated Indian population would lead to revolution. The Indians, however, held him in the highest respect for opening such schools. Unlike the schools already in existence, attendance at his schools was free of charge, as he met the total costs involved. His pundit told him that the local Indian population looked upon his action in setting up the schools as 'an act of great holiness'.[8] Some people saw the establishment of these schools as fulfilling a prophecy that the Hindus would turn to Christ in very large numbers. The Muslims, on the other hand, believed that after one hundred years of British rule, the son of a great king would drive the foreigners from their land.

Henry's schools proved very popular, but when a rumour spread that his intention was to seize all the children and force them to become Christians, the pupils stayed away. Help came from the teacher at Patna, who told those who were worried, 'We are men well known among you, and when we are made Christians then do you begin to fear.'[9] On one occasion when Henry visited Patna, he found the schoolroom empty. But when he stood up and assured the people that he had no intention of forcing Christianity on the pupils against their will, things were soon back to normal.

One day the general told Henry that his school 'made a very good appearance from the road; but you will make no proselytes'.[10] Despite the gossip, his schools became so popular that the classes sometimes numbered over 100 children. When new reading material was needed, Henry produced his translation of the Sermon on the Mount and his book of the parables. His moonshee, his pundit and the schoolteachers all objected, as this would encourage the rumours of his intention to impose Christianity on the children. The decision was made for the teachers to use the writings of an old Indian poet.

In a letter to Daniel Corrie, Henry encouraged him to establish schools: 'Your schools flourish; blessed be God! The Dinapore school is resorted to from all quarters, even from the other side of the river. The Bankipore school is also going on well. I do not institute more till I see the Christian books introduced. The more schools the more noise, and the more enquiry, and the greater suspicion of its being of a political nature... I bless God that you are brought to act with me on a broad and cautious plan; but I trust our motto will be, "constant, though cautious".'[11]

In another letter Henry urged Daniel to expand his schools: 'I long to hear of a Christian school established at Benares: it will be like the ark of God brought into the house of Dagon. But do not be in a hurry: let your character become known, and you may do anything. If nothing else comes of our schools, one thing I feel assured of — that the children will grow up ashamed of the idolatry and other customs of their country... But the translation of the Scriptures is the grand point. I trust we shall have the heavenly pleasure of dispersing the Scriptures together through the interior. Oh, the happiness and honour of being the children of God, the ministers of Christ!'[12]

Henry devoted much time and money to his schools — five of them in the area around Dinapore. He could see his educational plans progressing well, but it would have meant a great deal to him to have had Lydia at his side, helping and encouraging him in his work.

# 15.
# Translation under way in earnest

In a letter to Daniel Corrie Henry wrote, 'Sabat has been tolerably quiet this week; but think of the keeper of a lunatic, and you see me. A war of words broke out the beginning of last week, but it ended in an honourable peace...'

# 15.
# Translation under way in earnest

David Brown wanted Henry to resign from the East India Company and become the pastor of the Mission Church in Calcutta, but he declined as he wanted to take the gospel to the interior of India. Preaching the gospel to the Indian population was of greater importance to him than conducting services for the European population in Calcutta, where there were already several evangelical ministers. He was settling into his work in Dinapore and its surroundings and was pleased that he had been promised the assistance of two men in the translation work.

The Associated Clergy, having allocated him the task of the translation of the New Testament into Hindustani, Persian and Arabic, had agreed to provide him with two scholars who were expected to be a great help. One was the gentle, humble Mirza Muhammad Fitrut from Benares, and the other the proud, abusive Arab, Nathaniel Sabat, who was to prove to be a continual thorn in Henry's side. Beforehand, however, Henry had heard only good reports about the two men and he eagerly awaited their arrival.

One of the problems faced by Henry and the others involved in the translation work was that there was not one single, standardized language spoken by all the Indians. However,

Hindu temples at Benares, the home town of Mirza

Henry believed that, with the help of other missionaries with translation skills, this could be overcome. A good relationship existed between the missionaries, so that William Carey could write concerning them, 'I believe you will not find many in England who have less bigotry and more friendship.'[1]

While awaiting the arrival of his two assistants, Henry set to work studying Persian, Arabic and Sanskrit. He wrote to Dr Buchanan, who had contacts with Cambridge University, urging him to suggest the establishment of a faculty to study the languages of the Orient.

At that stage Henry himself was not fluent in Arabic or Persian, but he looked to the new men to guide him in the work. Mirza was well known for his brilliance in Hindustani, and Sabat came with glowing references from Dr Kerr of Madras. He was a professing Christian of whom Henry was assured that 'He will delight your heart, for he is a gentleman, a scholar, and a Christian.'[2]

He had great expectations of the two men, especially Sabat, for whom, as a Christian, he had the highest hopes: 'Thinking tonight of the qualifications of Sabat, I felt the conviction, both in reflection and prayer, of the power of God to make him another St Paul.'[3] Henry was told that Sabat came from a well-known Arabian family and for a time had taught Islamic law. He also had a reputation of knowing the literature of his homeland. More than anything Henry looked forward to enjoying Christian fellowship with Sabat.

Mirza arrived before Sabat and proved to be a kind, gentle scholar who was of great assistance to Henry. Both men looked forward to Sabat's arrival, which took place on 7 November 1807. With him came his pregnant wife and all their possessions.

Very soon Sabat proved to be a heavy burden to both Henry and Mirza. The day after his arrival was the Lord's Day, and while he was in the vestry, someone moved his chair, much to his disapproval. He turned and stomped out of the building in a temper and returned to his home. Later Henry called him aside and explained that the incident which had upset him was not intended as an insult to him.

In a letter to David Brown, Henry wrote, 'The very first day we began to spar. He would come into none of my plans, nor did I approve of his; but I gave way, and by yielding prevailed, for he now does everything I tell him. He wishes to have nothing to do with my Hindustani works, nor do I want him... He says himself that he can be of no use to me, now that I have Mirza, of whose capabilities he has a high opinion. I ... leave Sabat to his Persian.'[4]

Sabat and his wife lived in their own rented house, but he spent his working day with Henry. Sabat wrote to David Brown, complaining that he had to pay the rent for his house himself and that he had not been reimbursed the seven or eight hundred rupees it had cost him to travel to Dinapore. David sent Sabat's letter to Henry, who then confronted Sabat with his complaints. In the argument that followed Sabat said he would no longer work for Henry. However, Henry kept the peace and in a letter to David Brown wrote, 'I reasoned with him temperately, though it was not without difficulty that I kept my temper. I gave him to understand that we did not consider him as a hireling, but as a brother beloved, who had the cause as much at heart as ourselves... Nothing assuaged him but my promising to pay the rent, and also the expense of his journey when able ... but, as you say, he is an Arab — half savage.'[5]

Mirza Fitrut was an elderly Indian with a love of poetry, and that appealed to Henry. They had their skirmishes over some points of translation, but it was usually Mirza who gave way to Henry. Of this characteristic, Henry recorded: 'He is like a ball of wax, easy to be moulded into any shape; and whatever he sees me earnest for he will give up; so I alter as little of his translation as possible, lest through his absurd pliability he should give up the true idiom in my desire of having it literal.'[6]

Sabat and Mirza had frequent disputes and because Henry failed to support Sabat in every case, the latter told him an Arabian proverb: 'A friend is an enemy to his friend's enemy.'[7]

After much provocation, Mirza gave up and returned to Patna, but later, when Henry was transferred to Cawnpore, he was again asked to give assistance. He came, but Henry constantly had to exercise Christian love and wisdom to keep the peace between the two.

In describing his dealings with Sabat, George Smith wrote in his biography of Henry, 'In almost nothing does the saintliness of Martyn appear so complete as in the references in his *Journal* to the pride, the vanity, the malice, the rage of this "artless child of the desert", when it became apparent that his knowledge of Persian and Arabic had been overestimated.'[8]

According to Colonel MacInnes of Penang, Sabat 'never spoke of Mr Martyn without the most profound respect, and shed tears of grief whenever he recalled how severely he had tried the patience of this faithful servant of God. He mentioned several anecdotes to show with what extraordinary sweetness Martyn had borne his numerous provocations. "He was less a man," he said, "than an angel from heaven." '[9]

Mary Sherwood, the wife of Henry Sherwood, the pay-master of the 53rd Regiment of Foot, whose description of Corrie was recorded earlier, also provides information about Sabat. He claimed to be a member of the Arabian tribe of Koreish, which was a Muslim tribe.[10] His parents were shepherds with many sheep and camels. He spent time in the Persian army and later was the assistant secretary to the King of Cabul, where he became very friendly with Abdalla, who was also from the tribe of Koreish. Abdalla was a poet who, when translating a letter for the king, did so in poetical form. For this he was rewarded with a mouthful of pearls, according to the custom of the age. Sabat noticed that his friend, Abdalla, was not himself and thought he must have been suffering from lovesickness. His downcast temperament eventually resulted in his dismissal from his service of the king and his return to his home in Arabia.

Later, when Sabat was in Bokhara on the king's business, he spotted Abdalla and noticed that he was now clean-shaven.

When they spoke, Sabat was told by his friend that he had become a Christian. Sabat, a faithful Muslim, appealed to Abdalla to return to the faith of his ancestors, but without success. Sabat then reported the matter to the shah, who had Abdalla arrested. He was handed over to the religious leaders, the mullahs, who pleaded with him to renounce his faith in Christ and acknowledge that the promised 'Helper' of John 15:26 was Mohammed, not the Holy Spirit. However, his reply infuriated them when he quoted: 'Beware of false prophets, which come to you in sheep's clothing, but inwardly they are ravenous wolves' (Matthew 7:15).

After four days' imprisonment Abdalla was brought out before the crowds and threatened with death if he didn't recant, with an offer of the shah's pardon if he did. When he refused he was struck on the face, and blood flowed profusely from the mouth that had once been filled with pearls.

After his refusal to recant and become a Muslim, his left hand was cut off with a single powerful slash of a sword. When he again refused to deny Christ, his right hand was cut off. It was then that Abdalla looked at Sabat as if to ask, 'Why did you betray me? Why have you done this?' Abdalla refused to deny Christ, his Redeemer, and his suffering finally came to an end when he was decapitated and a martyr passed into paradise to receive his eternal reward.[11]

Now Sabat felt guilty and began to search the Scriptures to discover the reason for his friend's courageous faith. He obtained a Bible and, after much study, concluded that Jesus was the Christ foretold by the prophets. Believing he was 'born again', he made his way to Madras and there met Dr Kerr, who at first refused his demand to be baptized. After some heated discussion, however, Sabat was baptized. When the news that he had become a Christian reached his home one of his brothers was dispatched to kill him. The attempted assassination failed, and after many adventures Sabat eventually arrived in Serampore, where he assisted in translating the New Testament into Persian and Arabic.

Later, when he and his wife moved to Cawnpore, Mrs Sherwood met the man personally and recorded the following description of the wild-looking Arab:

> Every feature in the large disc of Sabat's face was what we should call exaggerated. His eyebrows were arched, black, and strongly pencilled; his eyes dark and round, and from time to time flashing with unsubdued emotion, and ready to kindle into flame on the most trifling occasion. His nose was high, his mouth wide, his teeth large, and looked white in contrast with his bronzed complexion and fierce black mustachios. He was a large and powerful man, and generally wore a skull-cap of rich shawling, or embroidered silk, with circular flaps of the same hanging over each ear. His large, tawny throat and neck had no other covering than that afforded by his beard, which was black.
>
> His attire was a kind of jacket of silk, with long sleeves, fastened by a ... girdle, about his loins, to which was appended a jewelled dirk [dagger]. He wore loose trousers, and embroidered shoes turned up at the toes. In the cold season he threw over this a wrapper lined with fur, and when it was warmer the fur was changed for silk. When to this costume is added earrings, and sometimes a golden chain, the Arab stands before you in his complete state of Oriental dandyism.
>
> This son of the desert never sat in a chair without contriving to tuck up his legs under him on the seat, in attitude very like a tailor on his board. The only languages he was able to speak were Persian, Arabic, and a very little bad Hindustani; but what was wanting in the words of this man was more than made up by the loudness with which he uttered them, for he had a voice like rolling thunder. When it is understood that loud utterance is considered as an ingredient of respect in the East, we cannot suppose that one who had been much in his

native courts should think it necessary to modulate his voice in the presence of the English Sahib Logues [i.e. the soft, cultured manner of speech of the English overlords].[12]

Despite Sabat's being welcomed as a Christian brother, Henry soon discovered that he lacked the 'fruit of the Spirit'. Indeed, he made Henry's life almost unbearable. Henry saw Sabat's sin as being 'vanity'.[13] When he accused Henry of pride, because he lived in a large house, Henry decided to put the house on the market and look for somewhere smaller. He also faced Sabat's criticism of Europeans in general, with his claims that the Arabians excelled in most forms of activity. When Sabat claimed that his intellect was far superior to that of the missionaries in Serampore, and that he could write about a text of Scripture in such a way that his arguments would be beyond their comprehension, Henry challenged him to make the attempt. The following day, when Sabat presented Henry with what he had written, Henry considered his reasoning to be like that of a schoolboy.

Sabat was under the delusion that when engaged in translating the Scriptures he was infallible and would not admit the possibility that there might be any errors in his translation!

One Saturday, Henry asked him to prepare the room used for Sunday worship for the next day's service. Within moments he found himself facing such a display of anger that he was reminded of the words in the epistle of James about the tongue being 'set on fire of hell'.[14] Sabat believed that he was no man's servant! He was still furious over the supposed insult when he arrived for the service the next day.

Sabat was a constant source of tension and in a letter to Daniel Corrie Henry wrote, 'Sabat has been tolerably quiet this week; but think of the keeper of a lunatic, and you see me. A war of words broke out the beginning of last week, but it ended in an honourable peace. After he got home at night he sent a letter, complaining of a high crime and misdemeanour in some servant; I sent him a soothing letter and the wild beast fell asleep.'[15]

Yet another problem erupted when Sabat complained that some of his possessions were being stolen from his house. When Henry offered him a room in his own home, Sabat agreed, but then demanded that his possessions be returned to his home as he would not live under the same roof as did Mirza. He claimed he was deprived of the honour due to him when the servants referred to him as 'the Arabian Moonshee', by way of distinguishing him from 'the Hindustani Moonshee'. Sabat didn't consider himself to be just another moonshee!

Henry observed Sabat's idleness and his lack of prayer and on many occasions he recorded in his journal comments about the proud Arab. In a letter to Daniel Corrie he wrote, 'My greatest trial is Sabat...'[16] Indeed, it appeared that Sabat was a trial to Indians as well as to Europeans. On one occasion when the owner of the house where he was living offended him, he and his wife set to work uprooting all the flowers, plants and shrubs from their garden, as a gesture of spite against the owner. When Henry rebuked them for what they had done, Sabat believed they had done nothing wrong. Behaviour like that concerned Henry, who wondered if Sabat really was a Christian.

As the weeks passed, Henry concluded that Sabat's translation of both the Persian and Arabic New Testaments left a lot to be desired. He concluded that to make satisfactory translations of the Scriptures it would be necessary to spend time in both Persia and Arabia. Later, when Sabat's work was checked by the missionaries in Calcutta, they were very critical of his Persian translation, even suggesting that he had plagiarized from earlier editions.

Sabat defended himself against these accusations. He then wrote a virulent attack upon Christianity, and departed for Penang. It was there that he wrote letters to the local newspapers again professing faith in Christ. Later he found work with the Sultan of Acheen on the island of Sumatra, but was taken prisoner by some who attempted to overthrow the government. From his prison house he wrote letters to the Penang newspapers, using his own blood as ink. Despite efforts to save his life, he was put to death by being sewn into a bag and cast into the depths of the sea. This was the man who had caused Henry so much heartache.

# 16.
# A busy schedule

'I was much pleased at the sight of Mr Martyn... [He] is one of the most pleasing, mild, and heavenly-minded men, walking in this turbulent world with peace in his mind and charity in his heart'
(Mary Sherwood).

# 16.
# A busy schedule

Henry found himself largely spiritually isolated. Among the officers it was Major Young and his wife who opened their home to the chaplain. They were Christians, and Henry frequently joined them at mealtimes, especially when Sabat had disrupted the day. When Major Young received a transfer and they had to leave Dinapore, this came as a great blow to Henry.

Henry's position meant that he was expected to play a part in the social life of the officers. This he found distasteful and in many cases he believed his involvement to be actually sinful. Following a gathering soon after his arrival, he wrote, 'Called on Colonel W. in the evening, but at night had a most awful sense of the general levity and unfaithfulness of my conduct as a minister. Oh, how will the lost souls with whom I have trifled, view me at the last day! O my God, rather let me be as the filth of the world, and the off-scouring of all things, than by conformity to the world be instrumental to their ruin!'[1]

There were times when, distressed by the lack of converts, he saw himself as the Achan in the camp (see Joshua 7). He longed to witness the conversion of the hard-hearted Indians, but knew that, humanly speaking, this was impossible: 'How shall it ever be possible to convince a Hindu or Brahmin of anything? These are people possessed by Satan, like the idols they worship, without any understanding.' He went on to say, 'Truly, if ever I see a Hindu a real believer in Jesus, I shall see something more nearly approaching the resurrection of a dead body...'[2]

Henry was frequently driven to pray about his own spiritual condition. He meditated upon the Scriptures and saw that true happiness was to be found in faithfully serving the Lord. He believed that he was indolent, although in reality this was far from the truth. Visits to the hospital caused him to be downcast as very few of the patients showed any concern for their spiritual well-being.

It was the companionship of the few Christian soldiers who regularly met with him for worship midweek and on Sunday evenings that was a true source of encouragement. These were what he called 'his men'. At first only a few braved the sarcasm, sneers and hatred of their fellow soldiers, but the numbers grew and on several occasions reached forty.

To avoid the critical comments of their godless comrades, many of the men would set off from their barracks in the opposite direction to Henry's house. Then they would make their way to the service by a roundabout route. Life was hard for Christians in the army! One day Major Young approached Henry in tears because of the persecution he was receiving from other officers and the men. He told Henry that he longed to be in England where he would not suffer such cruelty.[3]

When all were present Henry read and preached from the Scriptures. There was always a time of prayer and usually some singing of hymns of praise. Despite the hostility they faced, the men spoke to their unconverted friends about the Lord Jesus and on one occasion a soldier asked for prayer that God would soften the hearts of his comrades, that they might join him in times of worship. The next time he arrived accompanied by two of his friends. All present rejoiced in their God, who did indeed answer prayer.

On Sunday, 13 March 1808, several companies of the 67th Regiment and the company's European soldiers attended the public worship service, accompanied by their bands. That night when the usual seven or eight soldiers arrived at Henry's home, fourteen others also came along. That was truly a night of encouragement to all present.

Henry also faced the objections of his moonshee and pundit to various points of Christian faith and doctrine. The value of ceremonial washings and of pilgrimages was raised by the moonshee, who claimed that a pilgrimage to the temple at Mecca helped sanctify the heart. Henry rightly said that these things were of no spiritual value whatever. The moonshee also had contempt for the Christian doctrine of the Godhead, while the pundit rejected the biblical teaching about the birth of Christ, claiming that it was degrading to Christ to be born of a woman. The doctrine of election and the question of free will also proved contentious. While these discussions — which Henry described as 'warfare'[4] — were time-consuming, he prayed that they might lead to the conversion of both men.

Henry took every opportunity to speak to the local Indians concerning the way of salvation. When he presented a copy of the New Testament to the Rani of Daoudnagur, she thanked him for his gift but asked what she should do with the book — should she pray to it, or bow to it? Henry replied that she should pray to God for an understanding of the words in the book.

One situation that caused him concern was that of a British judge who had married an Indian woman, and had become a follower of her faith. He had built a mosque for his wife and openly renounced Christianity. Henry saw this as a bad example both to Europeans and to Indians and took the opportunity to rebuke the man, urging him to repent and turn to Christ.

When an earthquake shook the area, causing plaster to come crashing down in his house, he wrote, 'Would to God that their hearts might be shaken by the Spirit of God, through this awful phenomenon.'[5] Several months later the Ganges River flooded and so bad was the smell of the polluted water that he spent a week with a couple whom he refers to as 'Major and Mrs S—'.

A gang of thugs

When one of his servants was kidnapped by a band of thieves, Henry set out to demand the return of the man, at the risk of his own life. The gang of thieves released his servant, and Henry was able to resume his normal activities of pastoral and translation work.

Henry refused to be hurried in this work as he wanted to produce the very best of which he was capable. He read and reread his translations to such an extent that his eyes ached. To make matters worse, the weather was very hot, reaching 92° F (33° C) in the shade on his veranda, and the dust in the air nearly choked him.

There were serious concerns about his health, especially as he was showing signs of the lung disease that had killed his mother and sister. There were times when he fasted to such an extent that his friends feared for his health. Despite his illness, he conducted both morning and evening worship on the Lord's Day, and continued his daily visits to the hospital, where he read *Pilgrim's Progress* to the patients in serial form. At one point his headaches became so severe that he spent time with the Youngs, where he continued with his translation work.

In August 1807, during a visit to the hospital, he was overcome with severe pain in his lungs and throat. He was forced to return to his house and later, when he called at the Youngs' home, he found it impossible to read aloud because of the pain.

In a letter to Daniel Corrie dated 25 January 1808 he commented upon his health: 'Last Sunday I felt greatly fatigued with speaking, and for the first time perceived symptoms of injury, by pain in the breast.'[6]

At Easter 1808 he succumbed to the extreme heat: 'I was very dead and languid with the men at night. Much biliousness and feverish heat still in my body.'[7]

In early June, he recorded that he rose from his bed in severe pain which had kept him awake nearly all night. The next day, Sunday, he carried out his duties while suffering from a severe head cold. That evening, he was to meet as usual with the Christians from the barracks, but doubted that he would be able to cope. Yet the Lord was gracious and, several minutes before the gathering, he suddenly felt well enough to meet 'his men'.

Henry knew his health was deteriorating and confided in Daniel: 'My own health is good again; but the rains try my constitution. I am apt to be troubled with shortness of breath… While there is work, which we must do, we shall live.'[8]

He had several strange dreams which he believed signalled his approaching death. However, he was not afraid to die, as death meant 'awakening in a better world'.[9] On 19 September he wrote, 'Very ill … was attacked with a fever; now what may be the issue, God knows; Into thy hands, O Lord, I commit myself. Lord Jesus, receive my spirit.'[10]

In October he felt so ill from the extreme heat that he was obliged to cancel the worship services. At the end of December his health was worse, but those who loved the Lord still came to his house for instruction.

On 12 March 1809 Henry thanked God that at last the long-awaited church building was opened. It was a room eighty-one feet (24.6 metres) in length with a large veranda. The text he took for the opening service was: 'In every place where I record my name I will come to you, and I will bless you' (Exodus 20:24).

Sadly, he was not to get much use of the new building, as towards the end of March 1809 he received orders that he was being transferred to Cawnpore. He realized that travel in the very hot weather would be unwise and at first indicated that he would move in the rainy season, when the journey would be less stressful, but he subsequently changed his mind and set out for Cawnpore almost immediately.

A short time before his departure, he met Mr and Mrs Sherwood. They had met Henry's friend, John Parsons, who had given them a letter for him. No sooner had their budgerow

Mary Sherwood

dropped anchor at Dinapore, than Henry Sherwood set out to find Henry, who was to become a very close friend of the family.

Mary Sherwood described not only Henry Martyn's surroundings but also the man himself:

Mr Martyn's quarters at Dinapore were in the smaller square, as far as could be distant from our old quarters, but precisely the same sort of church-like abode, with little furniture, the rooms wide and high, with many vast doorways, having their green jalousied doors [doors with green shutters made from angled slats], and long verandas encompassing two sides of the quarters.

Mr Martyn received Mr Sherwood not as a stranger, but as a brother — the child of the same Father... I perfectly remember the figure of that simple-hearted and holy young man, when he entered our budgerow. He was dressed in white, and looked very pale, which, however, was nothing singular in India; his hair, a light brown, was raised from his forehead, which was a remarkably fine one. His features were not regular, but the expression was so luminous, so intellectual, so affectionate, so beaming with Divine charity, that no one could have looked at his features, and thought of their shape or form — the outbeaming of his soul would absorb the attention of every observer. There was a very decided air, too, of the gentleman about Mr Martyn... He was as remarkable for ease as for cheerfulness, and in these particulars his *Journal* does not give a graphic account of this blessed child of God.

I was much pleased at the sight of Mr Martyn. I had heard much of him from Mr Parsons; but I had no anticipation of his hereafter becoming so distinguished as he subsequently did. And if I anticipated it little, he, I am sure, anticipated it less; for he was one of the humblest of men...

Mr Martyn is one of the most pleasing, mild, and heavenly-minded men, walking in this turbulent world with peace in his mind and charity [love] in his heart.[11]

Mrs Sherwood wrote of his house, commenting that his home had no comforts and when she was troubled with pain in her face he had no pillow to give her, only a hard bolster on which to lay her head. He gave them his own room to use while they stayed with him.

Mrs Sherwood also described the time of daily worship in Henry's household, which he commenced by singing a hymn. She said he sang in 'a rich, deep voice...' Then he read and commented on a passage of Scripture and followed this with extempore prayer (spontaneous prayer, as opposed to that based on a prayer book or other formal prayers). His night-time devotions followed the same pattern.

Mrs Sherwood recorded that Henry spoke of the future, of a time when the gospel would have been spread throughout the four quarters of the earth. He also spoke of his longing for the day when Christ would return in power and glory.

Henry's single-hearted devotion to the Lord's service was such that he appeared to be quite untroubled by any distractions this world might have to offer. But on those occasions when he did relax in the company of friends, 'it was to play and laugh like an innocent, happy child, more especially if children were present to play and laugh with him'.

All too soon the Sherwoods left for their posting at Cawnpore, where Henry was shortly to follow.

# 17.
# A foolish decision

The Sherwoods heard the
footsteps of a party of
palanquin bearers
approaching their house...
Mr Sherwood went to the
door to find Henry
Martyn just outside, in the
extreme heat, in a state of
utter exhaustion.

# 17.
# A foolish decision

Henry made an unwise decision concerning his transfer to Cawnpore. He could have made the journey by budgerow, but decided to leave at once, travelling by palanquin. No doubt he wanted to see his new parish and settle into the work, but the journey would be 300 miles (around 480 kilometres) in April, one of the two hottest months of the year. Sabat and his wife travelled at a more leisurely pace by budgerow.

The first portion of the journey, from Dinapore to Allahabad, was made during the night to avoid the extreme heat of the day. The final stretch of 130 miles (approximately 210 km.), from Allahabad to Cawnpore, took two days and nights without any stops for rest. Henry described the hot wind as 'blowing like fire from a furnace'.[1] Every bone in his body ached, while the winds parched his mouth and skin.

Meanwhile in Cawnpore the Sherwoods were settling into their new home. Although the air outside was extremely hot and dusty, inside the servants worked the punkah, a fan, to keep the air circulating. The water carriers tossed water over the 'tatties' (door screens made of fragrant, mosslike grass) to keep them moist. This helped cool the air inside the house.

It was 30 April 1809[2] when the Sherwoods heard the footsteps of a party of palanquin bearers approaching their house. Mary Sherwood was writing a book, while Annie, a young orphan in their care, played by her side with a doll.

Henry Sherwood was working on the regimental financial books, and elsewhere in the house another little orphan, Sally, was playing with her toys, watched over by a servant. Hearing the sounds, Mr Sherwood went to the door to find Henry Martyn just outside, in the extreme heat, in a state of utter exhaustion.

Taking Henry by the hand, Henry Sherwood led him inside, where he promptly collapsed onto the floor in a dead faint. He was also feverish. Providentially, he could not have chosen a more appropriate house to receive help. No doubt he would have been cared for by any of the Europeans, but the Sherwoods' bungalow was the only one occupied by a Christian family. They made up a bed for him on a couch in the hall, that being the coolest spot in the house, and he spent several days there recovering from heat exhaustion. Of those days Henry wrote, 'Two days after my arrival, the fever which had been kindling in my blood broke out, and last night I fainted repeatedly.' He continued with words of thanksgiving to God: 'But a gracious God has again interposed to save my life, today I feel well again.'[3]

As his health began to improve he turned to his books, especially the Greek and Hebrew Scriptures. He told Mrs Sherwood about his studies of the Hebrew language and his plans to search for evidence to prove that all races had a common ancestry, which he could show to the Indians in the hope that this would help break down some of the barriers which made them so hostile towards the gospel.

Henry was not impressed with Cawnpore: 'I do not like this place at all. There is no church, not so much as the fly of a tent; what to do I know not, except to address Lord Minto [the governor general] in a private letter.'[4] Once again Henry felt isolated, except for the Sherwoods and the few men who came to his home to study the Scriptures. He spoke to the general in charge of the troops stationed in the town about the need of a place for worship. In an act of generosity he was told that he

Cawnpore

could use the Light Dragoons' riding school area if the weather prevented an outdoor service.

14 May was the Lord's Day and Henry conducted his first service in the oppressive heat, which was so severe that several officers and soldiers collapsed. This was followed by a service at the general's home for the soldiers' wives and other British citizens. Afterwards he visited the hospital, where he read the Scriptures to the men and prayed for them. Before long he also introduced them to John Bunyan's *Pilgrim's Progress*.

More than ever he felt the need for a more suitable place than the riding-school area in which to conduct services. In a letter to Daniel Corrie dated 15 May 1809, he commented: 'Yesterday I went to the Light Dragoons. They are the finest regiment I ever saw. We met in the riding-school. The effluvia [unpleasant odour] was such as would please only the knights of the turf. What must the Mohammedans think of us! Well may they call us dogs, when even in divine worship we choose to kennel ourselves in such places.'[5]

In the evening a group of soldiers who were professing Christians came to Henry for a time of worship, when they sang songs of praise together, had a time of prayer and listened to the reading and exposition of the Scriptures. These men had previously met in secret to worship God, but after Henry's arrival they were invited to the Sherwoods' bungalow. The men arrived for the meeting carrying a *mora* (a low seat) and their Bibles. When a group of officers caught them going to the Sherwoods' home, they were soundly abused for their 'unmilitary' behaviour, as if they were guilty of causing a disturbance, and Mr Sherwood had to intervene on their behalf. Afterwards, when Henry had his own rented bungalow, a room there was opened for these men, who came to be known as 'Henry's men'. Later still they met in the building that was being prepared as a place of worship.

Despite all the difficulties Henry still had a sense of humour. In a letter to Daniel Corrie, dated 22 May 1809, he wrote, 'I hear of a Mrs A. as one who is religious, and is even suspected of singing psalms of a Sunday. Such flagrant violations of established rules seem to mark her for one of our fraternity.'[6]

Much to the consternation of others, when Henry needed money for a house, he sent a coolie to collect his salary and bring it to him. When his friends heard what he had done, they expected the man to abscond with his wealth, but Henry's trust in the man was rewarded and he soon had the money in his hand.

On 29 May he left the Sherwoods' house for his new home between the sepoy parade grounds and the artillery barracks (sepoys were native Indians who served in the British army). It was situated at the end of an avenue of palm trees and aloes, where there were two bungalows, linked together by a passage-way. Henry and his household occupied the larger one and Sabat and his wife the smaller. There was a garden, laid out with trees and shrubs, and in the middle there was an open lawn area with a raised platform called a *cherbuter*, which Henry later used as a pulpit when preaching to the Cawnpore 'down and outs'.

On their first visit to Henry's home, the Sherwoods were conducted to the *cherbuter*, where they met other guests who were already seated. Mrs Sherwood described those present that evening.[7]

First there was Sabat, the Arab who, as we have already seen, was expected to provide valuable assistance in the translation of the New Testament into Arabic and Persian.

Secondly, there was the handsome young Roman Catholic Jesuit father, Padre Julius Caesar, whom Henry had met at Patna. This Italian priest was richly dressed in a skull cap and a robe of purple satin, which was tied around his body with a cord made from plaited silk. He also carried a rosary made up of precious stones. In addition to his native Italian he spoke French and Latin, making it possible for him to converse with Mr Sherwood as well as with Henry.

The third person was a handsome, well-educated Indian, dressed in his Hindustani clothing. The fourth man was a small, half-caste Bengali gentleman, with skin the colour of copper. He wore white nankeen trousers and could only speak Bengali.

The other members of the party were Mr Sherwood, wearing his scarlet-and-gold uniform, his wife, who was the only woman present, and Henry, who was dressed in his clerical coat of black silk.

As this group had no one language in common, a babel of voices could be heard speaking in eight different languages — English, French, Bengali, Hindustani, Persian, Arabic, Italian and Latin. Henry gave instructions for his servant to prepare some mutton patties, which he knew Mrs Sherwood enjoyed and, before they could leave, they all went into the bungalow and gathered round the table for a meal.

It was his pastoral duties, however, that occupied so much of his time. Once he rebuked the general for swearing, but he knew that the general didn't take his rebuke seriously. In a letter to Daniel Corrie he commented about his congregation: 'They sometimes take no more notice of me than a dog.'[8]

In the midst of his duties he received word from Charles Simeon that his sister Sally was very ill with consumption (tuberculosis). On 19 November he wrote, 'Oh my dear Sally, though I know you are well prepared, how does nature bleed at the thought of a beloved sister's drooping and dying. Yet still to see those whom I love go before me, without so much as a doubt of their going to glory, will, I hope, soothe my sorrow. How soon shall I follow? I know it must be soon ... death is settled in my lungs.'[9]

Henry's letter was never completed, as he received word in the meantime that Sally had died. He then wrote letters to Sally's husband and another to Charles Simeon, who had also written concerning Sally's death. In the midst of his sorrow he received a letter from Lydia offering to take up correspondence with him in place of Sally. This offer was joyfully accepted and he wrote to her at once, expressing his thanks to God for her decision.

Three weeks later he again wrote to Lydia, describing his state of health: 'Shall I venture to tell you, that our family complaint has again made its appearance in me, with more unpleasant symptoms than it has ever yet done? ... The symptoms I mentioned are chiefly a pain in the chest, occasioned, I suppose, by over-exertion the two last Sundays, and incapacitating me at present from all public duty and even from conversation.'[10]

As the months passed, Henry's thoughts turned frequently to Lydia, and his journal reflects a change in his plans. He inscribed in it on 8 July 1810 the following entry: 'My thoughts today are very much towards Lydia; I began even to be reconciled to the idea of going to England for her. "Many are the thoughts of a man's heart, but the counsel of the Lord, that shall stand." '[11]

About that time, Daniel Corrie's sister Mary arrived in India and rumours spread, even as far afield as England, that Henry was considering marriage to her. In a letter to Lydia, dated 14 August 1810, he put the rumour to rest: 'You thought it possible [your letter] might find me married, or about to be so. Let me begin therefore, with assuring you, with more truth than Gehazi did his master, "Thy servant went no whither"; my heart has not strayed from Marazion, or Gurlyn, or wherever you are. Five long years have passed, and I am still faithful. Happy would it be if I could say that I had been equally true to my profession of love for Him who is fairer than ten thousand, and altogether lovely.'[12]

In January 1810 Lydia heard that her former fiancé had married, releasing her from the vow she had taken. A few weeks later we read in her diary of a changed attitude towards Henry: 'Many sad presages of evil concerning my absent friend, yet I am enabled to leave all to God — only now I pray, if consistent with His will, his life may be spared, and as a means of it, that God may incline him to return again to this land. I never did before dare to ask this, believing the cause of God would be more advanced by his remaining in India; but now I pray, without fear of doing wrong or opposing the will of God, for his return.'[13]

Henry's parish duties often meant travel far from Cawnpore. There were marriages to conduct and babies to be baptized, which necessitated days of travel through rough, dangerous territory. And whenever he travelled by palanquin, the jolting caused him much pain.

On one occasion he was required at Pretabjush in Oude, which was still ruled by a nabob. (Nabobs were autocratic rulers exercising the power of life and death over their subjects.) Oppression and the insecurity of property had stripped the country of all its inhabitants. From Manicpore, where he moved inland about fifty miles to Pretabjush, he saw only two or three miserable villages. The road was just a winding footpath through a wood and, in consequence of the rains, even that was lost in a number of places. Indeed all the lowlands were under water. The journey, travelling by night, was not a pleasant one by any means. When Henry was ready to return to Cawnpore, the nabob assigned him four troopers for the journey, to protect him from the many violent gangs that plied their business in the region.

Wherever he went, Henry preached the gospel, but without any visible success. He longed and prayed for the power of God to accompany his preaching, so that sinners would repent.

Each day in his bungalow he led a time of worship with the household, and any visitors present were expected to take part. Mrs Sherwood wrote about the devotions she and her husband attended before they left for Calcutta: 'In the mornings we all used to set out together, children and servants, to go up from the river to the house... Having arrived at the bungalow the children and their servants went to the apartments appointed them, and I went into the hall to breakfast. There were always one or more strangers (gentlemen) present. We sang a hymn, and Mr Martyn read and prayed before breakfast, and we often sat long at breakfast.'[14] The conversation was always about spiritual matters.

Later, when Henry was ill and Daniel Corrie came to assist him, the Sherwoods took part in the meetings held for the Christian soldiers. There would be a time of worship in the new church building, which by then was nearing completion. Several hymns would be sung, the Scriptures read, followed by a devotional talk and a time of prayer. After that, everyone went to Henry's home to enjoy supper together. The time together usually finished with a hymn. Henry's favourite hymns were 'The God of Abraham praise' and 'O'er the gloomy hills of darkness'. The latter was one of hope and joy to all who longed to see the conversion of the heathen. Some of the wording, as sung by Henry and his friends, appears dated to modern ears, but the following verses well capture the spirit of the hymn:

O'er the gloomy hills of darkness
Look, my soul; be still, and gaze;
All the promises do travail
With a glorious day of grace;
Blessed jubilee!
Let thy glorious morning dawn.

Kingdoms wide that sit in darkness,
Grant them, Lord, Thy glorious light;
And from eastern coast to western
May the morning chase the night;
And redemption,
Freely purchased, win the day.

May the glorious day approaching
End their night of sin and shame,
And the everlasting gospel
Spread abroad thy holy name
O'er the borders
Of the great Immanuel's land!

Fly abroad, thou mighty gospel,
Win and conquer, never cease;
May thy lasting wide dominion
Multiply and still increase!
Sway Thy sceptre,
Saviour, all the world around
                              (William Williams, 1717-91).[15]

# 18.
# A new start

'I often went out with Mr Martyn in his gig ... and whoever went with him went at the peril of their lives. He never looked where he was driving, but went dashing through thick and thin, being always occupied in reading Hindustani ... or discussing some text of Scripture'
(Mary Sherwood).

# 18.

# A new start

Life in Cawnpore was made bearable because of the presence of the Sherwoods and the small group of Christian soldiers who regularly met for worship. After sunset Henry frequently visited the Sherwoods for the evening meal and the opportunity to talk with like-minded people. To get there he rode his horse, usually accompanied by his *sais*, the horse's groom, running by his side. Sitting his horse a little awkwardly, and with his coat pulled on anyhow, so that it looked as if it were slipping off his shoulders, he was instantly recognizable.

At night-time he often looked into the heavens and pointed out the constellations to those present, expressing the hope that in the world to come he would uncover the mysteries of the heavenly bodies.

After he had been in Cawnpore some time, the Sherwoods asked him to baptize Lucy, their new baby daughter. The family and servants gathered on the veranda to witness the ceremony. Mrs Sherwood suddenly realized that Lucy was being baptized in the same spot, and on the very same day, that their first child to be named Lucy had died twelve months earlier. She commented on this new child's baptism: 'Never can I forget ... the beautiful and earnest blessing [Mr Martyn] implored for my baby, when he took her into his arms after the service was concluded. I still fancy I see that child of God as he looked down tenderly on the gentle babe, and then looked upwards, asking of his God that grace and mercy for the infant which he truly accounted as the only gift which parents ought to desire.'[1]

Soon after Lucy's baptism the Sherwoods left for Calcutta, seeking medical advice. They wanted to know if it would be better for little Lucy if they were to return to England. However, the doctor urged them to avoid the damp English climate and to remain in India. During their absence, when Henry was largely ignored by the other Europeans in Cawnpore, his thoughts frequently turned to Lydia.

When the Sherwoods returned from Calcutta they observed that Henry was unwell, from what he called 'a fire burning in his breast'.[2] However, he could still laugh at some of the strange happenings in Cawnpore. Mrs Sherwood recorded what she called 'the adventures of a pineapple cheese'.[3] The Sherwoods had a special cheese which they brought out for supper each night they ate at home. Henry also had a similar cheese which he passed around to his guests. Noticing that both cheeses seemed to grow smaller at the same rate, Mrs Sherwood grew suspicious. When she mentioned this to Daniel Corrie's sister, Mary, who was staying in Cawnpore at the time, Miss Corrie agreed that she too had noticed it. Summoning her servant, Mary Sherwood demanded that he explain what was happening. The man knew he had been found out! Mrs Sherwood wrote that the servant 'joined his hands, crouched like a dog, and confessed the charge, crying, "Mercy! Mercy!" He was forgiven, though from that time the double duties of this celebrated cheese were put to a stop.'[4]

A second amusing incident occurred when it was discovered that the raisins and limes that the Sherwoods placed on the table when Henry was present had been sold to their servant at half price by Henry's servants.

Next to the Sherwoods, Henry's encouragement came from the few Christian soldiers who, as we saw in the previous chapter, regularly met for devotions in his house. The numbers varied but on 22 October 1809, with the visit of the 53rd Regiment, sixteen additional men came for worship. Sabat was

there as well. In Henry's journal we read, 'After a short discourse on "Behold the Lamb of God", we commemorated the
death of the Lord. It was the happiest season I have yet had at
the Lord's table … the rest of the day I felt weak in body, but
calm in mind, and rather spiritual.'[5]

He had agitated for a building that could be used as a
church, and on 3 April 1810 he was finally able to write to
David Brown, 'My church is almost ready for the organ and the
bell.'[6]

Henry's plan was to complete the translations of the New
Testament and some tracts into the languages spoken by the
Indians. He knew that his health was deteriorating and he
would not be able to preach to crowds for too long. Missionaries
throughout India longed to hear the name of Christ being
honoured by the native population. One of his favourite hymns,
a paraphrase of Psalm 72, was a prayer for the extension of
Christ's kingdom:

Jesus shall reign where'er the sun
Does his successive journeys run;
His kingdom stretch from shore to shore,
Till moons shall wax and wane no more.

The saints shall flourish in his days,
Dress'd in the robes of joy and praise;
Peace, like a river from his throne,
Shall flow to nations yet unknown.[7]

Before the Scriptures could be widely read the population
needed schools where reading was taught. Mrs Sherwood had
opened two schools — one for boys and the other for girls. As
he had done when based in Dinapore, Henry also opened a
school. It was near the rows of housing where the Indian
soldiers lived, and when Henry told the barrack-master that it
was his school, the suggestion was made that he should obtain
better quarters for the class. No doubt this was because the

An Islamic school in nineteenth-century India

teacher sat on the dusty floor at one end of a long shed, with the children sitting in the dust along the sides of the shed writing on wooden slates with chalk. Mrs Sherwood described the scene: 'Now, Cawnpore is about one of the most dusty places in the world. The Sepoy lines are the most dusty part of Cawnpore; and as the little urchins are always well greased, either with cocoa-nut oil or ... with rancid mustard oil, whenever there was the slightest breath of air they always looked as if they had been powdered all over with brown powder.'[8] The schoolmaster was an old man whose only way of showing who was in charge was to shout even louder than his pupils! Another class of about sixteen boys met in Henry's bungalow.

Henry, knowing the value of books to those translating the Scriptures, urged the establishment of a library in Calcutta of books that would be useful to those doing translation work. The missionaries in Calcutta decided to produce a new translation of the Scriptures in Hindustani. They were unsure what to do about *Pilgrim's Progress* as they found the story was beyond the comprehension of those who could read. Daniel Corrie approached Mary Sherwood, asking her to write a version of

*Pilgrim's Progress* specially for the Indians. Her book was the story of someone called Bartholomew and was founded upon fact.

Henry's life was very busy, but there were occasions when he found time to harness the horse to the gig and go for a drive, frequently taking one of the Sherwoods for an outing. When Mary Corrie was staying at Cawnpore, she was also sometimes invited along. Mrs Sherwood has left a record of those hazardous excursions: 'I often went out with Mr Martyn in his gig, during that month, when he used to call either for me or Miss Corrie, and whoever went with him went at the peril of their lives. He never looked where he was driving, but went dashing through thick and thin, being always occupied in reading Hindustani by word of mouth, or discussing some text of Scripture. I certainly never expected to have survived a lesson he gave me in his gig, in the midst of the plain at Cawnpore, on the pronunciation of one of the Persian letters; however, I did survive, and live to tell of it many years afterwards.'[9]

Sabat, who lived next door, continually complained about his wife ruling his life. Like many other middle-class Indian women of the time, she sat on cushions all day and was protected from mosquitoes by a net which hung from the roof and spread out around her. Frequently when night fell she made a bed from the cushions and fell asleep on the same spot. Several of her female servants cared for her, combing her hair, caring for her fingernails and passing on any gossip they had heard.

Her relationship with her husband, Sabat, was not one of love, but of hatred! She was a Muslim and violently objected to Sabat's efforts to get her to become a Christian. That would never happen! Sabat told Henry of his wife's attitude towards Christianity because he wanted Henry to believe that he suffered greatly as a result of living with Ameena. He reported the following conversation between them:

'Pray,' [she asked], 'will you have the goodness to inform me where Christians go after death?'

'To heaven and to their Saviour,' replied Sabat.

'And where do Mohammedans go?' she asked.

'To hell and the devil,' answered the fierce Arab.

'You,' said the meek wife, 'will go to heaven, of course, as being a Christian.'

'Certainly,' replied Sabat.

'Well then,' she said, 'I will continue to be a Muslim, because I should prefer hell and the devil without you, to heaven itself in your presence.'[10]

At first Henry noticed some signs, as he thought, that Sabat was making progress in the Christian life, but later he found that the Arab believed in the magical powers of some Hindustani magicians. They claimed they could make a mango plant blossom and produce fruit, all in the space of sixty minutes. Sabat said he knew this was true because he had seen it happen, and he wanted Henry to see it also. Henry agreed to watch the demonstration, and so the magicians came to the bungalow ready to perform their magic.

In a letter to Daniel Corrie Henry described what happened next: 'Sabat was about to be deceived again by suffering his attention to be diverted by the eggs, birds, etc., and the gibberish of the man, when I begged him to look at what the third accomplice was doing with the mango; he rose in great wrath (probably at having been their dupe before), and was about to demolish them and their *nobaut* [goods]; however, when he was appeased he said he should now be no more a believer in spells or charms.'[11] Life was often very tense between Henry and the quick-tempered Sabat.

Soon after arriving at Cawnpore, Henry found himself the centre of attraction to the beggars who would come at any time of the day to his bungalow hoping for a handout. When the numbers increased to such an extent that they were taking up too much of his time, he announced that they could only be given help on Sunday afternoon. Towards the end of 1809, Sabat rebuked Henry, telling him he had a ready-made congregation each Sunday afternoon, but failed to tell them of the salvation which was to be found in Christ, the Saviour of sinners. Henry felt ashamed. Had he not come out to India to preach the gospel? Yet here at Cawnpore God had given him a large number of the lowest-caste Indians, and he was doing nothing but feed their physical bodies. It was now time to feed their souls!

Mrs Sherwood described the motley crowd that surrounded the *cherbuter*:

These Fakirs and Yogis [Muslim and Hindu ascetics, with a reputation for sainthood, who lived by begging alms] are organized bodies, having their king or supreme in every district. They amount to hundreds in every large station... Even we English, in all our pretended wisdom, have been often deceived by them... I remember once seeing a man standing by the river side, who was said to have stood there in one attitude for many years, until his beard and his nails had grown to an enormous length, and the very birds had built their nests in his hair ... we did not suspect, what has since been discovered, that this appearance is always kept up by three or four persons, who combine together to relieve the guard, watching their opportunities to make the exchange when no eye is upon them.

A fakir

But horrid as these standing and sitting objects make themselves by wigs and false beards of matted hair, and a thick plaster of cow-dung, they are not worse [than] many that move about the country, demanding alms from the superstitious or ignorant people... Sometimes Mr Martyn's garden has contained as many as five hundred of these people on a Sunday evening, and as I dare not let my imagination loose to describe them, I will copy from my Indian journals what I have written of them.

... These devotees vary in age and appearance; they are young and old, male and female, bloated and wizened, tall and short, athletic and feeble; some clothed with abominable rags; some nearly without clothes; some plastered with mud and cow-dung; others with matted, uncombed locks streaming down to their heels; others with heads bald or scabby ... the features having become exaggerated, and the lips blackened with tobacco, or blood-red with the juice of the henna....

[There] are among them still more distinguished monsters. One little man generally comes in a small cart drawn by a bullock; his body and limbs are so shrivelled as to give, with his black skin and large head, the appearance of a gigantic frog. Another has his arm fixed above his head, the nail of the thumb piercing through the palm of the hand; another, and a very large man, has his ribs and bones of his face externally traced with white chalk, which, striking the eye in relief above the dark skin, makes him appear, as he approaches, like a moving skeleton. The most horrible, however, of these poor creatures are such as have contrived to throw all the nourishment of the body into one limb, so as to make that limb of immense size, while all the rest of the frame is shrivelled.[12]

A site on the River Ganges near Cawnpore where suttee was practised

The congregation responded to Henry's preaching with 'groans, hissings, blasphemies, and threatenings; the scene altogether was a fearful one'.[13]

Henry preached against sin and urged them to look to the Lord Jesus for salvation. He spoke out against the teaching that a washing in the Ganges River sanctified the person. He condemned the practice of a wife throwing herself upon her husband's funeral pyre. He questioned the belief that a cow was a sacred animal, and asked where they could find that taught in any book. He poured scorn on the situation in which cows were treated with such care while humans were dying from hunger. Questions were raised about these and other false teachings. At the conclusion of his address each person present was given a small coin — a *pice* — and Henry returned to his bungalow in a state of collapse. The British authorities kept close watch on these Sunday afternoon gatherings as they feared a riot or something that could start a civil war.

Henry was distressed when he saw no conversions resulting from his teaching in Cawnpore, but he did see some grounds for thanksgiving to God. At the end of 1810 he penned some thoughts about the year that had just ended: 'Nothing important has occurred this last year, but my removal to Cawnpore, and the commencement of my ministry, as I hope it may be called, among the Gentiles. This, with my endeavours to instruct the servants, has been blessed by the Lord, to the improvement of my temper and behaviour towards them, as I hope that I am more patient with them than before... This whole year also, I have been more or less engaged in investigating the nature of language... Ten years have elapsed, since I was first called by God, into the fellowship of the gospel...'[14] He continued, '... and ten times greater than ever ought to be my gratitude to the tender mercy of my God, for all that he has done for me... The chief thing I have to mourn over is my want of more power and fervour in secret prayer, especially when attempting to plead for the heathen. Warmth does not increase with me in proportion to my light.'[15]

Henry knew his health was failing, yet he had so much more work still to do. Frequently he meditated upon some words from a hymn:

Well, if our days must fly
We'll keep their end in sight,
We'll spend them all in wisdom's way,
And let them take their flight.

They'll waft us sooner o'er
This life's tempestuous sea,
Soon we shall reach the blissful shore
Of blest eternity.[16]

# 19.
# Time to leave Cawnpore

'On this occasion ...
brilliant light shone from his
eyes — he was filled with
hope and joy; he saw the
dawn of better things, he
thought, at Cawnpore, and
most eloquent, earnest, and
affectionate was his address
to the congregation'
          (Mary Sherwood).

# 19.
# Time to leave Cawnpore

Henry spent a great deal of time on what he called his 'philological mania', that is, his obsession with the study of languages and their relationships to each other.[1] He was attempting to show that all languages came from Hebrew. If he could prove this, scholars would be required to study the Old Testament, and he hoped that God would use this to bring about many conversions.

Translation work occupied much of his time, especially after Mirza resigned because of Sabat's rudeness to him. Later, however, Mirza returned to work with Henry and at last, on 29 June 1810, to the joy of both, the Hindustani New Testament was completed. The missionaries in Calcutta received the copy with acclaim, but it was not published until 1812, because a fire at the publishing company destroyed all the type. Henry had also translated both the *Book of Common Prayer* and the book of Genesis into Hindustani — all within five years of his arrival in India.

Sabat, on the other hand, who had arrived with the reputation of excellence in Persian and Arabic, proved a failure in his work. He himself was satisfied with what he had done, but Henry complained of his laziness and frequent absences. After David Brown and the others at Calcutta had seen some of Sabat's work, Henry received a letter to which he replied, 'I must own that I feel a little for poor Sabat on this occasion... I dare not show him the papers, without preparing him for the shock, and mean to get the Epistle to the Romans fairly away to you before the commencement of the storm. Rasheed says that the translator has not a facility in writing Persian, hence his style is destitute of ease and elegance. Yet it is intelligible, and the work not absolutely good for nothing.'[2]

Several days later, Sabat decided to go to Lucknow for a break from his routine. This gave Henry the opportunity to pass on to him the criticisms from the missionaries at Calcutta concerning his abilities as a translator. Before he left Henry handed him a sealed envelope with the instruction that he should not look at its contents until he had crossed the Ganges River.

Some time afterwards he received a reply from Sabat, which prompted Henry to write to David Brown, 'I have just heard from Sabat. Among other remarks he says, "Ah, and pity that a pearl should be set in the shop of an ironsmith. They said that I am a beginner in Persian, which I spoke, sucking milk." '[3]

The following year Henry pleaded with David Brown to take care in what he said to Sabat: 'Everybody would suppose Sabat improved: I fancy I see the worldly principle more predominant. Do not tell him any more that he is a learned man, the fact itself begins to be doubtful to me…'[4] And the more Henry looked at Sabat's work, the more he realized that his translation was of poor quality. All this time Henry's health was failing and Sabat's continual criticisms only made things worse.

Sabat even wrote a letter, very critical of Henry, to a friend at Lucknow, who worked for the British Resident (the local agent representing the governor general). When the resident saw the comments, he sent the letter to Henry, who in turn showed it to Sabat. When Sabat was asked to read out in English what he had written, there was a silence. He knew that Henry had read the letter and was ashamed. He could not even look Henry in the face. Calmly, Henry took the letter from him and, after indicating that he knew the contents, quietly told him to leave the room.

Ruins of the British Residency at Lucknow

In the midst of all these activities Henry offered to meet the cost of translating the New Testament into Hindustani out of his own pocket. He was also becoming more convinced that he needed to spend time in Persia and Arabia in order to produce accurate translations into those languages. His health was deteriorating to such an extent that he was unable to carry out all his duties.

On Sunday, 8 October 1809, he wrote to a friend, mentioning that he was suffering from severe headaches. In another letter, dated November 1809, he unburdened himself about his health: 'I am sorry to say that my strength for public preaching is almost gone. My ministrations [duties as a clergyman] among the Europeans at this station have injured my lungs, and I am now obliged to lie by except on the Sabbath days, and once or twice in the week... This rainy season has tried my constitution severely. The first attack was with spasms, under which I fainted. The second was a fever, from which a change of air, under God, recovered me.'[5]

Writing in his journal on 19 November, he drew a comparison between his sister Sally's illness and his own state of health: 'How soon shall I follow? I know it must be soon. The paleness and fatigue I exhibit after every season of preaching, show plainly that death is settled in my lungs.'[6] He knew that he too was carrying the disease that had caused the death of his mother and his sisters Laura and Sally. Sometimes he was unable to carry out his preaching duties on the Lord's Day, and on other occasions he spoke in a low voice, to spare the strain upon his lungs. Usually he was utterly exhausted by the end of the time he spent with 'his men' on a Sunday evening.

April 1810 was a difficult month health-wise, for we read in a letter written to David Brown, 'I do not know whether I may venture to tell you that I have a pain in my breast, occasioned, I fear, from over-exertion of my lungs on the Sundays; the Sunday before last it made its first appearance... Last Sunday it came on again at night, and I was obliged to leave my men in the midst. Today (Wednesday) it is not gone. Such a symptom in my constitution is alarming... Pray for me. Prayer lengthened Hezekiah's life, perhaps it may mine.'[7]

Three days later he recorded in his journal: 'These symptoms are alarming in such a consumptive constitution as mine; yet why shall I say alarming, if my time is come, in the will of God? At the apprehended approaches of death, my guilt and neglects rise to view, and make me often unhappy, but though cast down, I am not dismayed.'[8]

An accident occurred on 12 May 1810 which could easily have resulted in Henry's death. In the evening, as he was galloping along on his horse, the saddle came off and he fell heavily to the ground. By the grace of God he was only slightly hurt and was able to carry on with his work.

Early in June, his health took a turn for the worse, making him unable to carry out all his duties. Daniel Corrie and his sister Mary called in on their way to Daniel's new appointment to Agra. For a time he assisted Henry, and then approached the general asking that he might remain at Cawnpore for a time to help Henry and perhaps aid his recovery. The general, who

Agra Fort

didn't usually approve of such departures from normal practice, agreed that Daniel could help Henry for two or three months. Daniel lived with Henry, while Mary, his sister, stayed with the Sherwoods. Every day they met for a time of devotions and on the Lord's Day Daniel carried out Henry's normal duties.

During July 1810 Henry decided to return to England for a time, where he hoped to marry Lydia. It is interesting to note that just five months before this decision, Lydia had commenced to pray for his return.

A pinnace

Meanwhile in Cawnpore every effort was made to bring about an improvement in Henry's health, even using a small two-masted sailing vessel called a pinnace to ensure that he had some fresh air each day. Little Lucy Sherwood loved to be with him on these excursions, frequently sitting on his knee, pretending to be studying a book, just as Henry did. Those were happy days, but he feared his life was drawing to a close.

In a letter to Lydia begun on 14 August 1810 but not finished until 17 August, he wrote:

I am sorry to conclude with saying, that my yesterday's boasted health proved a mistake; I was seized with violent sickness in the night, but today am better. Continue to pray for me, and believe me to be

Your ever affectionate,

H. Martyn.[9]

The kindly general granted Henry six months' leave, in the hope that his health would improve during his absence. He began to make preparations to leave India. At first he was planning to return to England, but when it became clear that Sabat's work on the translation of the New Testament into Persian was not satisfactory, he decided he needed to spend time in Persia and Arabia in order to complete the work of translating the New Testament into the languages of those countries. This, he believed, would ensure a greater degree of accuracy.

While packing his belongings Henry decided to burn his personal papers, including his journal. By the grace of God, Daniel Corrie intervened just as Henry was about to throw away his journal, and appealed to his friend that it be kept safe and sound. After some discussion agreement was reached and the journal was left with Daniel, carefully packed and sealed, with the assurance that he would keep it until Henry's return.

Meanwhile, Henry had a rather romantic view of Persia. He did not think of it as a land of extremely high temperatures and dust. Mrs Sherwood claimed that his vision of Persia was coloured by his reading of its national poets: 'He often spoke of that land as a land of roses and nightingales, of fresh, flowing streams, of sparkling fountains, and of breezes laden with perfumes. Though these imaginations were far from the truth, yet they pleased and soothed him, and cheated him of some fears.'[10]

At last the time came for his departure from Cawnpore. 30 September 1810 was a day to remember. At 9:00 a.m. Henry was to preach his final sermon to his congregation, and he was to do so using the new church building for the very first time. For him and for others, this was a day of thanksgiving — the congregation filled the building and the regimental band was present to lead in both the singing and chanting.

Mary Sherwood wrote of him that day, 'Alas! He was known to be, even then, in a most dangerous state of health, either burnt within by slow inflammation, which gave a flush to his cheek, or pale as death from weakness and lassitude. On this occasion ... brilliant light shone from his eyes — he was filled with hope and joy; he saw the dawn of better things, he thought, at Cawnpore, and most eloquent, earnest, and affectionate was his address to the congregation.'[11]

John Sargent records some thoughts from that sermon: Henry thanked God at seeing 'a temple of God erected, and a door opened for the service of the Almighty, in a place, where from the foundation of the world, the tabernacle of the true God had never stood...' He went on to describe the scene that day: 'A mournful foreboding could not be suppressed, that he who had been the cause of its erection, and who now ministered in it for the first time, in the beauty of holiness, would minister there no more. They beheld him as standing on the verge of the eternal world, and ready to take a splendid flight. "My father, my father, the chariot of Israel and the horsemen thereof" [Elisha's words in 1 Kings 2 when Elijah was taken from him] were the sentiments with which many gazed on him.'[12]

Sargent continued by quoting the words of Mary Sherwood: 'He began in a weak and faint voice, being, at that time, in a very bad state of health; but, gathering strength as he proceeded, he seemed as one inspired from on high. Never was an audience more affected. The next day this holy and heavenly man left Cawnpore... He left us, with little hope of seeing him again, until, by the mercy of our Saviour, we meet with him in our Father's house.'[13]

On his return to his bungalow Henry sank down on his sofa, exhausted. When he felt a little better he asked his friends to gather about him and sing one of his favourite hymns:

O God, our help in ages past,
Our hope for years to come,
Our shelter from the stormy blast,
And our eternal home.[14]

In the afternoon he said his farewell to the mass of faces of Cawnpore's 'down and outs'. He was to leave this city believing that no one had been converted through his ministry there. He was not aware of a young man, Sheikh Saleh, who had come to saving faith as a result of his curiosity about what Henry was doing with the large congregation of Cawnpore's underprivileged.

Sheikh Saleh was born in Delhi about 1776, to well-educated parents, who made sure he had a good understanding of both Persian and Arabic. While living in Lucknow he found employment as a moonshee working for some British settlers. He was a fanatical Muslim whose zeal was so extreme that he was dismissed by his employers. Later he found work with a rajah who wanted the death of a rival living in Joudpore. Saleh and another person in the rajah's employ met the man, and the one who was to carry out the murder swore to him on the Koran that he had come in peace. Then, when the opportunity came, he stabbed his victim to death. This horrified Sheikh Saleh and he began to question his religion, which permitted such a wicked deed to be carried out.

Making his way to Cawnpore he, along with several others, secretly observed as Henry preached the gospel to his Sunday afternoon congregation. When he heard the gospel preached, Saleh wanted to know more, and asked his father if he could obtain work for him in Cawnpore. His father, who knew Sabat, arranged for the latter to employ his son in transcribing manuscripts. The gracious work of the Holy Spirit brought about a change of heart and, following Henry's departure from Cawnpore, Sheikh Saleh went to Calcutta. After some instruction from David Brown, he was baptized and admitted into the membership of the church, with a new name — Abdool Massee'h, which meant 'Bondman of Christ'. Not long afterwards, he went to Meerut and assisted John Parsons, who was chaplain there. He was instrumental in the conversion of the chief physician to the Rajah of Bhurtpore.

Later Abdool was ordained to the Christian ministry in the
Calcutta Cathedral by Bishop Heber. He faithfully served his
Lord until his death in 1827, dying with the words of a Persian
hymn upon his lips:

Beloved Saviour, let not me
In Thy kind heart forgotten be!
Of all that deck the field or bower,
Thou art the sweetest, fairest flower!

Youth's morn has fled, old age comes on,
But sin distracts my soul alone;
Beloved Saviour, let not me
In Thy kind heart forgotten be.[15]

After a time of prayer and fond farewells, Henry left Cawnpore for Calcutta on 1 October 1810, never to return. Mrs
Sherwood wrote that often she thought of him, remembering
the hymn 'There is a fountain filled with blood', and especially
the words:

E'er since, by faith, I saw the stream
Thy flowing wounds supply,
Redeeming love has been my theme,
And shall be till I die.

Then, in a nobler, sweeter song,
I'll sing thy power to save,
When this poor lisping, stammering tongue,
Lies silent in the grave.[16]

# 20.
# Moving on

'He is on his way to Arabia
where he is going in pursuit of
health and knowledge... He
has some great plan in his mind
... but ... the object is far
too grand for one short life,
and much beyond his feeble and
exhausted frame'

(Thomas Thomason, in a
letter to Charles Simeon)

# 20.
# *Moving on*

A seriously ill Henry left Cawnpore, and shortly afterwards India, but his name and the work he had accomplished there would be remembered for many years to come. His friend Daniel Corrie, who later became Archdeacon of Calcutta, visited Cawnpore in 1824 and again in 1833. He recorded in his journal his memories of the day when the church there was dedicated and of happy times of fellowship in the company of Henry Martyn, the Sherwoods and his sister Mary. He also mentioned some of the local people who treasured memories of Henry's time there: 'One poor blind man who lives in an outhouse of Martyn's ... affords a mournful pleasure in reminding me of some little occurrence of those times. A wealthy native too ... sent his nephew to express to me the pleasure he derived from his acquaintance with Martyn.'[1]

Daniel knew the true situation concerning Henry's health. He knew that Henry's desire was to complete the translations of the New Testament, and that he had said, 'I wish to have my whole soul swallowed up in the will of God.'[2]

Travelling down the Ganges River, Henry had the opportunity to relax, but that was not his style of living. Instead he spent time preparing sermons and doing translation work. Arriving at Allahabad, he wrote to Daniel expressing concern regarding his health. He reported that the cold wind found its way into his cabin and that he was forced to get out of bed because of the severe pains in his chest.

When he remembered that payment had not yet been made for the new gate at the entrance to the churchyard, he asked Daniel to conclude the transaction. Then he wrote, 'May you always go through it [that gateway] in faith, and return through it with praise.'[3] This letter concluded by indicating that it was then 7:20 p.m., the very time that Daniel would be at prayer with the Christian soldiers.

Henry's tender conscience was frequently attacked by the 'evil one' and on 4 October he was overwhelmed by an awful sense of his sins. In prayer he turned to his Saviour, the Lord Jesus Christ, and the peace of God flooded into his soul as he meditated upon the words of Psalm 51:7: 'Purge me with hyssop and I shall be clean; wash me, and I shall be whiter than snow.'

His journey to Calcutta was interrupted when he was needed to conduct baptisms and marriages. Often his thoughts turned to England, and especially to Lydia, to whom he commenced writing a letter. He wrote of the days when he had no company and of his deep love for her: 'My affection for you has something sacred in it, being founded on, or at least cemented by, an union of spirit in the Lord Jesus … as I must not indulge the hope of ever seeing you again in this world, I cannot think of you without thinking also of that world where we shall meet.'[4] He went on to explain that his departure from Cawnpore was in order to rest his voice. However, this didn't happen, as everywhere he went he was called upon to speak and preach, which brought on severe chest pains.

Upon reaching Benares he made arrangements to meet the Christian soldiers of the 67th Regiment. When he did he was greatly saddened: 'Many of the most hopeful were ashamed to look me in the face, and sorrow appeared in the faces of those who had remained faithful. About nine of these came to me in my boat, where we sang the hymn which begins, "Come ye

Benares

that love the Lord", after which I spoke to, and prayed with them, earnestly and affectionately, if ever I did in my life.'[5]

Arriving at Boglipore, he met with Antonio, a monk who had translated the Gospels for the people. Henry gave thanks for that, despite the fact that Antonio was not a Protestant. In his journal he wrote, 'The Lord bless his labours; and while he waters others, may he be watered himself!'[6]

On 25 October he had reason for rejoicing — his trip down the Ganges River had concluded, and now he was in the Hooghly River, soon to arrive at Aldeen.

After several stopovers, Aldeen appeared in the distance. His arrival at the Browns' home was joyful: 'Children jumping, shouting ... [conveyed] me in troops to the house. [The Browns] are a lovely family indeed, and I do not know when I have felt so delighted as at family worship last night.'[7]

Later he met the missionaries living at Calcutta, as well as Colonel Young and his wife, who had given him support while working at Dinapore. While in Calcutta he became involved in much discussion concerning the translation of the Scriptures.

On almost every Sunday he was in the pulpit, preaching the Word of God, and this brought on chest pains again. He continued to be sensitive to the comments of others. On one occasion he preached using the text: 'Now as [Paul] reasoned about righteousness, self-control, and the judgement to come, Felix was afraid and answered, "Go away for now; when I have a convenient time I will call for you"' (Acts 24:25), only to be told that some of his words were too personal. In his journal he recorded: '... and on reconsideration I thought it so myself, and was excessively distressed, at having given causeless offence.'[8]

He also decided to fulfil a promise he had made to Charles Simeon, and sat for a portrait. When David Brown saw it, he commented that it was a good likeness of his friend, but added, 'That is not the Martyn who arrived in India; it is Martyn the recluse.'[9] Some months later, when the package containing the portrait was opened by Mr Simeon, he was shocked by what he saw: 'I could not bear to look upon it, but turned away and went to a distance, covering my face, and in spite of every effort to the contrary, crying aloud with anguish... In seeing how much he is worn I am constrained to call to my relief the thought in Whose service he has worn himself so much.'[10]

In Calcutta, Henry was delighted to meet the new chaplain, Thomas Thomason, who had worked with Charles Simeon. He was already a married man, with children, when he made the decision to move to India and commence missionary work. An important factor in making that decision was everything he had heard about Henry Martyn.

In England Thomas had divided his Hebrew Old Testament into sections, one of which was always in his pocket for study.

His journey to India was not without peril, as the ship was wrecked. He rescued his wife, wrapped in a counterpane, and his children using sheets. However, he lost all his books and household goods. When Henry met him in Calcutta he was seated at a table catechizing the English children living in the region — 'fair English children, all of them elegantly dressed, standing around the desk and answering the good man's questions'.[11]

Both Thomas and his wife were shocked when they saw Henry's appearance. In a letter home, Mrs Thomason wrote, 'Dear, dear Martyn arrived and we had the unspeakable delight of seeing his face. He is much altered, is thin and sallow, but he has the same loving heart.'[12]

Henry Martyn in Bengal

In a letter to Charles Simeon, Thomas wrote of the differ-ence between Henry's portrait that he had seen in England before leaving for India and the man he met in India. He had seen the change: 'He is on his way to Arabia where he is going in pursuit of health and knowledge. You know his genius... He has some great plan in his mind of which I am no competent judge; but as far as I do understand it, the object is far too grand for one short life, and much beyond his feeble and exhausted frame... But let us hope that the sea-air may revive him... In all other respects he is exactly the same as he was; he shines in all the dignity of love; and seems to carry about him such a heavenly majesty, as impresses the mind beyond description. But if he talks much, though in a low voice, he sinks, and you are reminded of his being "dust and ashes".'[13]

Those who knew Henry realized that he might well die in executing his plans, but as he was held in such awe by his friends, no one dared try to prevent him leaving India. He met with the Calcutta translation committee, who heaped praise upon the Hindustani translation which was the result of his work with Mirza. After looking at Sabat's work they declared it to be useless. Now, more than ever, Henry was determined to set out for Persia and Arabia.

Life had been hard for Henry. He had been heartbroken by Lydia's refusal to come out to India and marry him; he had lived a life of stress because of the difficulties with Sabat, and his health caused him much concern. He had so much to do, yet the possibility that he might die very soon caused him to make plans to move on almost at once. He hoped that the sea journey to Persia would help him to improve his stamina.

Lord Minto, the governor general, and General Hewett, commander-in-chief of the armed forces in India, gave their permission for Henry to leave the country. After this he visited the Christian Armenians living in Calcutta and obtained letters of introduction to their brethren in Persia and elsewhere. He also obtained the names and addresses of Christians who could give him help if such was needed.

On 21 December 1810 Henry caught a cold which harmed his lungs. He believed that from that day on his health began to fail. His entry in his journal for that time shows that he was in no way a 'stained-glass window' saint who had risen above all normal human feelings, but had fears like everyone else. He wrote, 'Nature shrinks from dissolution, and conscience trembles at the thought of a judgement to come. But I try to rejoice in God through our Lord Jesus Christ.'[14]

All the time Henry was keeping watch for a suitable ship to take him to Persia. When he found a native *buggala* (a two-masted boat with a raised, highly ornamented stern, capable of carrying a cargo of up to 250 tons) about to sail to Bombay, he approached the captain, who refused him passage as he feared that the sailors might rebel with a Christian on board.

When he was asked to preach on 23 December, he believed that the sermon was one he himself needed to hear. His text was Psalm 9:17: 'The wicked shall be turned into hell, and all the nations that forget God.' He realized that the ultimate condition of the ungodly was hell, and that he was called to godly living wherever he went. He was also aware that the all-searching eye of God saw all that he did.

During his time in Calcutta the new year, 1811, dawned and again in his journal he reviewed the old year and looked forward to the new: 'The weakness which has come upon me in the course of the last year, if it should not give an entire new turn to my life, is likely to be productive of events in the course of the present year, which I little expected, or at least did not expect so soon. I now pass from India to Arabia, not knowing what things shall befall me there; but assured that an ever-faithful God and Saviour will be with me in all places whither-soever I go. May he guide and protect me, and after prospering me in the thing whereunto I go, bring me back again to my delightful work in India. It would be a painful thought indeed to suppose myself about to return no more. Having succeeded, apparently, through his blessing, in the Hindustani New

Testament, I feel much encouraged, and could wish to be spared in order to finish the Bible.'[15]

On the first day of the new year he addressed the gathering of those involved in the British and Foreign Bible Society. David Brown, who had conferred this honour on him, wanted his sermon published so that funds could be obtained to provide each of India's 900,000 professing Christians with a Bible.[16] Henry called upon Christian charity to give to the cause, saying, 'Asia must be our care, or, if not all Asia, India, at least, must look to none but us. Honour calls it as well as duty, your reputation for liberality requires that you render their assistance [that of the local population] unnecessary. Let us make haste then and anticipate their supplies, and thus prove to our friends and the world that the mother-country need never be ashamed of her sons in India.' He went on to speak of how, following displays of British military power, ministers of the gospel were endeavouring 'to fulfil the high destinies of heaven in favour of their country'. These men now 'called on their fellow citizens to cheer the [Indians] with the book of the promises of eternal life' and 'to impart freely to all men, that which, next to the Saviour, is God's best gift to man'. He urged his hearers: 'Imagine the sad situation of a sick or dying Christian, who has just heard enough of eternity to be afraid of death and not enough of a Saviour to look beyond it with hope. He cannot call for a Bible to look for something to support him, or ask his wife or child to read him a consolatory chapter... Oh give unto him what may comfort him in a dying hour! The Lord who loves our brethren, who gave his life for them and you, who gave you the Bible before them, and now wills that they should receive it from you, He will reward you. They cannot recompense you, but you shall be recompensed at the resurrection of the just. The King himself will say to you, "Inasmuch as ye have done it unto one of the least of these My brethren, ye have done it unto Me." '[17]

Early in the year, Henry met the Honourable Mountstuart Elphinstone, who was to take up the residency of Poona. This resulted in Henry's gaining a passage with him on the

*Hummoody*, owned by a Captain Kinsay, a Muscat trader, and sailed by a crew under the authority of his Abyssinian slave Nakhoda.

It was on 6 January 1811 that Henry preached for the last time in Calcutta. The following day, without saying farewell to his friends, he boarded Mr Elphinstone's pinnace and set sail down the river to Saugur, where they boarded the *Hummoody*. Very soon Henry was attempting to speak Arabic with the Arabian crew. When the ship made the open sea, he was again to suffer seasickness, which, as before, made him think about death and paradise. The journey down the Bay of Bengal also had its pleasant moments, however. He found his discussions with Mountstuart Elphinstone most enjoyable as both men enjoyed the classics. Frequently they sat on the poop deck talking about the countries beyond India. In a letter to Lydia, Henry wrote, 'One of my fellow-passengers is Mr Elphinstone, who was lately Ambassador at the Court of the King of Cabul, and is now going to be Resident at Poonah, the capital of the Mahratta Empire. So the group is rather interesting, and I am happy to say not averse to religious instruction — I mean the Europeans.'[18]

In turn Elphinstone enjoyed Henry's companionship and, in a letter to a friend, wrote, 'We have in Mr Martyn an excellent scholar, and one of the mildest, cheerfullest, and pleasantest men I ever saw. He is extremely religious and disputes about the faith with the Nakhoda, but talks on all subjects, sacred and profane, and makes others laugh as heartily as he could do if he were an infidel.'[19] In another letter he wrote of Henry, 'A far better companion than I reckoned on, though my expectations were high … a man of good sense and taste, and simple in his manners and character and cheerful in his conversation.'[20]

During this voyage Henry discovered that the ship's captain had been brought up by a missionary named Schwartz, who was known as 'the Lutheran apostle of South India'. He spent a lot of time learning all he could about this man whom he greatly admired.

On 18 January 1810 the island of Ceylon was sighted. The following day a canoe laden with fruit drew alongside, but the *Hummoody* didn't drop anchor until the ship reached Colombo. The captain urged all to go ashore there, see the places of interest and enjoy being on land again. It was here that Henry and Elphinstone found a garden with cinnamon trees and enjoyed the sweet perfume. Henry took some bark from a tree and posted it back to England with the hope that it would have retained some of its fragrance. When he met a crowd of people returning from a funeral, he could not enter into conversation with them as they spoke only Singhalese.

Soon the ship set sail once more, across the Gulf of Manaan and on to Cape Comorin. Frequently, as Henry watched sailing ships pass on their way from England to India, his thoughts turned to his many friends, especially Lydia, and to his native Cornwall. In a letter to her he wrote, 'Was it that …my thoughts wander too often on the beach to the east of T —? You do not tell me whether you ever walk there, and imagine the billows that break at your feet, to have made their way from India. But why should I wish to know? Had I observed silence on that day and thenceforward, I should have spared you much trouble and myself much pain. Yet I am far from regretting that I spoke; since I am persuaded that all things will work together for good… In my schemes of happiness I place myself of course with you, blessed with great success in the ministry, and seeing all India turning to the Lord.'[21]

When the ship dropped anchor on 26 January at Allepie, Henry was told that some 200 Portuguese and native fishermen were Christians. This made his heart glad!

Setting sail again, the ship moved out onto the ocean swell, only to cause him seasickness, but he looked to his Saviour for grace to cope. In his journal he wrote, 'In prayer, my views of my Saviour have been inexpressibly consolatory. How glorious the privilege that we exist but in Him; without Him I lose the principle of life, and am left to the power of native corruption — a rotten branch, a dead thing, that none can make use of. This mass of corruption, when it meets the Lord, changes its nature and lives throughout, and is regarded by God as a member of Christ's body. This is my bliss, that Christ is all. Upheld by Him, I smile at death. It is no longer a question about my own worthiness. I glory in God, through our Lord Jesus Christ.'[22]

The next port of call was the Portuguese colony of Goa, where Henry spent time with someone to whom he had been given letters of recommendation. With his friend Elphinstone he visited Old Goa, where there were convents and Roman Catholic churches. There they met a nun reading a book of prayers written in Latin. He wrote on one of the pages that it was possible to live in a convent, shut off from the world, and yet still have a love of the world in the heart. He found it impossible to hold a conversation with the local clergymen as they couldn't speak Latin. A highlight of the excursion was to stand beside the tomb of St Francis Xavier, one of the first to take Catholicism to India. Following this, Henry made his way to the Inquisition chamber. He was not permitted to enter as several prisoners were at that moment being examined.

A local colonel told Henry that there were approximately 200,000 professing Christians in Goa out of a population numbering 260,000.

When the ship weighed anchor and set sail for Bombay, Henry knew he would be involved in a totally different work from that which he had carried out in Cawnpore. Frequently he turned to God in prayer, asking for the sustaining grace he would need in Persia and beyond: 'I had an affecting season in prayer, in which I was shown something of my sinfulness. How desperate were my case without grace, and how impossible to hope even now without such strong and repeated assurances on God's part, of his willingness to save! Indeed it is nothing but his Spirit's power that enables me to believe at all the things that are freely given us of God. I feel happy when reading that the enjoyments of heaven consist so much in adoration of God. This is as my heart would have it. I would that all should adore, but especially that I myself should lie prostrate. As for self, contemptible self, I feel myself saying, let it be forgotten for ever, henceforth let Christ live, let Christ reign, let Him be glorified for ever.'[23]

After a time of rough seas the *Hummoody* dropped anchor at Bombay on 18 February — Henry's birthday. In his journal he wrote, 'This day I finished the thirtieth year of my unprofitable life; the age at which David Brainerd finished his course... I am now at the age at which the Saviour of men began his ministry, and at which John the Baptist called a nation to repentance. Let me now think for myself, and act with energy. Hitherto I have made my youth and insignificance an excuse for sloth and imbecility: now let me have a character, and act boldly for God.'[24]

Henry knew he had much to do in Bombay in preparation for the work he hoped to undertake in Persia and Arabia.

# 21.
# From India to Persia

'You will be happy to learn
that the murderous pirates
against whom we were sent,
having received notice of our
approach, are all got out of
the way, so that I am no
longer liable to be shot in a
battle, or to decapitation
after it'
(Henry Martyn in a letter
to Lydia Grenfell).

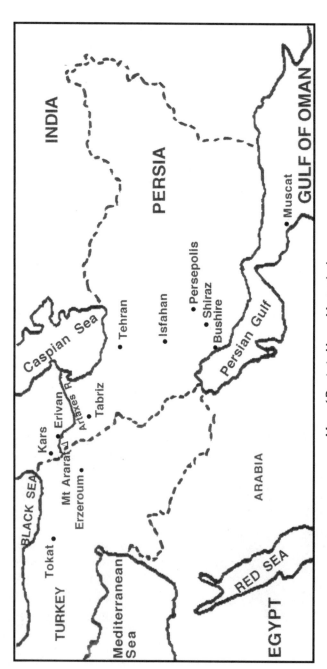

Map of Persia in Henry Martyn's day

# 21.
# From India to Persia

On 19 February 1811 Henry stepped ashore at Bombay to meet the governor, Jonathan Duncan, who provided him with a room for his five-week stay.

Bombay was then a small city with citizens from many surrounding countries. The deep harbour made it an ideal place for trade, while many missionary groups used it as a spring-board to take the gospel to the surrounding areas. While there, Henry took every opportunity to learn Arabic by mixing with people of many nationalities. He prepared a tract in Arabic for distribution to those who spoke that language. This tract was also to be given to Sabat, to encourage him to continue with his translation work. It was the study of Persian that occupied most of Henry's time as that was the language into which he would first translate the New Testament.

On one occasion, when he was at the home of the advocate-general for an evening meal, the discussion turned to religion. When his host denied the existence of hell, Henry took up that subject and others: 'I ventured to give him [the advocate-general], advice about the necessity of praying and keeping the Sabbath, etc., and acting up to the light that he had received, that he might receive more, proving to him that in the gospel, the apparent severity of God in punishing sin, appeared recon-cilable with the exercise of mercy.'[1]

A street in Bombay

The following day he dined with many guests of the governor at the latter's country residence. There he met Sir James Mackintosh and General Sir John Malcolm, who both knew the regions he intended visiting. These contacts were to prove very useful later on.

On Sunday, 24 February, he conducted public worship, his sermon based upon the text, 'But one thing is needed, and Mary has chosen that good part, which will not be taken away from her' (Luke 10:42), but found that he strained his lungs which caused him severe pain in his chest.

Later, at Government House, he again met Sir James Mackintosh who wrote of that meeting in his journal, 'Elphinstone introduced me to a young clergyman called Martyn, come round from Bengal on his way to Bussora, partly for health and partly to improve his Arabic, as he is translating the Scriptures into that language. He seems to be a mild and benevolent enthusiast... We had the novelty of grace before and after dinner, all the company standing.'[2] A week later he wrote of another meeting with Henry, 'Mr Martyn, the saint from Calcutta, called here. He is a man of acuteness and learning; his meekness is excessive, and gives a disagreeable impression of effort to conceal the passions of human nature.'[3]

On the same day Henry recorded what he thought of Mackintosh: 'Called on Sir J. Mackintosh, and found his conversation, as it is generally said to be, very instructive and entertaining. He thought that the world would be soon Europeanized, in order that the Gospel might spread over the world. He observed that caste was broken down in Egypt, and the Oriental world made Greek by the successors of Alexander, in order to make way for the religion of Christ. He thought that little was to be apprehended, and little hoped for, from the exertions of missionaries.'[4]

Towards the end of February, Henry wrote to his friends in both England and India. To Daniel Corrie he outlined his plans for the future, in a letter that was full of expressions of love for God and submission to his will. He said that he was willing to bear a courageous witness for the Lord Jesus. He knew that he would soon be on board ship for the next part of his journey and wrote, 'The sea, too, I loathe... Under the pressure of seasickness I resolved, that if ever I got back safe to India, it should not be a trifle that should move me from it again.'[5]

In the same letter he recorded an incident that illustrated his concern for the observance of the Lord's Day: 'Hearing last Saturday that some sons of Belial [evil men], members of the Bapre Hunt, intended to have a great race the following day, I informed Mr Duncan, at whose house I was staying, and recommended the interference of the secular arm. He accordingly sent to forbid it. The messengers of the Bapre Hunt were exceedingly exasperated; some came to church expecting to hear a sermon against hunting, but I merely preached to them on "the one thing needful". Finding nothing to lay hold of, they had the race on Monday, and ran Hypocrite against Martha and Mary.'[6]

The meeting with Sir John Malcolm was to prove particularly important to Henry. Sir John's first appearance before the Board of Directors of the East India Company took place when he was just twelve years old and seeking a cadetship. Asked what he would do if he ever came face to face with Hyder Ali (who defeated the British forces while they were at war with the French), he answered, in a burst of bravado, that he would 'cut off his heid'.

Sir John had travelled widely through India and Persia, seeking to stimulate trade between those nations and Great Britain. He spoke Persian fluently and had an outgoing personality that won him many friends, as Padwick records: '[He] "bribed like a king", scattered presents of "watches and pistols; mirrors and toothpicks; filagree boxes and umbrellas; cloths and muslins; with an unlimited supply of sugar, sugar-candy and chintz".'[7]

During his stay at Bombay Henry gained much knowledge about the places he expected to visit, and his friendship with Sir John Malcolm opened many doors that would otherwise have remained closed to him. Henry received letters of introduction to people in Bushire, Shiraz and Isfahan. One letter, written to Sir Gore Ouseley, the British Ambassador to Persia, gives us a picture of Henry as seen by a man of the world: 'His intention is, I believe, to go by Shiraz, Isfahan, and Kermanshah to Baghdad, and to endeavour on that route to discover some ancient copies of the Gospel, which he and many other saints are persuaded lie hid in the mountains of Persia. Mr Martyn also expects to improve himself as an Oriental scholar; he is already an excellent one. His knowledge of Arabic is superior to that of any Englishman in India. He is altogether a very learned and cheerful man, but a great enthusiast in his holy calling... I have not hesitated to tell him that I thought you would require that he should act with great caution, and not allow his zeal to run away with him. He declares he will not, and he is a man of that character that I must believe. I am satisfied that if you ever see him, you will be pleased with him. He will give you grace before and after dinner, and admonish such of your party as take the Lord's name in vain; but his good sense and great learning will delight you, whilst his constant cheerfulness will add to the hilarity of your party.'[8]

While waiting for a ship to leave for Persia Henry continued his translation work.

On 5 March, while visiting Elephanta Island, he met Feeroz, who was considered the most intelligent man in the region. Their discussions, which continued over several days, included such topics as the wise men who visited the baby Jesus and the way of salvation — whether it was through faith or works. They both agreed that repentance was essential, and later Henry was to realize that the old man had a good knowledge of Christianity. Feeroz said that the translations of the Scriptures were poor and out of date and that God had not created all things as Moses had claimed. When Henry showed him Sabat's translation of part of the Scriptures into Persian he replied that even if an Arab lived in Persia for twenty years he would not be capable of making an acceptable translation. He spoke out against those who had attempted to win converts using the sword, as the Portuguese had done.

Laden with letters of introduction to the authorities in Persia and some wandering tribes, Henry gained a berth on the *Benares* as a chaplain to the European members of the crew. Before the ship sailed he wrote letters to his many friends, and the one to Daniel Corrie is of interest: 'I have just time to send you a bit of a letter. It is now near six months since I left you and am not yet delivered from Bombay... My breath is not at all stronger, but I have no doubt it would be if I could flee the haunts of men. At this place I am visited from morning to night by the learned natives, who are drawn hither by an Arabic tract, which I was drawing up merely for Sabat, to help him in his book... At church on Sunday some of the 47th appeared; they put me in mind of my dear men at Cawnpore; my kind love to them all... General Malcolm has given me letters to great men at Bushire, Shiraz, and Isfahan... Perhaps I shall be taken up and hanged as a spy. As it is probable, nay almost certain, that I shall be detained at Bushire a month before I can receive the ambassador's permission to enter Persia, you may direct [letters] to me there, via Bombay.'[9]

The *Benares* and *The Prince of Wales* were on duty in the Persian Gulf to rid the area of the Arabic Joasmi pirates who frequented the waters of the Persian Gulf and Indian Ocean, plundering the ships sailing in that region, as well as playing a part in the cruel slave trade that was still carried on. The East India Company had tolerated the pirates until they captured a British ship. From that time on, they became the target of the British navy which in 1809–1810 attacked and captured their territory. Despite the area becoming peaceful, the British fleet continued to patrol the region to sink any remaining pirate ships that dared to attack a British vessel.

Henry was to take spiritual care of the forty-five sailors and twelve artillery men on board. He shared the cabin occupied by Captain Sealy and the captain's cousin, who was in charge of the ship's artillery. Both men met with Henry each night for a time of worship.

Again he faced the problem of seasickness and wrote in his journal words that have a familiar ring about them: 'Very sick and ill from the sea... At length, through the divine mercy, existence ceased to be a burden, and I began to revive.'

On 31 March, the first Sunday aboard, he conducted worship with the sailors. He found the crew inattentive but learnt it was partly because they all spoke different languages — French, Spanish, Portuguese and English. The rest of the day was given over to devotions, translation of the Scriptures into Persian and searching for evidence that all languages came from Hebrew. There were times when he spent hours studying just one word.

On 14 April, he could see in the distance the Persian coast which meant so much to him; it meant that he would soon be living in Persia, in order to produce the very best translation possible of the Persian Scriptures.

A week later, on 21 April, the *Benares* dropped anchor in Muscat Cove. Divine worship was cancelled because all hands were needed for work on the deck.

Going ashore he found the standard of living worse than in India, with only a few trees to be seen. When he indicated that he would like to go beyond the city limits, he was told that would be dangerous because of a war taking place. Consequently he returned to the safety of the *Benares*.

Most of the time he found the heat almost unbearable. During the night the temperature rarely dropped below 92° Fahrenheit (33°C). This was as a result of the many rocks in the area storing up the heat of the sun during the day.

During their stay at Muscat, the crew took on board fresh water and food, while Henry spent his spare time writing to his friends. He penned a letter to Lydia which he began with the words: 'I am now in Arabia Felix.'[10] After a brief outline of the voyage he wrote, 'You will be happy to learn that the murderous pirates against whom we were sent, having received notice of our approach, are all got out of the way, so that I am no longer liable to be shot in a battle, or to decapitation after it, if it be lawful to judge from appearances.'[11]

He also expressed his disappointment that he had not received any letters from her. He asked her to address any letters for him during the next twelve months to Bombay, and after that to Bengal, as he was expecting to return to India. After describing the benefits of the voyage, both to his health and his studies, and the joy of finding Christian fellowship where he had expected none, he sent greetings to the friends back in Cornwall with the words: 'The angels love and wait upon the righteous who need no repentance; but there is joy whenever another heir of salvation is born into the family. Read Ephesians 1. I cannot wish you all these spiritual blessings, since they already are all yours; but I pray that we may have the spirit of wisdom and knowledge to know that they are ours. It is a chapter I keep in mind every day in prayer.'[12]

He knew that his time at sea would soon end and then he would be making his way to Shiraz. However, he was pleased to know that a Persian sailor from *The Prince of Wales* would accompany him to Shiraz.

Before the ship sailed he wrote to David Brown a letter in which he explained the problems caused by the continual hot weather. He also said the cabin he shared with the captain made sleep difficult, not only on account of the heat, but because smoke from the galley wafted into the cabin. He told David he was lying on a couch and meditating upon the scripture: 'Behold, I am with you and will keep you wherever you go...' (Genesis 28:15). He went on to write, 'You will be happy to learn that the pirates whom we were to scourge, are got out of our way, so that I may now hope to get safe through the Gulf without being made to witness the bloody scenes of war.'[13]

The ship's departure was delayed, so Henry took the opportunity to go ashore with some of the British crew and, accompanied by a guard and an Arab guide, travelled out of town to see a huge pass in the mountains. Looking down, they could see in the distance a little valley with a green garden, which he learned was the work of a Hindu. During his time ashore he was able to speak about Christ, his Lord and Saviour, to the guide and his young slave, who showed great interest in all he had to say. After a time Henry returned to the *Benares*, but the next day the two men came to take their leave of him and he gave them a copy of the Gospels written in Arabic. The slave departed clutching the book, which he treated as a great treasure.

After the *Benares* sailed from Muscat the temperature dropped to a pleasant 84° F (29°C). The ship continued on its way, eventually sailing into Arabian waters, where to Henry's discomfort, the winds picked up. This led to a further bout of seasickness, but at least the extra speed meant that Persia would be reached much sooner.

Despite the seasickness, Henry was able to conduct worship on the Lord's Day, 19 May 1811. He preached from John 3:3: 'Jesus answered and said to [Nicodemus], "Most assuredly, I say to you, unless one is born again, he cannot see the kingdom of God." '

Henry was downcast as he contemplated his own sin, believing that he had neglected to carry out his spiritual duties as required by the Lord and that he had spent too much time thinking about Lydia, whose letters he had been reading.

21 May 1811 was a day for him to remember. It was the first time a missionary had set foot in Persia! When the anchor was dropped at Bushire, on the Persian side of the Persian Gulf, Henry recorded in his journal: 'Landed at Bushire this morning in good health; how unceasing are the mercies of the Lord; blessed be His goodness, may He still preserve me from danger, and, above all, make my journey a source of future good to this kingdom of Persia, into which I am now come.'[14]

Bushire was a small village of about 15,000 inhabitants, of Persian and Arabian stock. The temperatures were very hot, usually between 100° and 106° F (38°-41° C) in the shade! This was the hottest time of the year in Persia, an unwise time to travel. Despite the heat Henry hired a horse and rode out with some other travellers. When he became aware that his European clothes were attracting attention to him, he visited a tailor and ordered Persian clothing of a kind suitable to his social status. He was sure this would help him blend in amongst the people.

He soon found himself receiving formal social calls from the local community, including ones from the governor and an Armenian priest. On 25 May, Henry met a man who was considered to be the most learned man in Bushire. When this man was shown the various translations of the New Testament into Arabic, he pronounced Sabat's the best.

That afternoon, accompanied by two captains, the British Resident and the captain of the guard, Henry was presented to the governor, or khan, who treated him with much courtesy after being presented with a letter of recommendation from General Malcolm. He called Henry to sit beside him and share a *calean* (a smoking pipe resembling a hookah) with him. This was followed by coffee, and again the pipe circulated; then Henry was handed a cup of rosewater syrup. At times the silence in the room was broken only by the bubbling of the calean.

Later Henry was told that the governor was a murderer. Having invited some political opponents to a meal at his home under false pretences, he asked them to unbuckle their weapons as a sign of their friendship. At a signal some of his men then attacked and slaughtered them. He afterwards rode off with his soldiers to the towns from which his victims had come and killed or captured all the inhabitants. This had happened about two and a half years before Henry had come to Bushire.

On Sunday, 26 May, Henry conducted worship for the Europeans, and in the evening was invited to attend an Armenian service. He was not impressed by what he saw and heard: '... the same disagreeable succession of unmeaning ceremonies, and noisy chants, as at Bombay. I was introduced within the rails, and at the time of incense, I was censed [ritually perfumed with incense], as the padre afterwards desired me to observe, four times, whereas the laity have the honour done to them but once.'[15] To Henry the service was meaningless.

Other people to call upon him were a Jewish goldsmith and a boy who could read Hebrew fluently. This visit reminded him of the terrible situation in which the Eastern Jews found themselves. He had seen God's ancient people being persecuted by the Gentiles and wrote in his diary, 'O Lord, how long? Will Thine anger burn for ever? Is not justice yet satisfied? This afflicted people are as much oppressed in Persia as ever. Their women are not allowed to [wear the] veil, as all others are required to do; hence, if there be one more than ordinarily beautiful, she is soon known, and a khan or the king sends for her, makes her a Mahometan [Muslim], and puts her into the harem. As soon as he is tired [of her], she is given to another, and then to another, till she becomes the property of the most menial servant; such is the degradation to which the daughters of Israel are subjected.'[16]

Two days before leaving Bushire, Henry called on the acting British Resident, who warned him of the social and moral conditions of the land in which he would be staying for some time. After that he recorded: 'It is enough to make one shudder. If God rained down fire upon Sodom and Gomorrah, how is it that this nation is not blotted out from under heaven?'[17]

Henry was at times unwell, suffering from sunstroke, headaches and sleepiness. Frequently he fell asleep while trying to study, and awoke feeling weak and in pain. He was well aware that his health, which had shown some improvement as a result of the sea voyage, was now failing once more.

It was on the morning of 30 May that he took delivery of his Persian clothes, which were of a quality that marked him out as a gentleman to be treated with respect. At 10:00 p.m. that night he commenced his journey to Shiraz, a city well known for its intellectual community, which included some very fine poets.

# 22.
# The journey to Shiraz

When a trumpet sounded
everyone began to move.
The sound was so discordant
that Henry wondered
whether the trumpet had
holes in it... He saw horses,
mules, riders and luggage
moving across the plain, just
as he had imagined an
Oriental scene to be.

# 22.
# The journey to Shiraz

It was around 10:00 p.m. on 30 May 1811 that the caravan, or *kafila*, made up of some thirty horses and mules, set off for Shiraz. Some of the pack animals carried goods for Sir Gore Ouseley, the British Ambassador, who was then in Shiraz, while the others were weighed down with the possessions of Henry and the other travellers and their servants. Henry rode a type of pony known as a *yaboo* and his servant, Zechariah (or Zachary), an Armenian from Isfahan, rode a mule.

What lay before them was a journey of about 170 miles (over 270 km.), consisting of ninety miles (145 km.) of desert, where the temperatures made travel during the daylight hours impossible. The final eighty miles (130 km.) would involve climbing four steep inclines up the spurs of the Zagros Range, to the cooler region of Zaziroon. This was the most uncomfortable time of the year to make such a journey.

When a trumpet sounded everyone began to move. The sound was so discordant that Henry wondered whether the trumpet had holes in it, or the trumpeter was unused to playing it. He saw horses, mules, riders and luggage moving across the plain, just as he had imagined an Oriental scene to be. The moon shone brightly, and in the clear, hot air, he thought a great deal about the task that lay before him. He knew that God was watching over him, and so devoted much time to prayer, seeking the Lord's blessing.

That night Henry Martyn would have been unrecognizable to his English friends. Not only was he thinner, his features tired and drawn, but he was dressed in the fashionable clothing of a Persian intellectual. He described his appearance in a letter to Daniel Corrie: 'The Persian dress consists of, first, stockings and shoes in one; next, a pair of large blue trousers, or else a pair of huge red boots; then the shirt; then the tunic; and above it the coat, both of chintz, and a great-coat... On the head is worn an enormous cone, made of the skin of the black Tartar sheep, with the wool on.'[1] Henry had allowed his whiskers to grow and ate his food in true Oriental style, plunging his hand into the dish.

During the night all was quiet except for the sound of hooves and the tinkling of the bells worn by the mules and also by Henry's pony, the muleteer having insisted that Henry ride his own horse. Suddenly there came the sound of a muleteer singing in a melancholy tone:

Think not that e'er my heart could dwell
Contented far from thee:
How can the fresh-caught nightingale
Enjoy tranquillity?

O then forsake thy friend for naught
That slanderous tongues can say;
The heart that fixeth where it ought,
No power can rend away.[2]

The words reminded Henry of his friends in India and at home in Britain — especially Lydia.

That night the travellers covered about twenty-four miles, and before sunrise tents were erected under a tree, the only shelter they could find, at a place called Ahmedee. At first Henry tolerated the heat, as being no hotter than he had become used to in India, but as the day wore on the temperature rose until it reached 126° F. (52 ° F) Henry recorded in his

A group of Persians at the door of their tent

journal: 'When the thermometer was above 112° [44° C], fever-heat, I began to lose my strength fast; at last it became quite intolerable. I wrapped myself up in a blanket and all the warm covering I could get, to defend myself from the external air; by which means the moisture was kept a little longer upon the body, and not so speedily evaporated as when the skin was exposed: one of my companions followed my example, and found the benefit of it. But, the thermometer still rising, and the moisture of the body being quite exhausted, I grew restless, and thought I should have lost my senses. The thermometer at last stood at 126°; in this state I composed myself, and concluded that, though I might hold out a day or two, death was inevitable.'[3]

When the sun had set, Henry emerged from his small tent 'more dead than alive'.[4] He was concerned as to how he was going to cope. He had not slept well and had not had any food to eat, although he managed to get a little sleep while the horses and mules were being loaded for the journey. Soon the group moved off. Night had fallen and the cooler air revived him.

When they reached the next camping spot, Henry cut some branches from a date palm and wove them together to form a tattie. He then paid a local peasant to keep it wet, with the pleasing result that the temperature that day didn't rise above 114°F (45° C). He also decided to soak a large towel in water and wrap it around his head and body. He then dressed in all the clothing he had, trapping the cooling moisture next to his body, which made the journey a little more bearable. The extreme heat ruined his appetite and made him feel very weak, but he forced himself to eat some food and prepare himself for the next stage of the journey.

As he left the tent he felt something on his clothing, but did not know what it was. When his travelling companion (whom he refers to as Captain T—) saw that it was a dangerous scorpion, it was quickly flicked to the ground and killed by a heavy boot stamping on it. From then on everyone took great care to examine their clothing in case other scorpions had decided to take up residence. The risk of more scorpions also made sleeping even more difficult than before.

On the morning of 2 June the travellers reached a stream at the foot of a range of mountains about which Henry wrote, 'We seemed to have discovered one of Nature's ulcers. A strong suffocating smell of naphtha announced something more than ordinarily foul in the neighbourhood. We saw a river — what flowed in it, it seemed difficult to say, whether it were water or green oil; it scarcely moved, and the stones which it laved [washed over], it left of a greyish colour, as if its foul touch had given them the leprosy.'[5] There, in the midst of a grove of date trees, the weary travellers pitched their tents and turned in for the day. Henry woke up with a burning fever!

This was the Lord's Day, but there was no opportunity to hold a service, although the captain read a few hymns to Henry. Again it was rest during the day and movement after nightfall. Henry continued to wake up in a fever and, before setting out on the next stage of the journey, he once more wrapped the wet towel around his face and neck. This he believed gave him the strength to survive.

The travellers now began to climb up into the mountains. The uphill track was very narrow and a false step would certainly have meant death to horse and rider. As Henry was riding the muleteer's horse it led the way. There were times when they came to a fork in the track, but the horse always knew which way to go — it had been that way many times before.

Some hours later they came to a plateau where the horses could trot along, covering the ground more quickly. When the party stopped for a while, so that some officials could check their papers, Henry lay down and fell asleep.

Later they found a caravanserai, a resting-place constructed for weary travellers, which the *kafila* decided to use during the daytime. However, there was no means of keeping out the heat and the temperature there rose to 110° F (43° C) during the daytime.

At one place they met a man with blocks of ice which he was taking to Bushire. They bought the ice from him, which helped them cope with the heat.

The next part of their journey took them up another mountain range and on to Carzeroon, where Henry was unable to sleep due to headache, a racing pulse and skin that felt as if it was on fire. The only food they could buy in the town was some bread, milk and eggs, and even these were hard to find.

It was on 5 June at 10:00 in the evening that the travellers left Carzeroon to climb yet another mountain range. This was followed, as dawn broke, by a descent into a delightful valley where they could see fields of wheat and barley swaying in the gentle breeze. Here and there Henry could make out large oak trees, and with the temperature about 62° (16° C), he was reminded of an autumn morning in England.

The following day they reached another caravanserai at Peergan. Here they settled down for the day, eating the food that they had brought with them. While they were there Henry's servant Zachary fell from his mule; he was badly bruised and was much quieter than usual for some time afterwards.

At 1:00 am on 7 June the weary men again set out on another uphill journey. Henry was tired and felt miserable. The mosquitoes had kept him from sleeping and at this altitude he found the atmosphere too cold.

He was pleased when they arrived at the Dustarjan Valley, where it was decided to pitch tents beside a flowing stream, with water as clear as crystal. Of this spot Henry wrote, 'On the banks [of the stream] we observed the clover and golden cup: the whole valley was one green field, in which large herds of cattle were browsing. The temperature was about that of spring in England.'[6] He fell asleep for several hours, which refreshed him, and he awoke full of praise to God for his mercies.

Two days later, on 9 June, they arrived on the plain of Shiraz. On reaching the city gates they found them locked for the night, so they pitched their tents in a fragrant garden close to the city wall.

Some goods belonging to the ambassador, Sir Gore Ouseley were delivered to his camp, but much to Henry's disappointment, the ambassador himself was absent at the time. Henry and his fellow travellers made their way back to their tents and turned in for a good night's rest.

The next day they made their way through the city gate, and along the narrow streets until they reached the home of the wealthy and well-known citizen, Jaffier Ali Khan. Henry carried in his hand letters of introduction from his respected friend, General Sir John Malcolm. At long last he was in a centre where there was an educated elite, a Persian city of literature.

# 23.
# Life and work at Shiraz

In a letter to Lydia he described himself as he worked: 'Imagine a pale person seated on a Persian carpet, in a room without table or chair, with a pair of formidable mustachios, and habited as a Persian, and you see me.'

## 23
# Life and work at Shiraz

### Henry Martyn at Shiraz

#### I

A vision of the bright Shiraz, of Persian bards the theme:
The vine with bunches laden hangs o'er the crystal
    stream;
The nightingale all day her notes in rosy thickets trills,
And the brooding heat-mist faintly lies along the distant
    hills.

#### II

About the plain are scattered wide, in many a crumbling
    heap,
The fanes [shrines] of other days, and tombs where Iran's
    poets sleep:
And in the midst, like burnished gems, in noonday light
    repose
The minarets of bright Shiraz — the City of the Rose.

#### III

One group beside the river bank in rapt discourse are
    seen,
Where hangs the golden orange on its boughs of purest
    green;

Their words are sweet and low, and their looks are lit with joy,
Some holy blessing seems to rest on them and their employ.


IV

The pale-faced Frank [European] among them sits: what brought him from afar?
Nor bears he bales of merchandise, nor teaches skill in war;
One pearl alone he brings with him — the Book of life and death;
One warfare only teaches he — to fight the fight of faith.


V

And Iran's sons are round him, and one with solemn tone
Tells how the Lord of Glory was rejected by His own;
Tells, from the wondrous Gospel, of the Trial and the Doom,
The words Divine of Love and Might — the Scourge, the Cross, the Tomb.


VI

Far sweeter to the stranger's ear those Eastern accents sound
Than music of the nightingale that fills the air around:
Lovelier than balmiest odours sent from gardens of the rose,
The fragrance from the contrite soul and chastened lip that flows.


VII

The nightingales have ceased to sing, the roses' leaves are shed,
The Frank's pale face in Tokat's field hath mouldered with the dead:

Alone and all unfriended, midst his Master's work he fell,
With none to bathe his fevered brow, with none his tale
   to tell.

### VIII

But still those sweet and solemn tones about him sound
   in bliss,
And fragrance from those flowers of God for evermore is
   his:
For his the meed [honour], by grace, of those who, rich
   in zeal and love,
Turn many unto righteousness, and shine as stars above.
                                   (Henry Alford, 1810-71). [1]

Having handed over Sir John Malcolm's letter, Henry and his
servant Zachary were given a room and invited to breakfast
with Jaffier Ali Khan. At first coffee was served and caleans were
smoked. Then the food was served: curry and pilau dishes
[made from rice or wheat, vegetables and spices and usually
served with meat or fish] and a variety of sweets, which were
kept cool with snow and scented with rosewater. Henry, dressed
in his Persian clothes, ate the food in the same way as the
Persians did — with his hands.

After breakfast he was escorted to a summerhouse in the
garden where he met Jaffier's brother-in-law, Mirza Seid Ali
Khan, a fine scholar with a great understanding of the Persian
language, who agreed to assist Henry with his project. Mirza
Seid Ali was a member of the Sufi sect which taught that
everybody was part of God, and there was no difference
between good and evil in God's sight. This meant that there
was no need of laws.

Jaffier Ali was a wealthy man who had three great loves —
wealth, pleasure and literature. Both Jaffier and Mirza Seid Ali
spent much time with Henry explaining the Persian language
and outlining the nation's history. Later Henry heard nightingales singing, which reminded him of England.

Shiraz

He began writing letters to his friends, especially to Lydia, but felt all alone and disappointed that his friends failed to keep in contact with him. In one letter he wrote, 'In the morning [of 12 June 1811], I enjoyed much comfort in prayer. What a privilege to have a God to go to, in such a place, and in such company! To read and pray at leisure, seemed like coming home after being long abroad. Psalm 89 was a rich repast to me. Why is it not always thus with me?'[2]

He enjoyed the great variety of fruit that was available, and one day he received from the vizier, or prime minister, a gift of four mule-loads of melons. To David Brown he wrote, 'One thing is good here, the fruit; we have apples and apricots, plums, nectarines, greengages and cherries, all of which are served up with ice and snow. When I have said this for Shiraz, I have said all.'[3] He even went so far as to say that he would gladly exchange Shiraz for Aldeen.

Soon after his arrival, Zachary told Henry that he had overheard people wondering why the Englishman had come to

Shiraz. Some thought he was a convert to the Muslim faith, while others believed that he was part of a conspiracy to have the nation captured by the Indians, but no one guessed that his plan was to preach Christ, and so win converts to Christianity.

Jaffier made every effort to look after him, even putting up a tent for him in a garden outside the walls of the city, as a change from the town. John Sargent records that ' "Living amidst clusters of grapes, by the side of a clear stream," as he describes it, and frequently sitting under the shade of an orange-tree, which Jaffier Ali Khan delighted to point out to visitors, he passed many a tranquil hour, and enjoyed many a Sabbath of holy rest and divine refreshment. Of one of those Sabbaths, he writes July, 14 — "The first Sabbath morning I have had to myself this long time, and I spent it with comfort and profit. Read Isaiah, chiefly; and hymns, which, as usual, brought to my remembrance the children of God in all parts of the earth…" '[4] However, some weeks later when he spent a few days camping in a vineyard, the wind was so cold that he was glad to get back to the city, where he had a room in Jaffier's house.

When the cold weather set in, he didn't light a fire in his room, because the Persians built fireplaces without a chimney. It was a case of either having warmth from the fire and a room full of smoke, or wrapping himself in sheepskins to keep out the cold — he chose the sheepskins.

During his stay in Shiraz, he had no contact with women; even Jaffier's wife didn't make an appearance, but stayed in her own quarters, where she entertained female visitors. Henry found that he missed the presence of ladies at social gatherings, as he wrote to Lydia.

He purchased a horse and was soon in the habit of riding around the city walls in the mornings, while, as he told his friend Daniel Corrie, evenings were spent singing hymns and drinking a cup of milk and water, since there was no tea to be had. Zachary bought a fancy outfit of many colours for the horse as he wanted his master to appear to be an *amir* (a local chief). Despite his appearing to be a man of importance, some of the boys mocked him: 'But all my finery does not defend me from the boys. Some cry out, "Ho, Russ!"; others cry out, "Feringhee!" ['Foreigner!'] One day a brickbat was flung at me, and hit me in the hip with such force that I felt it quite a providential escape.'[5]

That was not the end of this story, as we read in another letter to Daniel: 'They continued throwing stones at me every day, till happening one day to tell Jaffier Ali Khan, my host, how one as big as my fist had hit me in the back, he wrote to the Governor, who sent an order to all the gates, that if anyone insulted me, he should be bastinadoed [beaten on the soles of the feet with a heavy stick], and the next day came himself in state to pay me a visit. These measures have had the desired effect; they now call me the Feringhee Nabob, and very civilly offer me the *calean*.'[6]

With the help of Mirza Seid Ali, Henry began translating the New Testament into Persian, on 17 June 1811, just over a week after arriving in Shiraz. In a letter to Lydia he described himself as he worked: 'Imagine a pale person seated on a Persian carpet, in a room without table or chair, with a pair of formidable mustachios, and habited [dressed] as a Persian, and you see me.'[7] He faced continual interruptions from visitors, but the time was not wasted, as he made sure they left with a good understanding of the work of the Lord Jesus Christ in the gospel, which is the power of God's salvation to all who believe.

Everything seemed different to Henry. The city gates were opened at sunrise and closed at sunset. The city was governed by the autocratic son of the shah, Prince Abbas Mirza. On 6 July, accompanied by the British Ambassador, Henry was invited to visit the prince. He described this meeting: 'Early this morning I went with the Ambassador and his suite to court, wearing, agreeably to costume, a pair of red cloth stockings, with green high-heeled shoes. When we entered the great court of the palace, a hundred fountains began to play. The Prince appeared at the opposite side, in his *talar*, or hall of audience, seated on the ground. Here our first bow was made. When we came in sight of him, we bowed a second time, and entered the room. He did not rise, nor take notice of any but the Ambassador, with whom he conversed at the distance of the breadth of the room. Two of his ministers stood in front of the hall, outside; the Ambassador's *Mihmander* [guard], and the Master of the Ceremonies, within, at the door. We sat down in order, in a line with the Ambassador, with our hats on. I never saw a more sweet and engaging countenance than the Prince's; there was such an appearance of good nature and humility in all his demeanour, that I could scarcely bring myself to believe that he would be guilty of anything cruel or tyrannical.'[8]

However, there was another side to the prince. When he gave an order, it was obeyed instantly! A short time before leaving the city, Henry made an entry in his journal, dated 8 April 1812, giving an example of his rule over the citizens of Shiraz: 'The Prince dining today at a house on the side of a hill, which commands a view of the town, issued an order for all the inhabitants to exhibit fireworks for his amusement, or at least to make bonfires on the roofs of their houses, under penalty of five *tomans* in case of neglect. Accordingly fire was flaming in all directions, enough to have laid any city in Europe in ashes. One man fell off a roof and was killed, and two others in the same way were so hurt that their lives were despaired of, and a woman lost an eye by the stick of a skyrocket.'[9]

Not all of Henry's time was spent translating the Scriptures or meeting officials. There was much to see in the region, and on one occasion he made his way to the ruins of the once-majestic city of Persepolis. Zachary and the two guards who accompanied them could not understand anyone wanting to visit old ruins and thought Henry must have left Shiraz for this remote place so that he could drink alcohol without the risk of being caught!

Despite being warned beforehand of the wickedness to be found in parts of Persia, he was 'completely disgusted'[10] with what he witnessed at times. On one occasion he went to see a play about the death of Hosyn, the eldest son of Mohammed. When the actors came to a scene in which one of them had to speak a few words in English, the man used the only English words he knew — vile swear words. Immediately Henry stood up, mounted the stage and then and there taught the actors some English words that were worth knowing — those of the Lord's Prayer.

He became aware of the strong anti-Christian feelings of the majority of the Persians. He heard reports of Christians being murdered and soon discovered that they were only tolerated if they were traders or people who were of use to the nation in some way. He also discovered that the observance of the Muslim faith was largely a matter of external show.

Despite all the company, he felt lonely in the lack of Christian fellowship. He had not received any mail and he began to feel that friends in both England and India had forgotten him. In a letter to Daniel Corrie he pleaded: 'I can hardly conceive, or at least am not willing to believe, that you would forget me six successive months; I conclude, therefore, that you must have written, though I have not seen your handwriting since I left Calcutta… What would I give for a few lines from you, to say how the men come on, and whether their numbers are increasing…'[11]

Several months later he was overjoyed to receive mail from Daniel Corrie. In a letter dated 12 December 1811 he wrote, 'Your letters of January 28 and April 22 have just reached me. After being a whole year without any tidings of you, you may conceive how much they have tended to revive my spirits. Indeed I know not how to be sufficiently thankful to our God and Father for giving me a brother who is indeed a brother to my soul, and thus follows me with affectionate prayers wherever I go…'[12] He added that he hoped to have the Persian New Testament completed within six weeks.

In September 1811 he made the decision to move to Isfahan, but this was prevented when he learned that war had broken out between the Turks and the Persians. He knew that he could complete the Persian translation in Shiraz with the aid of Mirza Seid Ali, but he faced continual interruptions from local people who wanted to talk with the English scholar. The number of visitors grew until, for the sake of his work, Henry had to decline seeing them all.

As the translation continued, Henry was asked many questions concerning Christianity. On one occasion a young man copying the account of the high priest striking the Lord Jesus across the face asked, 'Sir, did not his hand dry up?'[13] The doctrine of the Trinity caused heated discussion, but each time Henry pointed his questioners to the Scriptures.

In July 1811 he visited the Jewish synagogue. There was a service in progress when he arrived, but this was interrupted when Henry and the high-ranking Jaffier Ali Khan entered. Henry asked the man who was in charge if he knew the whereabouts of any ancient biblical texts. However, when Henry examined the manuscripts held there he was disappointed to find that none of the texts was of any great antiquity.

When the new year, 1812, arrived Henry wrote some thoughts in his journal: 'Spared by mercy to see the beginning of another year. The last has been in some respects a memorable year; transported in safety to Shiraz, I have been led, by the particular providence of God, to undertake a work the idea of which never entered my mind till my arrival here, but which has gone on without material interruption and is now nearly finished. To all appearance the present year will be more perilous than any I have seen, but if I live to complete the Persian New Testament, my life after that will be of less importance. But whether life or death be mine, may Christ be magnified in me. If he has work for me to do, I cannot die.'[14]

After eight months he could at last say that the Persian translation was completed. For this he thanked and praised God: 'I have many mercies for which to thank the Lord, and this is not the least. Now may that Spirit who gave the word, and called me, I trust, to be an interpreter of it, graciously and powerfully apply it to the hearts of sinners, even to the gathering

[of] an elect people from amongst the long-estranged Persians!'[15] In addition to the New Testament he translated the Psalms into Persian, a task which he described as 'a sweet employment'.

With the translation completed, Henry then had several scribes prepare two ornate copies for the Shah of Persia, four copies for his friends in India and several others to be sent to Cambridge University. However, it was not until 1814 that the copies for his friends in Serampore reached their destination and the printing of the Persian New Testament in India did not take place until 1816.

Despite Lydia's failure to correspond on a regular basis, Henry had continued to write regularly to her during his time in Shiraz. In his letter of 23 June 1811 we read:

My Dearest Lydia,

How continually I think of you, and indeed converse with you, it is impossible to say. But on the Lord's Day in particular, I find you much in my thoughts, because it is on that day that I look abroad, and take a view of the universal church, of which I observe that the saints in England form the most conspicuous part. On that day too, I indulge myself with a view of the past, and look over again those happy days, when in company with those I loved, I went up to the house of God with a voice of praise. How then should I fail to remember her who, of all that are dear to me, is the dearest? It is true that I cannot look back upon many days, nor even many hours passed with you... It was a momentary interview, but the love is lasting, everlasting. Whether we ever meet again or not, I am sure that you will continue to feel an interest in all that befalls me.

He then outlined the task that he faced and the spiritual need of the Persian population. He told of the interruptions to his work of translation, the long discussions on religious topics that took up his precious time and Mirza Seid's comments concerning Christ's love for his disciples: 'How he loved those twelve persons!' To that Henry replied, 'Yes, and not those twelve only, but all those who shall believe in Him, as He said, "I pray not for them alone, but for all them who shall believe on me through their word."' Henry commented, 'Even the enemy is constrained to wonder at the love of Christ.'

He concluded his letter with sorrowful words:

This is now the seventh letter I send you, without having received an answer.

Farewell!

Yours ever most affectionately,

H. Martyn. [16]

Henry continued to send letters to Lydia, outlining all he was undertaking, telling of God's protective care and of his love for her. He pleaded with her to continue to pray for him and the work he was doing.

He longed to see his friends in England once more and we also find Lydia writing in her diary of her wishes for his return. On 5 March 1810, just a few months before he began to think seriously of returning to England because of his health, she was praying that he might be 'restored to his friends and country; before, I never dared to ask anything but that the Lord would order this as His wisdom saw fit, and thought it not a subject for prayer. His injured health causes me to believe that India is not the place for his labours — and, oh, that his mind may be rightly influenced and the Lord's will done, whether it be his remaining there or returning.'[17]

Lydia's diary records that she had written to Henry on 3 April 1810. Later, on 30 November 1810, she noted that she had received another letter from him, this time explaining about his health problems. Lydia was so distressed by what she read that she feared that he might soon die.

Lydia mentioned the letters she received from him and the other times when she thought of him in distant India and, later, Persia. On 28 March 1811 she recorded in her diary: 'Heard from my dearest friend in India.'[18] This would have been Henry's letter written on 14-17 August 1810. On 1 February 1812 we read again that she had received another letter from him and had immediately written a reply.[19] Her next letters to him were posted on 30 August 1812 and 30 September 1812; sadly, both only arrived after his death.

## 24.
## Standing firm

He teased Mirza Seid Ali, who admired the Sufi master: 'There you sit immersed in thought, full of anxiety and care, and will not take the trouble to ask whether God has said anything or not. No: that is too easy and direct a way of coming at the truth...'

# 24.
# Standing firm

During his stay in Shiraz Henry often found himself engaged in controversy with Muslims, who tried to convince him that their faith was superior to Christianity. Indeed, he found his time for translation work was limited because of the many interruptions, his face-to-face debating with the leaders of the Muslims and his failing health. This is reflected in his journal entries, which became fewer and contained less information than previously. Information concerning his dealings with the Persian Muslims has to be found in the letters he wrote to friends.[1]

On 1 July 1811, Abdoolghunee, a Jew who had become a Muslim, declared that Mohammed,[2] and not Christ, was foretold in the Old Testament when the Lord told Moses, 'I will raise up … a Prophet like you … and will put my words in his mouth, and he shall speak … all that I command him' (Deuteronomy 18:18). He argued that, just as Moses was the lawgiver, so also was Mohammed. He maintained that the Europeans were descendants of Edom and that Mount Zion was to be found in Europe. The discussions which followed, involving this man and others, continued for some time, especially about the person and work of the Lord Jesus Christ.[3]

Abulhasan, another mullah (a Muslim learned in Islamic theology and law), who was present, suggested that a debate should take place between Henry Martyn and himself, with

Abdoolghunee as the adjudicator. Henry refused this as he was convinced that Abdoolghunee could not be an impartial judge.

Then there appeared a written defence of Islam by the chief mullah, Ibrahim ben al Hosyn (also known as Mirza Ibrahim).[4] He was concerned that Henry was in Shiraz to win converts to Christianity. He argued that the Koran was itself a miracle, far superior to the miracles of Moses or Christ, since the eloquent standard of the writing was beyond anything the Arabs could produce — and they were masters of such writings! He also argued that a further mark of the Koran's miraculous nature was that it would be used in the ages to come without alteration, while the miracles of Christ and Moses would fade into insignificance. He went on to claim that Mohammed himself had performed miracles. The publication concluded with words addressed to Henry: 'Thus behold, then, O thou that art wise, and consider with the eye of justice, since thou hast no excuse to offer to God. Thou hast wished to see the truth of miracles. We desire you to look at the great Koran: that is an everlasting miracle.'[5]

Although he wrote such a spirited defence of Islam, Mirza Ibrahim didn't himself attend the mosque for prayers or worship. The great man was held in such high respect by the citizens of Shiraz that no one saw anything strange about this. They simply assumed he was having his devotions in the quietness of his home.

When Henry had read the lengthy document, he began preparing three tracts defending and comparing the Christian faith with the false doctrines of Islam. His first reply to Mirza Ibrahim commenced with the gentle words: 'The Christian Minister thanks the celebrated Professor of Islamism for the favour he has done him in writing an answer to his enquiries, but confesses that, after reading it, a few doubts occurred to him, on account of which … he has taken upon himself to write the following pages.' The tract carried the signature, 'The Christian Minister, Henry Martyn.'[6]

John Sargent summarized Henry's argument as follows:

After replying to the various arguments of Mirza Ibraheem, Mr Martyn shows why men are bound to reject Mohammedanism [Islam] — that Mohammed was foretold by no prophet; that he worked no miracles; that he spread his religion by means merely human, and framed his precepts and promises to gratify men's sensuality, both here and hereafter; that he was most ambitious, both for himself and his family; that his Koran is full of gross absurdities and palpable contradictions; that it contains a method of salvation wholly inefficacious; which Mr Martyn contrasted with the glorious and efficacious way of salvation held out in the Gospel, through the divine atonement of Jesus Christ. He concludes by addressing Mirza Ibraheem in these words:

'I beg you to view these things with the eye of impartiality. If the evidence be indeed convincing, mind not the contempt of the ignorant, nor even death itself; for the vain world is passing away like the wind of the desert.

'If you do not see the evidence to be sufficient, my prayer is, that God may guide you; so that you, who have been a guide to men in the way you thought right, may now both see the truth, and call men to God through Jesus Christ, "who hath loved us, and washed us from our sins in his blood".' His glory and dominion be everlasting!'[7]

Henry's second tract took up the issue of salvation through the shed blood of the Lord Jesus Christ. He showed that salvation was not a reward given for good works or for repentance. He pointed his readers' eyes to Christ alone as the Saviour of sinners. He stated that it was faith in the Jesus Christ of the gospel that saved sinners. The New Testament, Henry argued, was the fulfilment of the Old Testament. He also wrote that the spread of the gospel throughout the world was itself a miracle.

Henry's third and final tract dealt mainly with the mystical teachings of the Sufi sect, who believed they were subject to no law, had no prophets and finally would be merged into the Deity. He showed 'that the love of God and union with Him cannot be obtained by contemplation, but only by a practical manifestation of His goodness towards us, accompanied by an assurance of our safety; and that this is fulfilled in Christianity not by the amalgamation of the soul with the Deity, but by the pouring out of God's Spirit upon His children, and by the obedience and atonement of Christ.'[8] He went on to explain by helpful analogies the principle of an innocent victim suffering on behalf of the guilty, to uphold the truth of the miracles per-formed both by Moses and by Christ, and closed by showing that secular history confirms the authenticity of the scriptural record.

When Henry visited Mirza Abulcasim, one of the leading Sufis in Persia, he found an old man with a silver beard, sitting in a courtyard garden. With him were a number of men who had sorrowful expressions on their faces, and all were silent. Henry at first sat down quietly, but after some time decided to speak as he didn't want to waste his time just sitting in silence.[9] He turned to Mirza Seid Ali and asked, 'What is this?'

'It is the custom here,' Seid Ali replied, 'to think much and speak little.'

Henry then enquired, 'May I ask the master a question?'

Mirza Seid Ali hesitated, but finally agreed that he could. Henry then begged Jaffier Ali to ask, 'Which is the way to be happy?' Jaffier asked the question according to Persian cus-tom. He commenced by saying that there was much misery in the world, and that educated people experienced it just as much as did the rest of mankind. He then asked Mirza Abulcasim what had to be done in order to escape misery.

The master replied by saying that he didn't know, but that it was often said that the subjugation of the passions was a sure and quick way to happiness.

After another pause, Henry asked the master how he felt about death — did he think of it with 'hope or fear, or neither'?

'Neither,' he replied. 'Pleasure and pain [are] both alike.'

When Henry asked him whether he had reached the state where he could be equally indifferent to both pleasure and pain, he replied, 'No'. Henry then enquired what grounds the man had for believing that anyone ever could arrive at such a state of mind. The master replied that he could not tell.

Then Mirza Seid Ali interrupted on behalf of the great master and asked Henry, 'Why do you think that pleasure and pain are not the same?'

His reply was straightforward: 'Because I have the evidence of my senses for it. And you also act as if there was a difference. Why,' he asked, 'do you eat, but that you fear pain?'

Henry had been told of the son of the mujtahid (a man recognized as an authority in Islamic law), who had deserted his father's teaching to sit at the feet of this Sufi teacher. He had left everything in the hope of finding happiness by the contemplation of God. Henry longed for an opportunity to speak to him of Christ and explain the way of salvation to him.

Later he teased Mirza Seid Ali, who admired the Sufi master: 'There you sit immersed in thought, full of anxiety and care, and will not take the trouble to ask whether God has said anything or not. No: that is too easy and direct a way of coming at the truth. I compare you to spiders, who weave their house of defence out of their own bowels; or to a set of people who are groping for a light at noonday.'[10]

Henry was becoming aware of the situation of the Jews in Shiraz, especially as they frequently turned away from their faith to Islam. Early in July 1811, when he was confronted by Abdoolghunee and a friend who had also converted to Islam, he told them very plainly that many of the Jews had become Muslims because the prince gave each new convert a set of fine clothes. Conversion paid well!

In an attempt to prove that the Old Testament prophecies pointed to Christ, Henry referred these men to Psalm 16. One of them replied by saying that 'None of the prophets saw corruption.' It was only later that Henry remembered the miracle that occurred when Elisha's bones were touched: 'Then Elisha died, and they buried him. And the raiding bands from Moab invaded the land in the spring of the year. So it was, as they were burying a man, that suddenly they spied a band of raiders; and they put the man in the tomb of Elisha; and when the man was let down and touched the bones of Elisha, he revived and stood on his feet' (2 Kings 13:20-21).[11]

On another occasion two Jews came to see Henry and the older of them asked the question: 'If Jesus was the Messiah, why did not the fiery wrath of God break out against them, as it did formerly for every small offence?' Before Henry could answer he added, 'But first, what do you think of God's severity to the Jews at other times?'

To this Henry replied, 'If my son [does] anything wrong, I punish him; but with the thieves and murderers out of doors, I have nothing to do.'

The man's son, who was also present, called to mind various passages from the Old Testament which supported what Henry had just said as he interjected, 'Yes, they were indeed a chosen generation.'

Henry then continued, in response to their first question: 'But did not the wrath of God break out against you at the death of Christ, in a more dreadful manner than ever it did?'

They mentioned the time of the captivity. Henry replied, 'But what was the captivity? It lasted but seventy years. But now seventeen hundred years have passed away; and have you a king? Or a temple? Are you not ... despised everywhere?' To this the Jews nodded their heads in agreement.

Henry went on to say, 'God has raised up a great prophet [Jesus] from the midst of you, and now you have gone after a stranger [Mohammed], of a nation who were always your enemies. You acknowledge Jesus, indeed; but it is only for fear of the sword of the Ishmaelite [a reference to the Arabs as the descendants of Ishmael].'

Another debate involved Henry facing the mujtahid, or professor of Islamic law, whose son he had met at the house of the Sufi master.[12] This man was considered the final authority in all matters concerning Muslim law, and Henry was invited to dinner at his house.

At about eight o'clock in the evening, he and Mirza Seid Ali were escorted to a courtyard to take their places on a platform about eight feet (2.4 metres) high, beside a pond. The mujtahid (who was somewhat overweight) was surrounded by a number of his friends, all well-educated men and including one of the Jews who had already had discussions with Henry about the Muslim faith. Seated on the platform, the professor placed Mirza Seid Ali on his right and Henry on his left.

Henry was surrounded by a show of learning and wealth and didn't know what to expect from the mujtahid, but when the latter began to speak, he realized he was dealing with a man of excellent fluency and clearness of speech. After speaking for almost an hour on the subject of the soul, the professor turned to the attributes of God. He continued to talk on a variety of religious subjects, and then said 'that philosophers had proved, that a single being could produce but a single being; that the first thing God had created was *Wisdom*, a being perfectly one with Him; after that, the souls of men, and the seventh heaven; and so on, till he produced matter, which is merely passive'.

When the mujtahid began to talk about the angels, asserting that man was superior to them, and that no being could be created that would be greater than man, the Jew spoke to Henry, quoting something in Hebrew. Henry was about to ask where in the Bible those words were found, but the mujtahid carried on with his discourse, ignoring the Jew's interruption. At last the Jew, who was tired of watching Henry sit without speaking, looked at him and asked, 'Why do you not speak? Why do you not bring forward your objections?'

After another lengthy speech, the mujtahid said to Henry, 'You see how much there is to be said on these subjects; several

visits will be necessary; we must come to the point by degrees.'
It was obvious that the man didn't want Henry to start his reply.

Eventually, however, the professor was obliged to take
notice of Henry. Turning to him, he began: 'Well, I must ask
you a few questions. Why do you believe in Christ?'

Henry replied, 'That is not the question. I am at liberty to
say, that I do not believe in any religion; that I am a plain man,
seeking the way of salvation.' He went on to say that it was, in
any case, quite unnecessary to prove the truth of Christ to
Muslims, because their religion accepted this as fact.

'No such thing,' the Professor replied. 'The Jesus we acknowledge is he who was a prophet, a mere servant of God,
and one who bore testimony to Mohammed; not your Jesus,
whom you call God.'

The man went on to claim that Mohammed had performed
miracles, which were witnessed by a Persian named Salmon.
Henry asked whether this Salmon had written an account of the
miracles he had seen. The professor had to admit that he had
not. Henry then added, 'Nor have you a single witness to the
miracles of Mohammed.' The mujtahid argued that despite
there being no accounts by witnesses of any miracle by Mohammed, there was sufficient evidence that such had occurred:
'For suppose five hundred persons should say that they heard
some particular thing of a hundred persons who were with
Mohammed, would that be sufficient evidence or not?'

'Whether it [is] or not,' Henry replied, 'you have no such
evidence as that, nor anything like it; but if you have ... we
must proceed to examine them, and see whether their testimony deserves credit.'

When the professor quoted a sentence from the Koran and
claimed it to be 'inimitable', Henry replied by quoting another
sentence and asked in what way it was inferior to the one from
the Koran. The professor declined to answer, claiming that a
knowledge of rhetoric was needed to understand his reasoning,
inferring that Henry was not capable of comprehending it.

It was midnight when dinner, or rather supper, was finally served. By now Henry felt tired and the professor was silent. Mirza Seid Ali wanted to hear more, but the professor declined to answer Henry's objections to his teaching and instead told a long story, concluding with the statement that it was pointless for Christians and Muslims to debate such matters, as they both had different beliefs, languages and histories. Henry did not comment on this remark, but responded to the tale by recounting a moral tale about a lion and a man, which had Mirza Seid Ali laughing all the way home.

On 15 August 1811 Henry was visited by Jani Khan, who was the head of all Persia's military forces. He was also chief of his own tribe, which was made up of 20,000 families. He had come from the king with a message to Jaffier Ali Khan, Henry's host. When he met Henry he asked a number of questions and they discussed various religious topics. Finally Jani asked, 'I suppose you consider us all as infidels?' 'Yes,' replied Henry, 'the whole of you.' Jani went away admiring his frankness.

Henry faced many insults and sneers from some of the local people. On 22 August 1811, one of the men engaged in making copies of the translation work showed some of his writings to one of the mullahs, a man named Acber, who wrote some very critical comments on the paper. When Mirza Seid Ali showed these very insulting remarks to some of his friends, they pleaded that they should not be shown to Henry, 'for fear I should disgrace them all through the folly of one man'.[13]

The next day, the prince's nephew, Ruza Cooli Mirza called, and hearing that Henry had written and spoken out against Mohammed, declared that the answer to such insults 'was the sword'.[14] His attitude changed, however, when Henry told him that the two great commandments of Christianity were: 'Thou shalt love the Lord thy God with all thy heart, and with all thy soul, and all thy strength; and thy neighbour as thyself.' The visitor then spoke in praise of the commandments, asking, 'What could be better?'[15]

During times of insult and opposition, Henry frequently encouraged himself by repeating the words:

If on my face, for Thy dear name,
Shame and reproaches be;
All hail, reproach, and welcome, shame,
If Thou remember me. [16]

One matter which was a continual cause of disagreement with the Islamic teachers was the deity of the Lord Jesus Christ. This doctrine was obnoxious to the Muslims, who saw Christ as nothing more than a prophet. Henry wrote that in discussions with the mullah Aga Mahommed Hasan, his visitor found fault with nothing in Christianity except the divinity of Christ. However, Henry stood firm on that doctrine saying, 'The more they wish me to give up this one point — the Divinity of Christ, the more I seem to feel the necessity of it, and rejoice and glory in it. Indeed, I trust, I would sooner give up my life than surrender it.'[17] In many of his discussions concerning the truth of Christianity, especially the deity of Christ and the doctrine of the Trinity, Henry humbly referred the person to the Scriptures.

On 16 January 1812 Henry recorded an incident concerning what someone had written about Christ, and his own response when he heard this obnoxious slur upon the Saviour:

Mirza Seid Ali told me accidentally, today, of a distich [a poetic couplet] made by his friend ... in honour of a victory obtained by Prince Abbas Mirza over the Russians. The sentiment was, that he had killed so many of the Christians, that Christ, from the fourth heaven, took hold of Mohammed's skirt to entreat him to desist. I was cut to the soul at this blasphemy. In prayer I could think of nothing else but that great day when the Son of God shall come in the clouds of heaven, taking vengeance on them that know not God, and convincing men of all their hard speeches which they have spoken against Him.

Mirza Seid Ali perceived that I was considerably disordered, and was sorry for having repeated the verse; but asked what it was that was so offensive. I told him that 'I could not endure existence if Jesus was not glorified — it would be hell to me, if he were to be always thus dishonoured.' He was astonished, and again asked, why? 'If anyone pluck out your eyes,' I replied, 'there is no saying *why* you feel pain — it is feeling. It is because I am one with Christ that I am thus dreadfully wounded.' ... This conversation took place while we were translating.[18]

While many of the local citizens visited Henry to discuss religion, several young men who were being trained to become doctors of Islam came to hear him speak in order to ridicule his teachings. One of these men, Muhammad Rahim, saw something in Henry's character and words that made him realize that he spoke the truth. Yet he was afraid to let it be known that he wished to become a disciple of Christ. When he heard that Henry was about to leave the city, however, he approached him, asking for a copy of the New Testament. Not only did Henry give him a copy, but on a blank page he inscribed the words: 'There is joy in heaven over one sinner that repenteth. Henry Martyn.'[19]

During his time in Shiraz Henry took every opportunity to glorify Christ. He spoke the gospel, lived the gospel and encouraged the people of the city to turn to the living God and his Son, Jesus Christ, the Saviour of sinners. However, Christians were generally treated with contempt by the Muslims at this time. The Armenian Christians frequently suffered abuse and assault, to such an extent that when they put on new clothes, they sewed patches on the sleeves, making them appear old; otherwise they would have had their coats taken from them by force.

Six years after Henry's stay in Shiraz, the city was visited by Sir Robert Ker Porter, who wrote, 'Faint with sickness and fatigue, I felt a momentary reviving pleasure in the sight of a hospitable city, and the cheerful beauty of the view. As I drew near, the image of my exemplary countryman, Henry Martyn, rose in my thoughts, seeming to sanctify the shelter to which I was hastening. He had approached Shiraz much about the same season of the year, A.D. 1811, and like myself was gasping for life under the double pressure of an inward fire and outward burning sun. He dwelt there nearly a year, and on leaving its walls the apostle of Christianity found no cause for shaking off the dust of his feet against the Mohammedan city. The inhabitants had received, cherished and listened to him; and he departed thence amidst the blessings and tears of many a Persian friend. Through his means the Gospel had then found its way into Persia, and, as it appears to have been sown in kindly hearts, the gradual effect hereafter may be like the harvest to the seedling... Besides, to a person who thinks at all on these subjects, the circumstances of the first correct Persian translation of the Holy Scriptures being made at Shiraz, and thence put into the royal hands and disseminated through the empire, cannot but give an almost prophetic emphasis to the transaction, as arising from the very native country, Persia Proper, of the founder of the empire who first bade the temple of Jerusalem be rebuilt, who returned her sons from captivity, and who was called by name to the Divine commission.'[20]

# 25.
# Off to Tabriz

As Henry could see the New Testament he had hoped to present to the shah lying on the ground near the premier's feet, he picked it up before anyone trampled on it and wrapped it safely in a towel, as they looked on, showing their utter contempt for him and his book.

# 25.
# Off to Tabriz

With his work in Shiraz completed, Henry's thoughts turned once more to the idea of returning to England, because of his continuing ill-health. There he hoped to marry the great love of his life, Lydia Grenfell. But first there was one more task he was anxious to perform in Persia.

He made the decision to travel to Tabriz, where the British Ambassador had his official residence. After sunset, at 10:00 p.m. on 11 May 1812, Henry, with his servant and all his possessions, joined a caravan for the eight-week journey across the Persian plateau to Tabriz. He carried with him some copies of the newly translated New Testament. Two, which were written in perfect calligraphy, were to be presented to Shah Fateh Ali Khan, and his son, Prince Abbas Mirza. To receive the approval of the shah would mean that the Scriptures would be read by the educated upper classes and it was Henry's hope that many of them would be converted as a result. He decided that while he travelled he would look over these two copies and correct any errors. A second Englishman with the party was Rev. William Canning, who was to take up the position as chaplain at the British Embassy in Tabriz.

During the first night on the road, Henry's saddle slipped and he fell heavily, but fortunately he was not injured. The journey involved riding during the night and early morning, with stops during the daytime at the many caravanserais that

The interior of a caravanserai

had been built for weary travellers. Often travel was in the rain,
which meant that Henry had to take special care of the manuscripts that were to be presented to the shah and his son.

Sometimes, on their reaching a caravanserai, it was found to
be in a state of ruin, with the result that the travellers had to find
accommodation elsewhere. Khooshee Zar Caravanserai was
such a one and the travellers had difficulty in finding shelter
there from the howling winds. Henry and the others were
forced to wait another day for the pack animals to catch up.

On 22 May they reached Isfahan, where Henry took the
opportunity to visit the Armenian bishops at Julfa. There he met
Matteus, a well-educated Armenian, and the Italian missionary,
Joseph Carabiciate, who was a native of Aleppo, but had been
educated in Rome. He was sixty-six years old and in good
health. He spoke Latin fluently, but was not interested in
discussing spiritual matters. He had grown tired of being
expected to work without receiving any monetary payment, and
was considering returning to Aleppo.

On the following Lord's Day, 24 May, at the invitation of the bishops, Henry attended the services at their churches. In one the three members of the congregation were outnumbered by the members of the clergy, which included two of the four local bishops. Henry was uncomfortable during the services, which was largely ceremonial — processions, the ringing of bells, the waving of banners and other rituals. Henry could not stand it and did not stay for the whole of the service at the Italian church, but he was told by those who did that 'The priest ate and drank all the consecrated elements himself, and gave none to the few poor women who composed his congregation, and who, the Armenians said, had been hired for the occasion.'[1]

When Henry left Julfa, he did so saddened by the spiritual ignorance of the bishops and clergy, and because there were no family devotions. However, he was pleased to see a copy of the Gospels translated into the local languages.

On 1 June 1812 the travellers left Isfahan for Tehran. That part of the journey reminded him of the English countryside: 'Continued winding through the mountains to Caroo, [which is] situated in a deep dell. Here were trees, green cornfields, and running streams; it was the first place I have seen in Asia which exhibited anything of the scenery of England.'[2]

On the following day, the travellers mounted their horses soon after midnight and set off through surroundings which appealed to Henry: 'It was a mild moonlight night, and a nightingale filled the whole valley with his notes. Our way was along lanes, over which the wood on each side formed a canopy, and a murmuring rivulet accompanied us, till it was lost in a lake.'[3]

On 8 June the party arrived at Tehran, which for protection was surrounded by an eleven-mile wall. The city was run down, but it was home to one of the shah's palaces, the legations of some European nations and the mission of the American Presbyterian Church. As it would be a couple of hours before the city gates were opened, Henry made himself comfortable and fell asleep.

Upon entering the city he made his way to the residence of the British ambassador, only to find him absent. As he did not want to lose any time, he decided to see if he could make the presentation of the New Testaments to the shah by himself.

The shah was camping near the city at the time, so Henry set out at nightfall to make his way to Carach. He sent a letter of introduction signed by Jaffier Ali Khan to the premier, Mirza Shufi, asking for his assistance in obtaining an audience with the shah. Mirza Shufi indicated that he would be welcome to attend on him.

When he arrived he found the premier lying upon a couch outside the shah's tent as he was ill. Beside him sat two men, named Mirza Khanter and Mirza Abdoolwahab. The latter was a secretary of state and a follower of the Sufi teachings.

These men didn't rise to greet Henry, as was the custom, as he took a seat. Nor did they offer him the calean. However, he spent two hours discussing religion and metaphysics with them.[4]

In the course of their discussions Henry was asked, 'Do you consider the New Testament as the word spoken by God?' His reply was: 'The sense [is] from God, but the expression from the different writers of it.'

The premier intervened to question him about his education and his knowledge of languages, saying that he spoke Persian very well.

The discussion continued with the question: 'We want to know what your learned men think about the state of the soul after death, till the resurrection?' Henry told them of several opinions on this.

Then they asked, 'But how ... does the spirit exist without a body?' 'Tell me', Henry replied, 'how the angels exist, and I will tell you.'

'In what sense,' they asked, 'do you believe the resurrection of the body; that every particle buried shall rise?' Henry told them of the metaphor found in the Scriptures of a grain of wheat being buried and producing a living plant.

'What are the principles of your religion?' Henry was asked. He replied, 'They are all centred in Jesus; not in his precepts, but in himself.'

Then a question was asked concerning the place of Christ: 'What are your opinions concerning Christ? Was he a prophet created?' 'His manhood was created,' replied Henry. 'His Godhead, of course, was not.'

The inquisition continued: 'Now we much wish to hear what are your notions on that extraordinary subject, the Trinity?' And so the discussion continued.

Three days later Henry was called to stand firm and confess Jesus Christ to be everything the Scriptures wrote of him. In the course of a debate held in the presence of the premier, several mullahs demanded that Henry 'should deny that Saviour who had bought him with his blood; but he "witnessed a good confession", and fearlessly acknowledged Jesus as his Lord'.[5]

On 12 June the debates came to a climax, with Henry facing eight or ten men ranged against him, including two mullahs whom he declared to be 'the most ignorant of any I have yet met with in either Persia or India'. These men rudely interrupted him when he was speaking and made unfounded statements about both the Old and New Testaments, neither of which they had ever seen for themselves.[6]

At one point, the premier, in whose presence the debate was taking place, intervened to say, 'You had better say, "God is God, and Mohammed is the prophet of God."' Without hesitation Henry replied, 'God is God, and Jesus is the Son of God.' In furious anger the men stood up as if they were about to attack him physically, exclaiming, 'He [i.e. God] is neither born nor begets!'[7] One of them shouted at Henry, 'What will you say when your tongue is burnt out for this blasphemy?'[8]

As Henry could see the New Testament he had hoped to present to the shah lying on the ground near the premier's feet, he picked it up before anyone trampled on it and wrapped it

Henry rescues his New Testament

safely in a towel, as they looked on, showing their utter contempt for him and his book.

Later that day, he penned his feelings: 'Thus I walked away alone to my tent, to pass the rest of the day in heat and dirt. What have I done, thought I, to merit all this scorn? Nothing, I trust, but bearing testimony to Jesus. I thought over these things in prayer, and my troubled heart found that peace which Christ hath promised to his disciples.'[9]

He knew that when he suffered the scorn and reproach of the ungodly he could say with the psalmist:

Oh, how great is your goodness,
Which you have laid up for those who fear you,
Which you have prepared for those who trust in you
In the presence of the sons of men!

(Psalm 31:19).

That evening a messenger came from the premier stating that the shah did not meet any Englishmen unless they were presented by the British Ambassador, or carried a letter of recommendation from him. He added that the British Ambassador would be at Sultania when the shah went there and that would be the ideal opportunity for Henry to present the shah with the copies of the New Testament.

The travellers set out for Casbin, where Henry hoped to receive a message from the ambassador. As they travelled along the roadway they found the people preparing anxiously for the shah to pass that way. The ordinary citizens feared the absolute power of the royal family, who had the power of both life and death over them. While royalty had the best of everything, many people lived a miserable life and dreaded the coming of the shah's soldiers who subjected them to violence and extortion.

On 20 June, when the travellers stopped at a small village to have breakfast, one of the local people asked Henry a number of questions about Christianity. As they continued on their way, he prayed for his friends in both England and India, who were often in his thoughts.

Travel on 22 June was more to Henry's liking: 'The weather was perfectly cool and agreeable, and all around were the pastures of the wilderness.'[10] Of the place where they stayed that night Henry recorded: 'We met with the usual insulting treatment at the caravanserai, where the king's servants had got possession of a good room, built for the reception of the better order of guests; they seemed to delight in the opportunity of humbling an European. Sultania is still but a village; yet the Zengan prince has quartered himself and all his attendants, with their horses, on this poor little village.'[11]

At their next stop they met merchants, some with large bales of cotton which had been grown locally, and others with iron and tea from distant places. They offered to sell Henry and his travelling companions some tea which had come from China. Henry tried to ask them about the places they had visited, but they only spoke Turkish.

The next day, 25 June, he and his companion, William Canning, woke after a restless night, with a high fever. They were so ill that neither man could possibly cope with travel. They stayed there for two days, during which time neither of them ate any food, but Henry knew that they had to move on to Tabriz as their money supply was almost exhausted. (The name 'Tabriz' — also spelt 'Tebriz' or 'Tabreez' — meant 'fever-dispeller' and the city was so called because of its healthy climate.) They begged the wealthier inhabitants to lend them even a few coins, showing them their letters of recommendation from General Malcolm, but they were refused help.

At the last moment a poor muleteer arrived from Tabriz and when he said he would act as security for Henry and his companion, they were loaned the sum of five tomans. The travellers could now rest more easily knowing they could purchase food. Henry wrote of that day, 'My mind was much disordered from headache and giddiness, from which I was seldom free; but my heart, I trust, was with Christ and his saints. To live much longer in this world of sickness and pain, seemed no way desirable; the most favourite prospects of my heart seemed very poor and childish; and cheerfully would I have exchanged them all for the unfading inheritance.'[12]

During the next two days three of the servants with Henry's party fell ill, while he himself showed no improvement in health: 'I passed the third day in the same exhausted state; my head, too, was tortured with shocking pains, such as, together with the horror I felt at being exposed to the sun, showed me plainly to what to ascribe my sickness.'[13]

During this bout of sickness, as he lay in bed, William Canning read Paul's Epistle to the Ephesians to him. While the others felt much better, Henry's condition again grew worse: 'My ague and fever returned, with such a headache, that I was almost frantic. Again and again I said to myself, "Let patience have her perfect work"; and kept pleading the promises, "When thou passest through the waters, I will be with thee," etc.; and the Lord did not withhold his presence. I endeavoured to repel all the disordered thoughts that the fever occasioned, and to keep in mind that all was friendly; a friendly Lord presiding; and nothing exercising me but what would show itself at last friendly. A violent perspiration at last relieved the acute pain in my head, and my heart rejoiced; but as soon as that was over, the exhaustion it occasioned, added to the fatigue from the pain, left me in as low a state of depression as ever I was in. I seemed about to sink into a long fainting fit, and I almost wished it; but at this moment, a little after midnight, I was summoned to mount my horse, and set out, rather dead than alive. We moved on... We had a thunderstorm with hail.'[14]

Even though Henry was so ill, the group kept travelling. He was so feverish that he had little recollection of what happened, but his thoughts again and again turned to England and his friends.

One day he was riding ahead of most of the party, with the baggage mules and the other travellers some distance behind. Arriving at a high bridge over the river, he sat down in the shade under the bridge, along with two camel drivers, to rest while the others caught up. Meanwhile the *kafila* crossed the river at a different point without his seeing them. Fortunately, William Canning turned back to search for his friend when he realized he was missing. Before long he found Henry's riderless horse and feared the worst. However, Henry quickly emerged from under the bridge and the two men set off to catch up with the others.

After a temporary improvement in his health, he soon fell ill again as the result of travelling in the hot sun for six hours and lack of food. In his journal for 4 July he wrote, 'I was presently in a high fever, which raged so furiously all the day, that I was nearly delirious, and it was some time before I could get the right recollection of myself. I almost despaired, and do now, of getting alive through this unfortunate journey. Last night I felt remarkably well, calm, and composed, and sat reflecting on my heavenly rest, with more sweetness of soul, abstraction from the world, and solemn views of God, than I have had for a long time. Oh for such sacred hours! This short and painful life would scarcely be felt, could I live thus at heaven's gate.'[15]

As Henry and one of the servants were both too ill to travel, they decided to remain where they were, but as they were now close to Tabriz, Henry sent a messenger to Sir Gore Ouseley, telling him to expect them in the near future. On the evening of the following day, 5 July, it was decided to move on to Tabriz, but it was not until 1:00 a.m. that they set out. Henry was again most unwell: 'I was again dreadfully disordered with headache and fever. We got into a wretched hovel, where the raging fever almost deprived me of reason.'[16]

During the night they lost their way. They asked some shepherds they met if one of them would act as a guide. However, not one was willing to do so, even though they were offered money.

Henry and his companions were forced to lie down in the open air and wait for the daylight. As a result he caught a cold, on top of the symptoms from which he was already suffering.

The next morning they set off for Wasmuch, where they had been promised that decent accommodation would be pre-pared from them. On their arrival the local people denied all knowledge of the arrangement and it took an hour of pleading before they were permitted to make use of the room.

Despite Henry's illness, they set out early the next morning for Tabriz, which they hoped to reach before sunrise. Arriving at the city gates in a very weak state, he asked for someone to guide him to the British Ambassador's residence.

## 26.
# The road to paradise

Henry found that Hassan
kept on going until nightfall,
passing village after village.
Eventually, as night was
closing in, Henry, who
needed to rest, dismounted
and, sitting down on the
ground told Hassan,
'I neither [can] nor [will] go
any further.'

# 26.
# The road to paradise

On 5 July the British Ambassador, Sir Gore Ouseley, and his wife welcomed a very sick Henry Martyn into their residence, and cared for him as they would have done a son. Sixteen days later his fever broke, leaving him still very ill.

In 1810, Sir Gore had been appointed as the British Ambassador to the court of the shah. He was well liked by the Persians and won their gratitude when, in 1813, he negotiated a peace treaty between their nation and Russia. Henry had hoped that he could have personally presented the shah and the crown prince with the specially prepared copies of the New Testament, but sickness made that impossible. It was Sir Gore who promised to make the presentation, which he faithfully carried out.

He also took a copy with him when he visited St Petersburg. The president of the Russian Bible Society, Prince Galitzin, asked for permission to publish the Persian version of the New Testament. The proof reading was done by Sir Gore Ouseley, with the assistance of Jaffier Ali Khan. That edition came off the press in 1815, well before the one published in Calcutta, which did not appear until the following year.

Despite being very ill, when Henry heard that a Tartar was about to leave for Constantinople, he raised himself from his sickbed, sat at a table and wrote several letters concerning his future plans.

Having received Lydia's letter written in February he wrote:

Tabriz, 12 July, 1812

My dearest Lydia,

I have only time to say that I have received your letter of February 14. Shall I pain your heart by adding, that I am in such a state of sickness and pain, that I can hardly write to you? ... Whether I shall gain strength enough to go on, rests on our heavenly Father, in whose hands are all my times. Oh, his precious grace! His eternal unchanging love in Christ to my soul, never appeared more clear, more sweet, more strong. I ought to inform you that, in consequence of the state to which I am reduced by travelling so far overland, without having accomplished my journey, and the consequent impossibility of returning to India the same way, I have applied for leave to come on furlough to England. Perhaps you will be gratified by this intelligence; but oh, my dear Lydia, I must faithfully tell you, that the probability of my reaching England alive is but small...

Why have you not written more about yourself? However, I am thankful for knowing that you are alive and well. I scarcely know how to desire you to direct [mail]. Perhaps Alexandria in Egypt will be the best place; another may be sent to Constantinople; for though I shall not go there, I hope Mr Morier will be kept informed of my movements. Kindest love to all the saints you usually mention.

Yours, ever most faithfully and affectionately

H. Martyn.[1]

He wrote a longer letter to Charles Simeon, outlining his future as he saw it. He mentioned writing a letter to Charles Grant and the Board of Directors of the East India Company, seeking permission to take sick leave and return to England for a time. He gave a brief account of his illness and declared that he thought it improbable that he would reach England. He could see the end of his life approaching and wrote, 'Nothing seemingly remains for me to do but to follow the rest of my family to the tomb.'²

He once again made unwise decisions concerning travel in his state of health. The first stage of his planned return to England would involve riding a horse some 1,500 miles (in excess of 2,400 km.) to Constantinople. This would have been foolish even for a person who was in good health.

On 20 August he was gladdened when he heard from Mirza Aga Meer that his correspondence with Mirza Ibrahim (see chapter 25) had been read to the shah. As a consequence the shah ordered Mirza Boozong, a leading mullah, to prepare a written answer.

Despite warnings from Sir Gore Ouseley concerning his health, Henry was determined to set off for England, by way of Constantinople. Mr Morier, the embassy secretary, certainly agreed with Sir Gore's concern for his health. He wrote, 'We had not long been at Tabriz before our party was joined by the Rev. William Canning and the Rev. Henry Martyn. The former was attached to our Embassy as chaplain; the latter, whom we had left at Shiraz employed in the translation of the New Testament into the Persian language, having completed that object, was on his way to Constantinople. Both these gentlemen had suffered greatly in health during their journey from Shiraz. Mr Martyn had scarcely time to recover his strength before he departed again.'³

The ambassador, who believed the road to Constantinople was the safest route to travel, gave Henry letters of introduction to the governors of Yerevan, Kars and Erzeroum and the British Ambassador at Constantinople. Henry also carried personal letters from Cajo Aratoon, Sir Gore Ouseley's agent, to the Armenian patriarch and Bishop Nestus at Ech-Miazin. The prince provided him with a guard, known as a *mihmander*, and provided him with horses for the journey.

On 28 August 1812, a few days before his departure, Henry wrote to Lydia. Part of the letter reads as follows:

I wrote to you last, my dear Lydia, in great disorder. My fever had approached nearly to delirium, and my debility was so great, that it seemed impossible I could withstand the power of disease many days. Yet it has pleased God to restore me to life and health again; not that I have recovered my former strength yet, but consider myself sufficiently restored to prosecute [proceed with] my journey... In three days, therefore, I intend setting my horse's head towards Constantinople, distant about thirteen hundred miles...[4]

Sabat, about whom you enquire so regularly, I have heard nothing of this long time... I am pronounced to be the only man in Bengal who could have lived with him so long. He is, to be sure, the most tormenting creature I ever yet chanced to deal with — peevish, proud, suspicious, greedy...

Soon we shall have occasion for pen and ink no more; but I trust I shall shortly see thee face to face. Love to all the saints.

Believe me to be yours, ever
Most faithfully and affectionately,

H. Martyn.'[5]

The route Henry was to follow had been built by the Romans and was still in good repair. However, the horses were not of the best, but came from stock requisitioned from the poor peasants by the government.

At sunset on 2 September a small group of men passed through the western gate of Tabriz, on their way to Constantinople. Henry was accompanied by two Armenian servants, one a groom and the other to act as translator when they came to Turkey. The first stopover was at Sangla. They arrived there at midnight, delayed because a packhorse stumbled and fell.

At 3:00 p.m. the small group of travellers were again on their way, Henry feeling somewhat better after a good rest. In his diary he wrote, 'My health being again restored, through infinite and unbounded mercy, I was able to look round the creation with calm delight. The plain of Tabriz, towards the west and south-west, stretches away to an immense distance, and is bounded in these directions by mountains... Oh! it is necessary to have been confined to a bed of sickness, to know the delight of moving freely through the works of God, with the senses at liberty to enjoy their proper objects.'[6] And so the travellers continued, sometimes finding suitable places to rest, but on one occasion compelled to stay in dark, dingy rooms beside a stable, where the smell from the animals made him unwell.

On 5 September they arrived at Gurjur, where good accommodation was found. Despite the fresh air, good road and the fact that he was feeling well, he mourned over his sins: 'Here I was well accommodated, but had to mourn over my impatient temper towards my servants; there is nothing that disturbs my peace so much. How much more noble and godlike to bear with calmness, and observe with pity, rather than anger, the failings and offences of others. Oh that I may, through grace, be enabled to recollect myself in the time of temptation! Oh that the Spirit of God may check my folly, and at such times, bring the lowly Saviour to my view.'[7]

Now it became a wearisome journey, constantly on the move along the road to Constantinople, especially once the leadership of the party was assumed by the Tartar Hassan Aga, who made it a rushed journey, pressing on with no concern for Henry's health.

When the travellers arrived at Nackshan, Henry was, after a long delay, found accommodation in a corner of a wash-house belonging to a wealthy inhabitant. The packhorses were late arriving, so Henry had to go without breakfast. He rested during the daylight hours. At midnight he woke the rest of the party, when they set off once more.

On 7 September, he saw Mount Ararat in the distance, and recorded: 'On the peak of that hill the whole church was once contained; it has now spread far and wide, even to the ends of the earth, but the ancient vicinity of it knows it no more. I fancied many a spot where Noah perhaps offered his sacrifices...'[8]

On 11 September the weary travellers arrived at Hosyn Khan, where the governor's residence was more like a palace. Shortly after his arrival, Henry received a summons to meet him. For a time the governor ignored his presence, and continued reading the Koran. He then called for a cloak of costly material which he put on, claiming it was cold, and had the doctor take his pulse, all to impress Henry with his wealth and consequence. However, when the governor had Sir Gore Ouseley's letter read to him, he at last began to show some interest and to pay some attention to Henry.

Later in the afternoon Henry was again invited to the Hosyn Khan, where the governor received him in his courtyard garden, or 'paradise'. Henry recorded the scene which met his eyes: 'A fountain, in a basin of white marble, was playing before him, and in it water-grapes and melons were cooling; two time-pieces were before him, to show the approach of the time of lawful repast [it being the Muharram, the first month in the Islamic calendar]; below the window, at a great depth, ran a broad and rapid stream, over rocks and stones, under a bridge of two arches, producing an agreeable murmur: on the side of the river were gardens, and a rich plain; and directly in front, Ararat.'[9]

This meeting was in private and lacking in formality, but the governor was too weary to engage in conversation. Henry raised the matter of religion, commenting that 'he was in one paradise now, and was in quest of another hereafter', but his remark met with no response.[10] Before Henry left, the governor kindly provided him with a *mihmander*, four horses and a guard.

The next day, as not all the horses were ready, Henry rode ahead and came to Ech-Miazin, which means 'Three Churches'. Making his way to the largest church and producing the Armenian letter of recommendation addressed to the patriarch, he was escorted to the latter's residence, where he found two bishops having breakfast. On the table he saw pilaus, kebabs and other foods served to the accompaniment of wine and arrack (an alcoholic spirit made in Eastern countries from the sap of the coco palm or from rice).

Henry was well received by Serope (who had studied for eight years in Europe and, having seen some of the errors of Roman Catholicism, was now seeking to bring about reforms in his own church), one of the bishops and the Armenian monks, but all too soon it was time to leave. Serope presented him with an English bridle and saddle and a sword, as the roads in Turkey were infested with more dangers than in Persia. Henry's servant was armed with both a gun and a sword and the monks sent a man of their own, Melcom, who was also armed, to accompany the travellers.

It was at 6:00 a.m. on 17 September that Henry, 'accompanied by Serope, one bishop, the secretary, and several servants of the monastery',[11] left Ech-Miazin. The monks who accompanied him soon returned to Ech-Miazin, however, leaving him with Melcom, who was responsible for guarding the money, two baggage horses with their owners and two men from the governor's palace.

That day the *mihmander* rode ahead to Quila Gazki, where he obtained some good accommodation for Henry. On the next stage of the journey they met a man armed with a very long spear and Henry narrowly escaped injury when the man's horse almost collided with Henry's after being startled by a gunshot aimed at some partridges. The headman of the next village, who was reading a book, asked Henry if he knew what book it was — 'Nothing less than the great Koran!'[12]

The following night they camped at Fiwick, a small Armenian village where the population was largely Turkish. The head man visited Henry, but failed to offer him or any of his Armenian companions any accommodation for the night, although the Muslims in the party were taken care of. Fortunately, he was given a room at the home of an Armenian, but found sleep difficult as the room was, in his own words, 'a thoroughfare for horses, cows, buffaloes, and sheep'.[13]

On 21 September the travellers arrived at Kars, which had a look of about it that reminded him of Europe. The homes were built of stone, and carts were moving along the streets. On a high rock there was a fort, and it was also here that Henry saw the biggest graveyard he had ever seen. He estimated that there must have been thousands of gravestones. His letter of recommendation from Sir Gore Ouseley secured a promise of horses for the journey and a guard of ten men.

The next day, however, when he and his companions were ready to set out, the promised horses were nowhere to be seen and the only guard present was Hassan Aga, a Tartar. He soon proved to be a very cruel man, belting the pack-horses with his long whip.

When the journey at last got under way, the Tartar moved ahead of the rest of the travellers and took possession of a coffee room at the next stopping place. This room had a raised area with cushions on one side, and cushions on the floor on the other, but the rest of the floor area consisted of bare stones and timbers. Henry had caught cold from the chilly wind that had blown the day before, so the Tartar ordered that some wood be gathered, and soon a large fire was blazing in the room. It was difficult to rest here, because Henry found that he was sharing a bench with the Tartar and there were a number of other people also using the room.

It appeared that the Tartar was regarded as the most important person present and when the meal was brought to the table, he sat down to four or five delicacies. Henry asked for eggs, but to his horror the ones brought were rotten, while for butter he was offered ghee (a kind of butter made from the milk of a buffalo). All night people from the village came into the coffee room to talk and smoke. The night was extremely cold, as there was a hoar frost, which, together with the noise and smoky atmosphere, meant that Henry found sleep almost impossible.

On 24 September the travellers wound their way over hills and through valleys in sultry weather. When they found a pool of water formed from a nearby hot spring, everyone took the opportunity to rest. The warm water was very refreshing and the porches around the pool reminded Henry of the Pool of Bethesda (see John 5). The Tartar, Hassan Aga, took his calean with him into the pool and, with the water up to his chin, enjoyed a smoke.

On 29 September, when the group arrived at a small village, Henry knew he was ill, suffering from fever and a high temperature. As Hassan Aga's son was ill, he was sent home. Hassan certainly didn't show the same kindness to Henry — it was a case of 'Get the horses ready and move on!'

The following day, after arriving at Purnugaban, everyone tried to settle down to rest. Henry's only nourishment for the day had been tea. He was feeling depressed because of a severe headache and loss of appetite. Despite feeling so unwell, he was still able to fix his mind on the words of Scripture: 'My soul rests in Him who is as an "anchor of the soul, sure and steadfast", which, though not seen, keeps me fast.'[14]

1 October proved to be a long, hard day. The travellers departed from Purnugaban at 7:00 a.m., not arriving at their next resting place until 8:00 pm. Henry then found out that the plague was raging in Constantinople, causing the death of many thousands. He could only write, 'Thus I am passing inevitably into imminent danger. O Lord, thy will be done! Living or dying, remember me!'[15]

At Chifflick, the next stop along the way, Henry fell ill in the cool of the night with a raging fever. When Hassan sent word to him in the early hours that they should be on their way once more, he was in bed, unable to move because he felt so ill. Hassan was furious, but Henry waited until after breakfast before setting out at 8 a.m., with Hassan forcing the party to ride fast to make up for the time lost because of Henry's illness.

When they reached Sherean they obtained new mounts and again Hassan set off, determined to ride all day and all night. It was raining and as Henry once again became feverish he wondered how he could keep himself alive. When they came to a village Hassan refused to stop, but at 1.00 a.m. they found two men sheltering under a wagon who had a fire going. Henry was able to dry some of his clothes and, in an effort to control his fever, he drank plenty of water. All too soon they set out again in the darkness through the wind and rain, but Henry thanked God for some relief from his suffering.

Arriving at the next town, Hassan came to Henry in a state of great alarm. Some time before, he had ridden a horse belonging to a man from this town until it dropped dead, much to the annoyance of the governor, who had threatened to make an example of him. He begged Henry to rescue him if he was arrested, but in fact nothing happened.

As soon as possible, Hassan had Henry back on his mount and they were on their way to a village which he claimed was some four hours distant, but Henry found that Hassan kept on going until nightfall, passing village after village. Eventually, as night was closing in, Henry, who needed to rest, dismounted and, sitting down on the ground, told Hassan, 'I neither [can] nor [will] go any further.'[16] This infuriated Hassan, but Henry remained where he was until at last he spotted a light in the distance. Mounting his horse once more, he announced that he was going to make his way towards that light, and the others could do as they pleased.

When they finally arrived at the village Hassan made no effort to find Henry any suitable accommodation. Someone suggested that he should rest on a verandah which was open to the weather. His Armenian servant, Sergius, came to his rescue, insisting that his master wanted somewhere comfortable, where he could be alone. The question was then asked: 'And why must he be alone?'[17] The local people seemed to think that only a very proud man would want to be on his own.

Eventually, when some money was produced, they took Henry to a room in a stable, but Hassan and several others followed, intending to sleep in the same room. Henry, who by now was very ill, wrote in his journal of that night: 'My fever ... increased to a violent degree: the heat in my eyes and forehead was so great, that the fire almost made me frantic. I entreated that it might be put out, or that I might be carried out of doors. Neither was attended to: my servant, who, from my sitting in that strange way on the ground believed me delirious, was deaf to all I said. At last I pushed my head in among the luggage, and lodged it on the damp ground, and slept.'[18]

The next morning he was only slightly improved, but soon Hassan had everyone mounting their horses, ready for the day's travelling. He showed no concern for the very sick Englishman. The next stopping place was a small village at the end of a mountain pass. Some comfortable accommodation was found for Henry, but he wrote that, soon after sunset, 'The ague [an illness involving fever and fits of shivering] came on with a violence I had never before experienced: I felt as if in a palsy; my teeth chattering, and my whole frame violently shaken... The cold fit, after continuing two or three hours, was followed by a fever, which lasted the whole night, and prevented sleep.'[19]

The next morning, 6 October, Henry was able to catch up on some rest as no horses were available. He sat down and meditated upon God: 'I sat in the orchard, and thought, with sweet comfort and peace, of my God; in solitude my company, my friend and comforter. Oh! when shall time give place to eternity! When shall appear that new heaven and new earth wherein dwelleth righteousness! There, there shall in no wise enter in anything that defileth: none of that wickedness which has made men worse than wild beasts — none of those corruptions which add still more to the miseries of mortality, shall be seen or heard of any more.'[20]

That was the final entry Henry made in his journal!

# 27.
# *Home at last!*

For that dear Name [the
name of Christ]
Through every form of
danger, death, and shame,
Onward he journeyed to a
happier shore,
Where danger, death, and
shame assault no more
(Thomas Babington
Macaulay).

# 27.
# Home at last!

On 14 October 1812, Henry had his servant, Sergius, make a list of all his writings and promise to take them to Constantinople if he died. This Sergius faithfully did, handing them to Mr Isaac Morier, explaining that they had come from his master. Sergius also said that the Armenian clergy had given his master a Christian burial. It seems obvious that Hassan, the leader of the travellers, must have pushed Henry beyond what his body could stand, for Henry Martyn was taken into the heavenly paradise at Tokat on 16 October 1812 — at just thirty-one years of age.

Henry Martyn was gone, but he left behind a name that should never be forgotten, for he gave the Scriptures to the people of India and Persia in their own languages.

Constance Padwick quotes an appropriate section of a poem from the *Divan-i-Shams-i-Tabriz*, translated by R. A. Nicholson:

Up, O ye lovers and away!
'Tis time to leave the world for aye;
Hark, loud and clear from heaven
The drum of parting calls — let none delay;
The cameleer hath risen amain,
Made ready all the camel train,
And quittance now desires to gain:
Why sleep ye travellers, I pray?

Behind us and before there swells
The din of parting and of bells;
To shoreless space each moment sails
A disembodied spirit away.
O heart, towards thy heart's love wend,
And O friend, fly toward the Friend. [1]

In his zeal to spread the good news of his Redeemer, Henry
had made some unwise decisions. To travel overland to Cawnpore from Dinapore in the midst of summer was foolish,
particularly as he could have deferred his journey to a more
suitable time of the year. Then, after his arrival in Persia, to
travel from Bushire to Shiraz with temperatures rising to 126° F
(52°C) would have been madness for anyone, but especially for
a sick man. This was followed by his decision to travel to
Constantinople on horseback, a distance of around 1,500 miles.

Henry wanted to present the shah personally with his
precious copy of the Persian New Testament, but the journey
from Tehran to the shah's camp, which was off his direct route,
served no purpose, for he knew that the shah would not receive
a lone Englishman unless he was presented by the British
Ambassador. Then the speedy journey from the royal camp to
Tabriz very nearly resulted in Henry's death when he became
very sick with a high fever and fits of shivering.

Indeed, from the time he left England, Henry suffered much
ill health. On board the ship to India he was frequently so ill
with seasickness that he longed for death and for paradise
where he would be with his Lord (see Luke 23:43). He knew
that his lungs were already infected with the tuberculosis that
had killed his mother and his two sisters. He finally died from
that same disease.

Despite the plague raging in Tokat, that was not what was
responsible for his death; he entered the plague-ridden city
already suffering from the disease that finally took his life. How
often he had prayed: 'Oh! when shall time give place to
eternity?'[2]

Tokat in 1812

Following his death he was buried by the Armenian priests, who treated him with the respect and honour that would have been accorded to one of their bishops.

In 1842 Rev. George Percy Badger, an Anglican chaplain, was sent to work amongst the Nestorian tribes of Kurdistan. When in Tokat, he and his wife visited the place where Henry's body had been laid to rest. When they found the grave, with the help of the Armenian priest who had conducted the funeral service, Mr Badger stood beside it and 'lifted up a secret prayer that God in his mercy would raise up many of a like spirit to labour among the benighted Mohammedans of the East'.[3]

In 1844 Dr Henry J. van Lennep was in Tokat attempting to find the exact place of Henry's grave. This proved to be a difficult task. The graveyard was bare of vegetation except for two wild pear trees, which were almost dead because the ground was so dry. After much searching, Dr van Lennep finally came upon a small slab of limestone, about twenty inches by forty inches (50 by 100 cm.), which bore an inscription in Latin:

REV. VIR.
GUG. MARTINO.
SACER. AC. MISS. ANGLO.
QUEM. IN. PATR. REDI.
DOMINUS.
HIC. BERISAE. AD. SB. VOC.
PIUM. D. FIDEL. Q. SER.
A.D. MDCCCXII
HUNC. LAP. CONSAC.
C. I. R.
A.D. MDCCCXIII.

Ten years later, Dr van Lennep was appointed to carry out missionary work in Tokat and returned to the scene. By now the grave was even more difficult to find, since in the meantime rain had caused the whole area to be covered in thick mud. The weeds grew profusely between the graves, making the graveyard nothing more than a jungle of undergrowth. With a plan drawn on his earlier visit and the help of friends, he soon located the spot where he remembered finding Henry's grave, but there was now no sign of it. The headstone was not found until they had dug to a depth of about two feet (about 60 cm.). Having cleared away the soil and rubble, the Christians in Tokat hoped to be able to keep the grave in good condition, but within a few months they found that it was once again completely covered by soil.[4]

George Smith explains that it must have been because of Dr van Lennep's difficulty in finding Henry Martyn's grave that a poem about him included the lines:

No stone marks the spot where these ashes are resting,
No tear has e'er hallowed thy cold, lonely grave,
But the wild warring winds whistle round thy bleak
    dwelling,
And the fierce wintry torrent sweeps o'er it with its wave.[5]

A decision was made to reinter Henry's remains in the new missionary cemetery in Tokat. When this was carried out, no evidence was found of a coffin, indicating that Henry had been buried in the Oriental manner — wrapped in a shroud and placed in the grave.

The Board of Directors of the East India Company had made the decision to meet the cost of a four-sided obelisk made from local marble and inscribed in English, Armenian, Turkish and Persian, with the same inscription on each side. The English text read as follows:

REV. HENRY MARTYN, M.A.
CHAPLAIN OF THE HON. EAST INDIA COMPANY,
BORN AT TRURO, ENGLAND, FEBRUARY 18, 1781,
DIED AT TOKAT, OCTOBER 16, 1812.
HE LABOURED FOR MANY YEARS IN THE EAST, STRIVING TO
BENEFIT MANKIND BOTH IN THIS WORLD AND THAT TO COME.

Obelisk marking Henry's grave in the missionary cemetery at Tokat

HE TRANSLATED THE HOLY SCRIPTURES INTO HINDUSTANI
AND PERSIAN,
AND PREACHED THE GOD AND SAVIOUR OF WHOM THEY TESTIFY.
HE WILL LONG BE REMEMBERED IN THE EAST, WHERE HE WAS
KNOWN AS A MAN OF GOD. [6]

There is no doubt that Henry's death was mourned by his friends and the nation of his birth. The news arrived in England at the time when the British Parliament was debating the charter of the East India Company, with regard to missionary work. The parliament gave missionaries the legal right to preach the everlasting gospel throughout India. Cambridge University took action to ensure that Henry Martyn's memory would not be forgotten. The church honoured him as a great servant of God, who had given his life in making possible the publication of the New Testament in the languages of the people of India and Persia. He was a noble saint, of whom Lord Macaulay wrote:

Here Martyn lies. In manhood's early bloom,
The Christian hero finds a Pagan tomb.
Religion, sorrowing o'er her favourite son
Points to the glorious trophies that he won,
Eternal trophies! not with carnage red;
Not stained with tears by helpless captives shed,
But trophies of the Cross. For that dear Name,
Through every form of danger, death, and shame,
Onward he journeyed to a happier shore,
Where danger, death, and shame assault no more. [7]

Marcus Loane, a former Anglican Archbishop of Australia, wrote that when he was in Tokat in 1986 he was unable to visit the site of Henry Martyn's grave as a school had been built over the graveyard. With a little investigation, he found the obelisk that once marked Henry's final resting place in a museum opposite the cemetery; the name had been defaced on each side, but the English inscription was readable.

# 28.
# News of a death

'He was in our hearts, we honoured him; we loved him; we thanked God for him; we prayed for his longer continuance amongst us; we rejoiced in the good he was doing — we are sadly bereaved!'

(Rev. Thomas Thomason, missionary in India).

# 28.
# News of a death

Gradually news of Henry Martyn's death spread throughout the Christian world. It is interesting to read the comments made by his friends (and others) when they heard of Henry's death.

## The Sherwoods

When the Sherwoods heard of the death of their dear Christian friend and one-time pastor, Mary wrote in her journal, 'We were all most deeply affected, and I then resolved, if all were well, and that if it pleased God ever to give me a son, I would bestow on him the revered name of Henry Martyn.'[1]

Later, when the Sherwoods were indeed blessed with a son, Mary wrote of his baptism, 'We christened him, after our lamented, departed friend, Henry Martyn. The ceremony was performed in the little chapel in our garden, Mr Corrie being one godfather. When the beloved name was pronounced, tears were in the eyes of all present. Where was he now who was so dear to all of us, the bright ray of light which had once so gladdened our eyes and warmed our hearts?'[2]

## Lydia Grenfell

But what about the woman he loved so dearly, yet was prevented from marrying by the objections of her mother and her
own foolish vow, made when she broke off her first
engagement?

On 12 December 1812 she recorded that a letter had arrived
from India — that being Henry's last but one, which had been
posted on 12 July 1812. From her notes we read that she was
concerned at that time about his state of health: 'Heard from
Tabriz from Mr M., with an account of his dangerous state of
health and intention of returning to England if his life was
spared. This intelligence affected me variously. The probability
of his death, the certainty of his extreme sufferings, and distance
from every friend, pressed heavily on my spirits; I was enabled
to pray and felt relieved. Of his return no very sanguine expectations can be entertained. Darkness and distress of mind have
followed this information. I cannot collect my thoughts to write,
or apply as I ought to anything. Oh, let me consider this as a call
to prayer and watchfulness and self-examination. Lord, assist
me!'[3]

On 26 December she recorded that frequently throughout
the day her thoughts turned to her 'dear friend'. She wrote that
she could not 'think of him as having gained the heavenly
crown, but as struggling with dangers and difficulties. Secure in
them all, of Thy favour, and defended by Thy power, he is safe,
and pass but a few years or days, and he will enter into the rest
of God. Let me, too, follow after him as he follows Christ.'[4]

Lydia was becoming more concerned about the faithful man
who loved her and had proposed to her more than once. On 4
January 1813 we find her still praying for Henry's well-being,
unaware that he had died and passed into the presence of the
Lord and Saviour he served. Still believing that he was alive
and coming home to England, she wrote in her diary, 'The state
of my beloved friend less occupies my mind than I sometimes

think is reconcilable with a true affection for him; but the truth is, the concerns of my soul are the more pressing.'[5]

Soon after recording those words, on 1 February 1813, she wrote, 'My beloved friend remembered every hour, but today with less distressing fears and perplexity of mind.'[6]

Word of Henry's death reached Lydia on 14 February 1813, but it was not until 20 February that she recorded the fact in her diary: 'Heard on the 14th of the removal of my most tender, faithful, and beloved friend to the joys of heaven. Oh, I could not wish his absence from them prolonged. What I only wished was, and now I am reconciled to that too — I wished to have been honoured of God so far as to have been near him, or that some friend had been. Lord, if this was wrong, forgive me. I will endeavour, yea, I am enabled to say of this too, "Thy will be done." Great has been the peace and tranquillity of my soul, such nearness to God, such a hold of Christ, such hope in the promises, such assurance of bliss and immortality, as I cannot express, and may have to forget.'[7]

What a difference a wife could have made to Henry! He needed the restraining hand of a loved one to order his way and prevent him undermining his health, but this was not to be.

During his last days on earth, his thoughts no doubt turned to his friends in England and India, especially Lydia. A few weeks before his death he had written to her and spoken of his proposed return to England: 'Do I dream? That I venture to think and write of such an event as that! ... Soon we shall have occasion for pen and ink no more; but I trust I shall shortly see thee face to face.'[8]

Lydia's love for Henry was not so strong that she would marry him. One of her nieces wrote of the time when she received the news of his death: 'The circumstances of his affecting death, and my aunt's *intense* sorrow, produced an ineffaceable remembrance on my own mind. I can never forget the "upper chamber" in which she took refuge from daily cares and interruptions — its view of lovely Mount's Bay across fruit-trees and whispering white cœlibes — its perfect neatness, though with few ornaments. On the principal wall hung a large print of the Crucifixion of our Lord, usually shaded by a curtain, and at its foot (where he would have chosen to be) a portrait of Henry Martyn.'[9]

Lydia did not forget the godly, faithful man who had loved her dearly, for his name appears in her diary in entries written years after his death.

Twelve months after receiving the news of his death, Lydia recorded: 'A twelvemonth, this day, since I heard of the death of my dear friend. My thoughts revert to this event, but more to the mercies of God to me at that season.'[10]

Henry's name is mentioned in her diary later on various occasions, one of the last being 2 April 1826, where she wrote of being present at a worship service where she heard of the abounding love and grace of the Lord Jesus Christ preached from the text: 'Now then, we are ambassadors for Christ, as though God were pleading through us: we implore you on Christ's behalf, be reconciled to God. For he made him who knew no sin to be sin for us, that we might become the righteousness of God in him' (2 Corinthians 5:20-21). She commented, 'The text was that I once heard preached from by the blessed Martyn, whose spirit I pined to join in offering praises to God after sermon.'[11]

Sadly, Lydia's mental condition became very fragile and before her death from breast cancer on 18 September 1829, at the age of fifty-four, she spent a year in a mental asylum where she was treated for 'dementia'.


## Daniel Corrie

It was Daniel Corrie who had spent time with Henry at Cawnpore when he was very ill. Of his friend he wrote, 'A more perfect character I never met with, nor expect to see on earth. During the four years we were fellow-labourers in this country [India], I had no less than six opportunities of enjoying his company; and every opportunity only increased my love and veneration for him.'[12]

Daniel and Henry were the closest of friends, who supported each other during their disappointments and struggles with the Evil One. Hearing of Henry's death, Daniel wrote to his brother-in-law, Mr C. Shaw, in response to a letter 'containing the affecting intelligence of Martyn's death, to us afflictive, to him happy beyond expression. I could find nothing but lamentations to express — lamentations for us, not for him. He was meet [suitable] for "the inheritance of the saints in light". My master is taken from me; oh, for a double portion of his spirit! [see 2 Kings 2].The work of printing and distributing the Scriptures will henceforth go on more slowly.'[13]

In a letter to Charles Simeon Daniel wrote, 'Could he [Henry Martyn] look from heaven and see the Abdool Massee'h, with the translated New Testament in his hand, preaching to the listening throng … it would add fresh delight to his holy soul.'[14]

Years later Daniel Corrie, now a bishop, wrote of a visit he made in 1824 to Cawnpore, when he was the Archdeacon of Calcutta: 'I arrived at this station on the day fourteen years after sainted Martyn had dedicated the church. The house he occupied stands close by. The view of the place and the re-membrance of what had passed greatly affected me… I had to assist in administering the sacrament, and well it was, on the whole, that none present could enter into my feelings, or I should have been overcome.'[15]

Again he writes, 'How would it have rejoiced the heart of Martyn could he have had the chief authorities associated, by order of Government, to assist him in the work of education; and how gladly would he have made himself their servant in the work for Jesus' sake! One poor blind man who lives in an outhouse of Martyn's, and received a small monthly sum from him, often comes to our house, and affords a mournful pleasure in reminding me of some little occurrence of those times. A wealthy native too, who lived next door to us, sent his nephew to express to me the pleasure he derived from his acquaintance with Martyn. These are all the traces I have found of that "excellent one of the earth" at the station.'[16]

Nine years later Daniel Corrie again visited Cawnpore, which at that time had two chaplains. He wrote, '*October 6*. I attended Divine service at the church bungalow, and stood up once more in Martyn's pulpit. The place is a little enlarged. The remembrance of Martyn and the Sherwoods, and Mary [his sister], with the occupations of that period, came powerfully to my recollection, and I could not prevent the tears from flowing.'[17]

## Charles Simeon

On 12 February 1813 Charles Simeon, in correspondence with Rev Thomas Thomason in Calcutta, wrote, 'The day before yesterday a letter arrived from Mr Isaac Morier, of Constantinople, announcing that on October 16 (or thereabouts) our beloved brother entered into the realms of glory, and rested for ever in the bosom of his God... But what an event it is! How calamitous to his friends, to India, and to the world! Methinks I hear God say: "Be still and know that I am God." ... I had been forming plans in my mind with a view to the restoration of his health in England, and should now have been able to carry into execution whatever might have been judged expedient; but I am denied the joy of ministering to him!'[18]

## Thomas Thomason

Thomas Thomason also felt dearly the loss of his close friend and fellow missionary. He wrote when hearing of Henry's death, 'He was in our hearts; we honoured him; we loved him; we thanked God for him; we prayed for his longer continuance amongst us; we rejoiced in the good he was doing — we are sadly bereaved! Where such fervent piety, and extensive knowledge, and vigorous understanding, and classical taste, and unwearied application, were all united, what might not have been expected? I cannot dwell upon the subject without feeling very sad. I stand upon the walls of Jerusalem, and see the lamentable breach that has been made in them; but it is the Lord — He gave, and He hath taken away.'[19]

## John Sargent and Samuel Wilberforce

John Sargent believed that the world should know of the sacrificial, missionary work carried out by Henry Martyn. He had for a long time been Henry's close friend, the two of them having attended Cambridge University together. Daniel Corrie had forwarded to him the first portion of Henry's journal and other papers. With the arrival of the second portion, John announced that he was to commence writing a biography of Henry Martyn. After Lydia Grenfell's death he included in his work copies of Henry's letters to her, but no copies of her letters to Henry were to be found.

The Rev. Samuel Wilberforce began editing Henry's journal, which is an account of his walk with his God and Saviour.

The work of John Sargent and Samuel Wilberforce, taken together, provides us with an account of Henry's life from 1803 until a few days before his death.[20]

## Sir James Stephen

Sir James Stephen said that 'Martyn's is the one heroic name which adorns the annals of the English Church from the days of Elizabeth to our own... Tidings of the death of Henry Martyn reached England during the parliamentary debates on the renewal of the East India Company's Charter, and gave new impetus to the zeal with which the friends and patrons of his youth were then contending for the establishment of an episcopal see at Calcutta, and for the removal of all restraints on the diffusion of Christianity within its limits.'[21]


## The pope

Much praise was heaped upon the memory of Henry Martyn, but not by all. In 1816 the pope issued two edicts concerning Henry's Persian New Testament. The Roman Catholic bishops in the areas where the New Testament would be used were warned 'that Bibles printed by heretics are numbered among the prohibited books by the rules of the Index (Nos. II and III), for it is evident, from experience, that from the Holy Scriptures which are published in the vulgar tongue [i.e. the language of the people], more injury than good has arisen through the temerity of men.'[22]

How glad we can be that the Holy Spirit is more powerful than such edicts from proud men!

# 29.
# Brilliance and sadness

'I know no parallel to these achievements of Henry Martyn ... the born translator. He masters grammar, observes idioms, accumulates vocabulary, reads and listens, corrects and even reconstructs. Above all, he prays...'
(Canon W. J. Edmonds).

# 29.
# Brilliance and sadness

There were two men who caused Henry a great deal of distress, one of them being Sabat. Despite the difficulty of living with the proud Arab, Henry displayed his saintly character. As we noted earlier, one of his biographers wrote, 'In almost nothing does the saintliness of Martyn appear so complete as in the references in his *Journal* to the pride, the vanity, the malice, the rage of this "artless child of the desert", when it became apparent that his knowledge of Persian and Arabic had been overestimated.'[1]

Yet till his dying day, Sabat 'never spoke of Mr Martyn without the most profound respect, and shed tears of grief whenever he recalled how severely he had tried the patience of this faithful servant of God. He mentioned several anecdotes to show with what extraordinary sweetness Martyn had borne his numerous provocations. "He was less a man," he said, "than an angel from heaven." '[2]

Despite the distress Henry suffered through the behaviour of Sabat, he could still write that 'Not to esteem him a monument of grace, and to love him, is impossible.'[3]

The second person to cause him much suffering was Hassan, who constantly demanded that the travellers move on, regardless of the heat or Henry's serious illness. It was he who appears to have been ultimately responsible for the time and place of Henry's death. Unlike Sabat, he never admitted he had been at fault or commended Henry for his godliness or restraint in dealing with him; on the contrary, he simply didn't care about the Englishman's welfare.

And, in the midst of all his other trials and tribulations, Henry faced Lydia's rejection of his love.

There can be no doubt of Henry Martyn's brilliance in the field of language translation. He had a God-given gift such as few have ever received. Kellsye Finnie compiled a list of Henry's translations. He translated the New Testament, the Anglican Prayer Book and the Anglican Marriage Service into Hindustani. He translated the parables for use in his schools. He also ensured that the Persian translation of the New Testament was the finest possible, translated the Psalms into Persian and kept a close watch on Sabat as he worked on the Arabic translation of the New Testament.[4]

Finnie goes on to quote the words of Canon W. J. Edmonds, a missionary to the Urdu-speaking Muslims in Pakistan: 'I know no parallel to these achievements of Henry Martyn ... the born translator. He masters grammar, observes idioms, accumulates vocabulary, reads and listens, corrects and even reconstructs. Above all, he prays. He lives in the Spirit, rises from his knees full of the mind of the Spirit.'[5] Indeed, Henry Martyn read books of grammar in much the same way that many people today would read popular works of fiction or watch their favourite TV show. It was Canon Edmonds, quoted above, who wrote, 'He read grammars as other men read novels, and to him they were more entertaining than novels.'[6]

Henry's joy in the work of translation is reflected in many entries in his journal. One example is found in the section covering 25-31 August 1807, where we read the following entries:

*25 August.* Translating the epistles; reading Arabic grammar and Persian...

*27- 29 August.* ... Studies in Persian and Arabic the same. Delight in them, particularly the latter, so great, that

I have been obliged to pray continually, that they may not be a snare to me.

*31 August.* … Resumed the Arabic, with an eagerness which I found it necessary to check…[7]

Often he became excited over just one word and frequently after staying up late at night could hardly wait for it to be the morning, when he would again resume his study.

Henry's great desire was to preach the gospel, but he wanted first to have the Bible and other Christian literature available to give to those who paid attention to his words. And there can be no doubt that his translation work, used by the Holy Spirit, won many to a saving faith in the Lord Jesus Christ.

The first publication of his Persian New Testament was in 1815. Sir Gore Ouseley, the British Ambassador to Persia, had visited Russia, where he told the president of the Russian Bible Society, Prince Galitzin, of Henry Martyn's work. At once it was decided to publish 5,000 copies, Sir Gore Ouseley and the Rev. R. Pinkerton making themselves available to correct any errors in the proof copies.

Another event not to be overlooked was the day when Sir Gore Ouseley stood before Fateh Ali Khan, the Shah of Persia, and presented him with Henry's specially prepared copies of the Persian New Testament. On 20 September 1814 Sir Gore wrote to the Right Hon. Lord Teignmouth, who at that time was president of the British and Foreign Bible Society:

My dear Lord,

Finding that I am likely to be detained here some six or seven weeks, and apprehensive that my letters from Persia may not have reached your Lordship, I conceive it my duty to acquaint you, for the information of the society of Christians formed for the purpose of propagating the Sacred Writings, that, agreeably to the wishes of our poor friend, the late Rev. Henry Martyn, I presented in the name of the Society (as he particularly desired) a

انجیل لوقا                                    ۱۶۲

از اورشلیم آغازشده بتوبه و امرزش کناهان درهمه قبایل باسمش کرده شود * وشماشا
هدان این چیزها هستید* و اینک من وعده پدر خود را بشما میفرستم و شما در شهر اورشلیم
توقّف نمایید تا وقتی که از عالم بالا بقوّت ملبس شوید * پس ایشان را بیرون اورده تا بیت
عینه دستهای خود را بلند کرده انهار ادلجویی مینمود * و او هنوز ایشان را ادلجوی مینمود که
از ایشان جدا کشته بسوی اسمان بلند شد * و انها او را سجده نموده بافرح بسیار بسوی
اورشلیم برکشتند * و پیوسته در هیکل مانده خدا را حمد و سپاس مینمودند امین *

انجیل یوحنا

فصل اوّل

بود درا بتدا کلمه و انکلمه نزد خدا بود و ان کلمه خدا بود * و همان درابتدا نزد
خدا بود* و هر چیز بوساطت او موجود شد و بغیر از وهیچ چیز از چیز های که موجود شده
است و جود نیافت * در او حیات بود و ان حیات روشنائ انسان بود * وان روشنائ
در تاریکی میدرخشید و تاریکی درنمییافتش * شخصی بود که از جانب خدا فرستاده
شده که اسمش یحیی بود * و او برای شهادت امد تا انکه شهادت بران نور دهد تا
انکه همه بوساطت او ایمان اورند * و او خود روشنائ نبود بلکه امده بود که بران
روشنائ شهادت بدهد * و روشنائ حقیقی انست که هر کس را باجهان درمیاید منوّر
میگرداند * و این درجهان بود و جهان بوساطت ا و پدید کشت و جهانش
نمیشناخت * و بسوی خاصان خویش امد و ایشان نه پذیر فتندش * و چندی که
پذیر فتندش ایشان را رتبه داد که فرزند ان خدا بشوند و ایشان بودند که با سمش
ایمان اوردند * و تولّد ایشان از اخلاط و از خواهش جسمانی و خواهش نفسانی
نبود بلکه مجبّرد از خواهش خدا بود * و ان کلمه مجسّم شده درمیان ما قرار کرفت

Facsimile of the opening page of John's Gospel from the first edition of
Henry Martyn's Persian New Testament, published by the Russian Bible
Society
*(Reproduced by permission of the Syndics of Cambridge University Library)*

copy of his translation of the New Testament into the Persian language to His Persian Majesty, Fateh Ali Shah Kajar, having first made conditions that His Majesty was to peruse the whole, and favour me with his opinion of the style, etc.

Previous to delivering the book to the Shah, I employed transcribers to make some copies of it, which I distributed to Hajji Mahomed Hussein Khan, Prince of Maru, Mirza Abdulwahab, and other men of learning and rank ... who ... would, I felt certain, give it a fair judgement, and, if called upon by the Shah for their opinion, report of it according to its instrinsic merits.

The enclosed translation of a letter from His Persian Majesty to me will show your Lordship that he thinks the complete work a great acquisition, and that he approves of the simple style adopted by my lamented friend Martyn and his able coadjutor, Mirza Sayyed Ali... Should the Society express a wish to possess the original letter from the Shah, or a copy of it in Persian, I shall be most happy to present either through your Lordship.

I beg leave to add that, if a correct copy of Mr Martyn's translation has not yet been presented to the Society, I shall have great pleasure in offering one that has been copied from and collated with the original left with me by Mr Martyn, on which he had bestowed the greatest pains to render it perfect.

I also promise to devote my leisure to the correction of the press, in the event of your thinking proper to have it printed in England, should my Sovereign not have immediate occasion for my services out of England.

> I am, etc.
>
> Gore Ouseley.[8]

The shah, having received his copy of the Persian New Testament, sent a letter to Sir Gore, indicating the opinion he held of the work:

In the Name of the Almighty God, whose glory is most excellent.

It is our august command that the dignified and excellent, our trusty, faithful, and loyal well-wisher, Sir Gore Ouseley, Baronet, His Britannic Majesty's Ambassador Extraordinary (after being honoured and exalted with the expressions of our highest regard and consideration), should know that the copy of the Gospel, which was translated into Persian by the learned exertions of the late Rev. Henry Martyn, and which has been presented to us by your Excellency on the part of the high, dignified, learned, and enlightened Society of Christians, united for the purpose of spreading abroad the Holy Books of the religion of Jesus (upon whom, and upon all prophets, be peace and blessings!), has reached us, and has proved highly acceptable to our august mind.

In truth, through the learned and unremitted exertions of the Rev. Henry Martyn, it has been translated in a style most befitting sacred books, that is, in an easy and simple diction. Formerly, the four Evangelists, Matthew, Mark, Luke, and John, were known in Persia; but now the whole of the New Testament is completed in a most excellent manner: and this circumstance has been an additional source of pleasure to our enlightened and august mind. Even the four Evangelists which were known in this country had never been before explained in so clear and luminous a manner. We, therefore, have been particularly delighted with this copious and complete translation. If it please the most merciful God, we shall command the Select Servants, who are admitted to our presence, to read to us the above-mentioned book from the beginning to the end, that we may, in the most minute manner, hear and comprehend its contents.

Your Excellency will be pleased to rejoice the hearts of the above-mentioned dignified, learned, and enlightened Society with assurances of our highest regard and approbation; and to inform those excellent individuals, who are so virtuously engaged in disseminating and making known the true meaning and intent of the Holy Gospel, and other points in sacred books, that they are deservedly honoured with our royal favour. Your Excellency must consider yourself as bound to fulfil this royal request.

Given in Rebialavil, 1229.

(Sealed) FATEH ALI SHAH KAJAR.[9]

Not until Judgement Day will the spiritual achievements that the Lord brought to fruition through the labours of that humble young man of God be fully known.

# 30.
# Henry Martyn: the man

'There came to this city
[Shiraz] an Englishman,
who taught the religion of
Christ with a boldness
hitherto unparalleled in
Persia, in the midst of much
scorn and ill-treatment...
He was a beardless youth,
and evidently enfeebled by
disease...'
              (Muhammad Rahim).

## 30.
# Henry Martyn: the man

Henry Martyn was brought to a saving faith in the Lord Jesus Christ while he attended Cambridge University. Guided by Charles Simeon, an evangelical minister of the Church of England, he set about making preparations to serve the Lord in India. He willingly sacrificed a congenial life in the academic atmosphere of Cambridge for the harsh climate and trials of missionary work in India and Persia. He put his love for the Lord Jesus and the natives of the Orient before his love of Lydia Grenfell. He died at the young age of only thirty-one.

He was a brilliant scholar, yet he enjoyed playing with the children he met in the missionary compounds. He had a love for sinners that drove him to surrender his life to the translation of the Scriptures, and to live in far-distant lands. His health was always second in importance to his labours for the Lord.

He trusted people whom others dismissed as not worthy of notice and preached the gospel to the down-and-outs of society in Cawnpore. He spent much time and money opening schools for the youngsters in those places where he served the East India Company. Sabat, that proud son of Arabia, who made Henry's life so difficult, was tolerated when others would have sent him on his way!

Henry was a humble man, who didn't parade his achieve-ments before the world in which he moved, and his journal is more a diary of his spiritual walk with his Saviour than a list of his accomplishments.

Intolerance and abuse came from many quarters, but he stood firm for the faith he held so precious. When in Persia, facing the hostility of the Muslims, he stood firm for the honour of his Saviour and the gospel. He did not live to see the fruit of his labours and died a lonely death. Yet he knew, and no doubt experienced, what the psalmist had written: 'Precious in the sight of the LORD is the death of his saints' (Psalm 116:15).

In Cambridge University the name of Henry Martyn is still honoured. He was one of their greatest sons, but more importantly, he was one of the Lord's most diligent servants. Cambridge University has on display the portrait of Henry painted in 1810 and sent to Charles Simeon. In turn Simeon bequeathed it in 1836 to the university, which has a hall and library bearing the name 'Henry Martyn'. His service, rendered to his spiritual Commander, was, and still remains, a call for Christians to give their lives in Christ's service.

In his day, Charles Simeon would frequently point to the portrait of Henry that hung in his home and say, 'There, see that blessed man... No one looks at me as he does; he never takes his eyes off me, and always seems to be saying, "Be serious; be in earnest; don't trifle, don't trifle." '[1]

Henry Martyn's life and witness led to conversions that he never knew about and of people he never met. In 1841 George Fowler published a book entitled *Three Years in Persia*, in which a chapter is devoted to memories of Henry Martyn. He tells the story of one whose conversion was unknown to Henry :

It is gratifying to find from a paper in the *Asiatic Regis-ter*, the writer of which spent a few weeks at Shiraz, that the love and work of this distinguished missionary, although he saw no fruits from them, have in one instance proved that his labour has not been in vain in the Lord. He relates that in that city he met with an interesting character, Muhammad Rahim, who had been educated for a mullah; a man of considerable learning, and much attached to the English. He found him reading a volume of *Cowper's Poems*, and was astonished at the precision with which he expressed himself in English; this led to the subject of religion, when he acknowledged himself to be a Christian, and related the following circumstance.

In the year of the Hegira 1223 there came to this city an Englishman, who taught the religion of Christ with a boldness hitherto unparalleled in Persia, in the midst of much scorn and ill-treatment from the mullahs as well as the rabble. He was a beardless youth, and evidently enfeebled by disease; he dwelt among us for more than a year. I was then a decided enemy to infidels, as the Christians are termed by the followers of Mohammed, and I visited this teacher of the despised sect, for the purpose of treating him with scorn, and exposing his doctrines to contempt. Although I persevered in this conduct for some time, I found that every interview not only increased my respect for the individual, but diminished my confidence in the faith in which I was educated. His extreme forbearance towards the violence of his opponents, the calm and yet convincing manner in which he exposed the fallacies and sophistries by which he was assailed (for he spoke Persian excellently), gradually inclined me to listen to his arguments, to enquire dispassionately into the subject of them, and finally to read a tract which he had written in reply to *A Defence of Islam*, by our chief mullahs. The result of my examination was a conviction that the young disputant was right. Shame, or rather fear, withheld me from this opinion; I even avoided the society of the Christian teacher, though he remained in the city so long. Just before he quitted Shiraz I could not refrain from paying him a farewell visit. Our conversation, the memory of which will never fade from the tablet of my mind, sealed my conversion. He gave me a book; it has been my constant companion; the study of it has formed my most delightful occupation; its contents have often consoled me. Upon this he put into my hand a copy of the New Testament in Persian; on one of the blank leaves was written, 'There is joy in heaven over one sinner that re-penteth. HENRY MARTYN.'[2]

This man was not the only one in India and Persia who came to saving faith through the work of Henry Martyn.

Today no tomb marks Henry's final resting place, but his name is listed in the Lamb's Book of Life as one who gave his all, doing his Master's bidding. Non-Christians cannot under-stand what really motivated the Rev. Henry Martyn to leave the safety of England and travel to India, but Christians certainly know: he loved his God and wanted to see sinners brought to a saving faith in the Redeemer.

Someone has written:

What is the meaning of the Christian life?
Is it success? Or vulgar wealth? A name?
Is it a weary struggle — a mean strife
For rank, low gauds [showy objects of purely ornamental
    value], ambition, or for fame?
What sow we for? The world? For fleeting time?
Or far-off harvests, richer, more sublime?

The brightest life on earth was one of loss;
The noblest head was wreathed with sharpest thorn
Has *he* not consecrated pain — the Cross?
What higher crown can Christian brows adorn?
Be we content to follow on the road
Which men count failure, but which leads to God![3]

Today Henry Martyn is in the presence of the Lord, having trod that narrow, rough path, following in the footsteps of his Redeemer.

# Appendix
## A sermon preached by Henry Martyn

If ... God was under no
obligation to do anything
for us ... there is no way
of accounting for his
being willing to save us
but by saying that he
chose that it should be so.
It was mere sovereign
grace that moved him to
have compassion on us.

# Appendix
# A sermon preached by Henry Martyn

*'For God so loved the world, that he gave his only begotten
Son, that whosoever believeth in him should not perish, but
have everlasting life'* (John 3:16).

When we wish to express strong feelings, or excite particular
attention, we are apt to go for words to the extremities of time,
space and being. Thus, when the apostle John would commu-
nicate to us the thought under which his own mind laboured —
namely, the incalculable number of the remarkable things Christ
said and did — he expressed it by saying that, if they were
written every one, he supposed the world itself could not
contain the books that should be written. In the book of the
Acts, Moses is described to have been in his childhood 'beautiful to God', as it is in the original — the meaning of which is, as
it is rendered, 'exceedingly beautiful'. Whenever men are in
transports of passion, they go for terms of endearment, or
expressions of anger, beyond the little sphere in which their
thoughts circulate when their tempers are quiet. A man furious
with anger is never easy, nor seems to have expressed the
feelings of his heart, till he has brought on something about
God, his soul and the word which is used to denote its everlasting misery. Flinging about firebrands and death, he seems

during the existence of the paroxysm to be endued with super-natural strength. He is like those furious spirits of whom it is feigned that they plucked up mountains by the roots and hurled them at each other. It appears, then, that strong feelings and vivid conceptions are generally efforts to reach beyond created being and finite duration. It is natural therefore, conversely, that the same emotions should in their turn be excited by the mention of all the great things that belong to religion. We make these observations that our minds may be duly prepared for the consideration of this text, which, besides the important matter contained in it, is remarkable for bringing into notice such persons and things only as are in their nature at the very summit of being and of thought. The persons introduced are God and Christ and the whole world, and none else; the subjects treated about are endless happiness and misery, and nothing less.

The first word that meets us as we approach the text is 'God'. The name of God is heard by different men differently. The heathen hears it without any emotion at all; he has been accustomed to attach the idea to some inferior being, who surpasses him in power, not in purity — to one who can sport and play and sin. He has been used to listen to songs in which the praises of his god and all manner of obscenity are mixed up together — at least transitions are made from one to another so readily that the poor idolater cannot suppose that they are very unsuitable to each other. Of such a being's future judgement for sin he cannot be afraid, nor feel more at hearing his name than at hearing of any other unimportant thing.

Not so the man brought up in a Christian land. He may be a profane man, and call upon the Almighty as often as he is surprised, without thinking of God at all; he may hear others do the same with equal indifference, but at the serious mention of the sacred name, some awful thoughts will come over his mind and he will think of a mighty Being who created him and can destroy him. His thoughts, though indistinct, as they ever must be in all, will correspond to the accounts which the Scriptures give of his majesty, as being the first and the last, the only self-existent Creator and Governor of all, dwelling in inaccessible light, yet present everywhere and knowing everything. Conceptions of a Being of this kind allow nothing light and trifling to be connected with them. Moreover, the most thoughtless amongst us cannot help believing God to be a holy Being; they know also that there is a judgement to come, and conscience tells them they are not prepared for it. Hence, the mention of his name makes them uneasy, and they will compose their minds and give attention when something is said about God, but they are prepared to hear something which is sure to be disagreeable. Disagreeable or not, it cannot be unimportant.

The sentence, therefore, having begun with the name of God, let us go on to see what else may be said in it. 'God so loved'— love! Does God love? Can God love? This soft affection is found among creatures, and in exact proportion to its extent and power does peace and harmony prevail. When we love, does love and harmony prevail. When we love, and are loved, we are ourselves happy and make others so. But can it be said of God that he loves — of him whom you represent as a jealous God, a great and dreadful God, who cast down the angels and reserves them in everlasting chains unto the judgement of the great day, and will turn the nations into hell if they forget him? Yes, though he has done these things, and must do them again, yet he loves.

You will wonder how such opposite attributes as love and unbending justice can consist together; or else will begin to suspect that the love of God, of which we are speaking, is only the love which he feels for those who are worthy of it. Let us advance a step farther in the text, and see: 'God so loved the world' — the world of which St John saith that it 'lieth in wickedness' [1 John 5:19]. No sign of worthiness appears here: we were once 'foolish, disobedient, deceived, serving divers [various] lusts and pleasures, living in malice and envy, hateful and hating one another' — that is, detestable ourselves and detesting one another. Nothing amiable appears yet. But perhaps they still retained some respect for God, though they were so full of hatred to one another. But the Lord looked down from heaven, and behold, there was none doing good, no not one — all the imaginations of the heart were only evil continually. It was not the mere infirmity of nature that led men into such an extent of depravity, but radical enmity in the heart. The heart in its natural state is not merely an enemy to religion, but enmity itself against God, being made up of malice and ill will, and spiteful opposition to God for imposing the restraints of his laws upon us and preparing a place of punishment. We accounted him unjust and tyrannical — we had rather he were less holy, and still more that he did not exist at all.

Now God, we are sure, must have been privy to these thoughts. Had we attempted it, we could not have concealed them. His eye is fixed on the heart; he knows, and ever has known, all that is passing there, is fully acquainted with the malignity of every thought. But perhaps God thinks more lightly of these things than we would have it understood that he does; and if he had punished them, the punishment would not have been very terrible. But you will notice one expression of our text — that they 'should not perish'. The idea of perishing leaves no room for that of recovery. Absolute ruin then would have been the consequence, if justice had taken its course. Thus we need not go beyond our text to find proofs of our being unworthy of God's love. When he undertook to introduce a new dispensation whereby they might be saved, he found them perishing. But in the government of a good and righteous God, no creature could have perished without deserving it. If men deserved to perish, they could not be worthy of his love.

Possibly this thought may occur to some, that men fill so high a place in the universe that the preservation of them might be an object of importance; that perhaps God might take measures for preventing their excision, in order to preserve the integrity of his universal empire. But, alas, the earth with its grandeur is but a speck before God! Could then the destruction of it, with all its inhabitants, diminish ought [anything] of God's glory? Would there not remain multitudes enough of holy creatures, yea, of millions of worlds, to glorify him? Or if we were to suppose the whole universe, with all its wonders, to be blotted out and brought to nothing, would not he remain the same great God, infinitely happy in himself alone? Could he not, if he pleased, call forth another world with the same ease as when he spake this into being?

But in truth, so far is the salvation of men from being necessary to God's glory that he would have been glorified by our destruction. As our earth [sank] in ruins, the inhabitants of heaven might praise God in the same strains as those in which they will praise him at the fall of his other enemies; for thus they will sing in heaven at the final execution of judgement: 'We give thee thanks, O Lord God Almighty, which art, and wast, and art to come; because thou hast taken to thee thy great power, and hast reigned' [Revelation 11:17]. And again they will glorify him for the ruin of his enemies: 'Great and marvellous are thy works, Lord God Almighty; just and true are thy ways, thou King of saints' [Revelation 15:3]. Thus might the song of triumph be sung at the destruction of the race of men. They might have sung as we perished, 'Just and true are thy ways!'

If, then, God was under no obligation to do anything for us, but, on the contrary, might have justly left us to perish; if he might in righteous judgement have sent 'indignation and wrath, tribulation and anguish, upon every soul of man' [Romans 2:8,9], because they were enemies and rebels, there is no way of accounting for his being willing to save us but by saying that he chose that it should be so. It was mere sovereign grace that moved him to have compassion on us.

He might have left it undone with perfect justice, propriety and honour to himself; that he has done it at all, in any manner, is an interposition unexpected and extraordinary. If it is an act of mercy that God should suspend our punishment, what shall we say then, when God hath so loved the world as to 'give his only begotten Son'? He loved us, but could not resign his rights, or put up with a partial fulfilment of his will! A person must be found capable of bearing the sins of men; and where was such an one but in the bosom of God himself? If God will save sinners, he must give none other than his own Son! His love to the world may be great, but will it draw from him a gift like this? 'Take now thy son,' said God to Abraham, 'thine only son ... whom thou lovest ... and offer him [up] there' [Genesis 22:2]. This was the severity of the trial — that Abraham was to give up his only-beloved child. We pretend not to define accurately the relation which subsists between the Father and the Son; so far we may be certain from these names that Christ is at least as dear to his Father as a child to an earthly parent. If this be the case, can the Father give him? Is there any example of such generosity on earth, that we may be encouraged to hope? Was ever a person known to give his fortune to another who had no claim upon him; or to give the life of one of his own children for the sake of a friend? Much less would he do it for the sake of a person indifferent to him; still less for one who had used him ill; still less if he was still raging with enmity — least of all would he give an only child for such a person in such circumstances. To do any, the least, of all these things would argue a most unaccountable regard, when so many obstacles cannot prevent its exercise.

But what, can 'the fellow of Jehovah' [Zechariah 13:7] be given to man? Shall he who is God, equal with the Father, God over all, blessed for ever, shall the Alpha and Omega, the beginning and the ending, which is and which was and is to come — shall he leave his glory and sojourn with mortals? Must the Ancient of Days put on a mortal tabernacle? What fellowship hath light with darkness? What agreement between dust and glory? Will the Father consent that one of the persons of the blessed Trinity be thus debased? 'No,' he might say, 'if this be the only condition, let them perish!' But God so loved the world that he gave his only begotten Son.

'Herein is love, not that we loved God, but that he loved us, and sent his Son to be the propitiation for our sins' [1 John 4:10]. 'Herein is love,' as if there were love in nothing else. May we not say that to give us a being among rational creatures, therein is love; to have our life carried so many years as a taper in the hands of providence, therein is love; to have food and raiment [clothing] and kind friends, therein is love; to give us heaven, therein is love? No; *'herein* is love', that God gave his Son. He gave him unasked for; man would never have conceived such a request, or if he had, would not have dared to urge it. God foresaw how he would be treated, yet he gave him notwithstanding, to shame and to spitting, to pain and to sorrow, to a suffering life and a disgraceful death, for 'God *so* loved the world' — *such* anxiety, *such* desire and concern was there in the heart of God for the salvation of sinners!

The farther we advance in the text, the more conspicuously will this truth appear. God gave his Son, that *'whosoever believeth on him should not perish'*. The plan of salvation by Jesus Christ is altogether peculiar: in it men are considered as all alike perishing, as well the virtuous as the profligate, because they have both broken that law which allows of no violation and provides no remedy. But the Son of God having appeared on the theatre of the world and suffered the penalty due to us, God sends forth this message into the world, and at this moment is delivering it to you, that he is willing to grant pardon and bliss to the sinner who comes to him through Christ. Whosoever will venture to rest the whole weight of his concerns for eternity on this rock shall find that it will not fail him; whosoever, pursued by avenging justice, will flee to this city, shall be safe — yea, if he be a murderer, he shall be safe; whosoever believeth — it matters not what he has been; only let him be convinced that he deserves punishment, and plead the death of Christ — the sentence of death shall be reversed and a free pardon granted; he shall not perish, as he otherwise would have done; he shall not perish, though Satan would persuade him that he will; he shall not perish, though his remaining sinfulness threatens him every moment. He is 'kept by the power of God through faith' [1 Peter 1:5], and therefore he shall not perish.

The common objection of cavillers [those who make petty objections] here obtrudes itself: 'Is not this the dangerous doctrine of salvation by faith alone?' Would to God that they who thus idly speak would conceive rightly of their guilt, corruption and danger! If they saw themselves on the brink of everlasting perdition, where they all are by nature, they would no longer think of their works as meriting favour, or purchasing an interest in Christ, but would cry, 'Save Lord, or I perish!'; they would then see that if pardon be not by faith only, they are lost. They suppose we lay stress on faith in contradistinction to other good works, whereas it is only an act of the mind whereby it gives up all hopes founded on itself and reposes on the mercy of God in Christ. May the sinner after this live as he will? Or does he wish such a thing? Perish the thought! There is such a word as gratitude in his vocabulary: knowing why Christ came, it is his business to become more holy from day to day, and for this purpose the Spirit of God is given him.

But we are unwilling to pass the time in answering objections. It is a disgrace to human nature that any should be found quarrelling with that way of salvation which has originated solely in the transcending mercy of God. Yet so it is: how many in the world never understand or believe! It is 'the savour of death unto death' to them [2 Corinthians 2:16]. Many others there are who have indeed no objections to make, but love sin too well to forsake it for Christ. Oh, think a moment of your abominable selfishness and base ingratitude! If God spared not his own Son but gave him up for you, why should you refuse to resign anything at the call of God?

Let those who believe in Christ remember that they are warranted to expect every real blessing: such as assurance of pardon, heavenly-mindedness, everything consolatory, sanctifying and adoring. For, 'He that spared not his own Son, but delivered him up for us all, how shall he not with him also freely give us all things?' [Romans 8:32]. All is yours, for 'ye are Christ's' [1 Corinthians 3:22-23]. If God has parted so freely with that which is so far dearer to him than anything else, how shall he deny you anything afterwards? If he has so freely given you the greater miracles, how can you suppose he should deny you the less? And if he has given you this gift when you were alienated from him, it is not to be imagined that he will deny you any inferior mercy when you are in a state of amity with him. 'If, when we were enemies, we were reconciled to God by the death of his Son, much more, being reconciled, we shall be saved by his life' [Romans 5:10].

Oh, what numerous, connected, well-secured, precious and everlasting blessings and joys have we in our Lord Jesus Christ! Let us recur, with gratitude ever new, to the glorious theme and take a view of it in its lengths and breadths and depths and heights; let us proclaim to all around the glad, the glorious, the joy-inspiring news of a Saviour born; let us blow the great trumpet, and make it known among the nations that the year of jubilee is come. Come, ye sinners, draw near to the fountain of living waters: drink, drink deep of the sacred stream, drink in eternal life. When millions of years shall have passed away, your joys will be but beginning; and when millions more shall have passed away, they shall be no nearer ending.

Let us then join the choir of angels and adore, with songs of the highest praise, the love and mercy of our God — let there be a new song in our mouths and in our hearts, even praises to our God. Let our meditation of him be sweet, and let our souls, which he hath redeemed, rejoice in God our only Lord. While also we are rejoicing in the bounty of God, let us delight to imitate it. God gave his Son to them who had no claim: hesitate not to give to those whose helpless penury is a claim upon you. Give liberally, give cheerfully; so all the Christmas song will belong to you — you will have a right to sing, not only 'Glory to God in the highest!', but 'Peace on earth, and goodwill towards men!'

# ℕotes

**Chapter 1 — Dangerous times**
1. D. Bentley-Taylor, *My love must wait — The story of Henry Martyn*, IVP, 1978, p.8.
2. G. Smith, *Henry Martyn, Saint and Scholar — First modern missionary to the Mohammedans, 1781-1812*, The Religious Tract Society, London, 1892, p.5.
3. *Ibid.*
4. For a biography of Samuel Walker see Tim Shenton, *A Cornish Revival — The Life and Times of Samuel Walker of Truro*, Evangelical Press, 2003.
5. J. C. Ryle, *The Christian Leaders of the Last Century*, T. Nelson and Sons, 1899, p.314.
6. *Ibid.*, p.318.
7. C. Padwick, *Henry Martyn, Confessor of the Faith*, Church Missionary Society, London, 1925, p.39.
8. K. Finnie, *Beyond the Minarets — A biography of Henry Martyn*, STL Books, 1988, p.15.

**Chapter 2 — School and university**
1. R. T. France, 'Henry Martyn' in *Five Pioneer Missionaries*, Banner of Truth Trust, 1965, p.236.
2. J. Sargent, *The Life and Letters of Henry Martyn*, Banner of Truth Trust, 1985, p.5.
3. *Ibid.*, p.7.
4. *Ibid.*, pp.8-9. It is worth recording the words of John R. C. Martyn, who writes, 'Henry behaved like a typical self-opinionated undergraduate, short-tempered even towards his father' (*Henry Martyn (1781–1812), Scholar and Missionary to India and Persia*, The Edwin Mellen Press, Great Britain, 1999, p.11).

**Chapter 3 — A man of God**
1. Quoted from the *Memoirs of the life of Gilbert Wakefield* (1792), p.148, by Hugh E. Hopkins, *Charles Simeon of Cambridge*, W. B. Eerdmans Publishing Company, 1977, p.24.

2. D. A. Winstanley, *Early Victorian Cambridge* (Cambridge, 1955), p.91, quoted by Hopkins, *Charles Simeon of Cambridge*, p.25.

3. Hopkins, *Charles Simeon of Cambridge*, p.27.

4. Padwick, *Henry Martyn, Confessor of the Faith*, p.64.

5. Hopkins, *Charles Simeon of Cambridge*, p.62.

6. Padwick, *Henry Martyn, Confessor of the Faith*, p.65.

7. Hopkins, *Charles Simeon of Cambridge*, p.21.

8. Bentley-Taylor, *My Love Must Wait*, pp.14-15.

9. Sargent, *Life and Letters of Henry Martyn*, p.15.

10. H. Martyn, *Journal and Letters of the Rev. Henry Martyn, B.D.*, Seeley and Burnside, England, 1837, vol. 1, 16 December 1804, p.203.

11. Sargent, *Life and Letters of Henry Martyn*, p.19.

12. Smith, *Henry Martyn, Saint and Scholar*, p.21.

13. Padwick, *Henry Martyn, Confessor of the Faith*, pp.78-9.

14. Sargent, *Life and Letters of Henry Martyn*, p.17.

15. *A Frenchman in England*, translated by S. C. Roberts (Cambridge, 1933), in Hopkins, *Charles Simeon of Cambridge*, p.21.

16. Martyn, *Journal and Letters*, vol. 1, 17 January 1803, p.28.

17. France, 'Henry Martyn', p.245.

## Chapter 4 — A new curate

1. Martyn, *Journal and Letters*, vol. 1, 20 October 1803, p.63.

2. *Ibid.*, vol. 1, 23 October 1803, p.65.

3. *Ibid.*, vol. 1, 6 November 1803, p.66.

4. Sargent, *Life and Letters of Henry Martyn*, p.48.

5. Martyn, *Journal and Letters*, vol. 1, 13 September 1803, p.53.

6. *Ibid.*, 30 October 1803, p.65.

7. *Ibid.*, vol. 1, 1 January 1804, pp.75-6.

8. *Ibid.*, vol. 1, 3 January 1804, p.76.

9. George Smith writes, 'There was a tradition in the family of his half-brother John, that Henry and his sisters litigated with him, and farther lessened the patrimony. However that may have been, while in India, Henry set apart the proceeds of his Fellowship at St John's for the maintenance of his brother's family, and bequeathed all he had to his children' (*Henry Martyn, Saint and Scholar*, p.41).

10. Padwick, *Henry Martyn, Confessor of the Faith*, p.106.

11. Sargent, *Life and Letters of Henry Martyn*, p.57.

12. Martyn, *Journal and Letters*, vol. 1, 15 April 1804, p.110.

13. *Ibid.*, vol. 1, 29 July 1804, p.145.

14. *Ibid.*, vol. 1, 10 August 1804, p.157.

15. *Ibid.*, vol. 1, 27 August 1804, p.152.

16. L Grenfell, *Extracts from the Religious Diary of Miss L. Grenfell of Marazion, Cornwall*, Lake and Co., 1890, 26 August 1804, pp.13-14.

## Chapter 5 — Farewell, Cambridge

1. Martyn, *Journal and Letters*, vol. 1, 6 December 1804 p.198.
2. *Ibid.*, vol. 1, 8 October 1804, p.168.
3. *Ibid.*, vol. 1, 10 November 1804, p.188.
4. *Ibid.*, vol. 1, 12 January 1805, p.216.
5. *Ibid.*, vol. 1, 15 January 1805, p.217.
6. *Ibid.*, vol. 1, 18 February 1805, p.231.
7. *Ibid.*, vol. 1, 7 March 1805, p.237.
8. *Ibid.*, vol. 1, 18 March 1805, p.240.
9. *Ibid.*, vol. 1, 3 April 1805, p.244.

## Chapter 6 — Never to return

1. Padwick, *Henry Martyn, Confessor of the Faith*, p.101.
2. *Ibid.*, p.102.
3. *Ibid.*, p.103.
4. Martyn, *Journal and Letters*, vol. 1, 12 May 1805, p.251.
5. *Ibid.*, vol. 1, 7 June 1805, pp.262-3.
6. Sargent, *Life and Letters of Henry Martyn*, p.86.
7. Martyn, *Journal and Letters*, vol. 1, 8 June 1805, pp.263-4.
8. *Ibid.*, vol. 1, 4 July 1805, p.272.
9. Sargent, *Life and Letters of Henry Martyn*, p.91.
10. Grenfell, *Diary*, 25 July 1805, pp.21-2.
11. Martyn, *Journal and Letters*, vol. 1, 10 August 1805, p.289.
12. Grenfell, *Diary*, 10 August 1805, p.25.

## Chapter 7 — Hard times

1. Sargent, *Life and Letters of Henry Martyn*, p.96
2. *Ibid.*, pp.97-8.
3. Martyn, *Journal and Letters*, vol. 1, 23 August 1805, p.301.
4. *Ibid.*, p.302.
5. Sargent, *Life and Letters of Henry Martyn*, pp.98-9.
6. Martyn, *Journal and Letters*, vol. 1, 30 August 1805, p.306.
7. *Ibid.*, vol. 1, 8 September 1805, p.313.
8. *Ibid.*, vol. 1, 15 September 1805, p.318.
9. Sargent, *Life and Letters of Henry Martyn*, p.105.
10. Martyn, *Journal and Letters*, vol. 1, 22 September 1805, p.322.
11. Sargent, *Life and Letters of Henry Martyn*, p.109.
12. Martyn, *Journal and Letters*, vol. 1, 29 September 1805, p.326.
13. *Ibid.*, vol. 1, 3 October 1805, p.329.
14. *Ibid.*

## Chapter 8 — San Salvador: a pleasant stopover

1. Martyn, *Journal and Letters*, vol. 1, 6 October 1805, p.331.
2. *Ibid.*, vol. 1, 10 October 1805, p.334.

3. *Ibid.*, vol. 1, 9 December 1805, pp.369-70.

4. *Ibid.*, vol. 1, 12 November 1805, p.353.

5. Sargent, *Life and Letters of Henry Martyn*, p.117.

6. *Ibid.*, p.123.

7. Martyn, *Journal and Letters*, vol. 1, 25 November 1805, p.359.

## Chapter 9 — The Cape of Good Hope at last!

1. Martyn, *Journal and Letters*, vol. 1, 4 December 1805, p.365.

2. *Ibid.*

3. *Ibid.*, vol. 1, 20 December 1805, p.377.

4. *Ibid.*, vol. 1, 26 December 1805, p.382.

5. *Ibid.*

6. *Ibid.*, vol. 1, 29 December 1805, pp.384-5.

7. Sargent, *Life and Letters of Henry Martyn*, p.127

8. *Ibid.*, p.134.

9. *Ibid.*, 23 January 1806, p.135.

10. *Ibid.*, 30 January 1806, pp.137-8.

## Chapter 10 — India ahoy!

1. Sargent, *Life and Letters of Henry Martyn*, p.139.

2. *Ibid.*, p.141.

3. Martyn, *Journal and Letters*, vol. 1, 7 March 1806, p.415.

4. *Ibid.*, vol. 1, 19 April 1806, p.435.

5. Sargent, *Life and Letters of Henry Martyn*, p.143.

6. Martyn, *Journal and Letters*, vol. 1, 11 April 1806, p.431.

7. Smith, *Henry Martyn, Saint and Scholar*, p.144, footnote.

8. Sargent, *Life and Letters of Henry Martyn*, pp.144-5.

9. Martyn, *Journal and Letters*, vol. 1, 28 April 1806, p.438.

10. Sargent, *Life and Letters of Henry Martyn*, p.145.

11. Martyn, *Journal and Letters*, vol. 1, 6 May 1806, p.440.

## Chapter 11 — Starting work

1. Martyn, *Journal and Letters*, vol. 1, 9 May 1806, p.442.

2. Sargent, *Life and Letters of Henry Martyn*, pp.148-9.

3. M. Sherwood, *The life of Mrs Sherwood*, Darton and Co., London, 1857, p.372.

4. Martyn, *Journal and Letters*, vol. 1, 17 May 1806, p.447.

5. Bentley-Taylor, *My love must wait*, p.63.

6. Martyn, *Journal and Letters*, vol. 1, 19 May 1806, p.449.

7. *Ibid.*, vol. 1, 20 May 1806, p.450.

8. *Ibid.*, vol. 1, 8 June 1806, p.455.

9. Smith, *Henry Martyn, Saint and Scholar*, p.153.

10. Jessie Page, *Henry Martyn: His life and labours — Cambridge, India, Persia*, The Edwin Mellen Press, p.67.

11. Sargent, *Life and Letters of Henry Martyn,* p.156.
12. Martyn, *Journal and Letters,* vol. 1, 24 May 1806, p.451.
13. *Ibid.,* vol. 1, 9 July 1806, p.466.

Chapter 12 — 'My dearest Lydia'
1. Grenfell, *Diary,* 10 August 1805, p.25.
2. *Ibid.,* 1 November 1805, p.31.
3. Martyn, *Journal and Letters,* vol. 1, 30 July 1806, pp.473-8.
4. *Ibid.,* vol. 1, 1 September 1806, p.491.
5. Sherwood, *Life,* p.322.
6. Sargent, *Life and Letters of Henry Martyn,* p.158.
7. Martyn, *Journal and Letters,* vol. 1, 17 October 1806, p.504.
8. *Ibid.,* vol. 1, 17 August 1806, p.447.
9. *Ibid.,* vol. 1, 8 November 1806, p.509.
10. Sargent, *Life and Letters of Henry Martyn,* p.176.
11. Its author was Valmiki, a Hindu of the Bombay coast. It tells the exploits of Rama who, aided by Hanuman, the monkey-god, conquered Ceylon and brought back his queen, Sita, whom Rawana, the giant and tyrant of that island, had carried away.
12. Sargent, *Life and Letters of Henry Martyn,* p.179.
13. Padwick, *Henry Martyn, Confessor of the Faith,* p.176.
14. Martyn, *Journal and Letters,* vol. 1, 2 December 1806, pp.515-16.

Chapter 13 — Henry's first Indian parish
1. Martyn, *Journal and Letters,* vol. 1, 28 November 1806, p.512.
2. *Ibid.,* vol. 1, 29 November 1806, pp.512-13.
3. *Ibid.,* vol. 1, 10 December 1806, p.520.
4. Sargent, *Life and Letters of Henry Martyn,* p.185.
5. Martyn, *Journal and Letters,* vol. 1, 30 December 1806, p.526.
6. *Ibid.,* vol. 1, 31 December 1806, p.527.
7. Sargent, *Life and Letters of Henry Martyn,* pp.187-8.

Chapter 14 — Satan's kingdom under attack
1. Martyn, *Journal and Letters,* vol. 2, 3 May 1807, p.56.
2. *Ibid.,* vol. 2, 22 February 1807, p.22.
3. *Ibid.,* vol. 2, 20-23 January 1808, p.149.
4. Sargent, *Life and Letters of Henry Martyn,* pp. 224-5.
5. Martyn, *Journal and Letters,* vol. 2, 31 July 1808, p.208.
6. *Ibid.,* vol. 2, 1-6 August 1808, p.209.
7. *Ibid.*
8. *Ibid.,* vol. 2, 13 January 1807, p.5.
9. *Ibid.,* vol. 2, letter, 6 April 1807, p.46.
10. *Ibid.,* vol. 2, letter to Daniel Corrie, 23 March 1807, p.35.

11. Sargent, *Life and Letters of Henry Martyn*, p.217.
12. *Ibid.*, pp.204-5.

Chapter 15 — Translation under way in earnest
1. Padwick, *Henry Martyn, Confessor of the Faith*, p.199.
2. Martyn, *Journal and Letters*, vol. 2, 13 July 1807, p.89.
3. *Ibid.*, vol. 2, 24 September 1807, p.109.
4. *Ibid.*, vol. 2, 10 November 1807, p.123.
5. *Ibid.*, vol. 2, 4 December 1807, pp.131-2.
6. *Ibid.*, vol. 2, 22 February 1808, p.160.
7. *Ibid.*, vol. 2, 26 April 1808, p.185.
8. Smith, *Henry Martyn, Saint and Scholar*, p.227.
9. *Ibid.*, pp.227-8. Quoted from J. Sargent, *Memoir of the Rev Thomas Thomason, M.A.*, 2nd edition, London, 1857.
10. Many Arabs claimed this as it gave them a higher social standing.
11. Sherwood, *Life*, p.343.
12. *Ibid.*, p.346.
13. Martyn, *Journal and Letters*, vol. 2, 7 January 1808, p.143.
14. *Ibid.*, vol. 2, 13 February 1808, p.157.
15. *Ibid.*, vol. 2, 28 March 1808, pp.172-4.
16. *Ibid.*, vol. 2, 2 May 1808, p.190.

Chapter 16 — A busy schedule
1. Martyn, *Journal and Letters*, vol. 2, 24 June 1807, p.23.
2. *Ibid.*, vol. 2, 4 January 1808, p.139.
3. *Ibid.*, vol. 2, 13 July 1807, p.90.
4. *Ibid.*, vol. 2, 3 February 1807, p.14.
5. *Ibid.*, vol. 2, 1-4 June 1808, p.196.
6. *Ibid.*, vol. 2, 25 January 1808, p.150.
7. *Ibid.*, vol. 2, 15 April 1808, p.183.
8. *Ibid.*, vol. 2, 9 August 1808, p.210.
9. *Ibid.*, vol. 2, 28 August 1808, p.214.
10. *Ibid.*, vol. 2, 19 September 1808, p.215.
11. Sherwood, *Life*, pp.317-21.

Chapter 17 — A foolish decision
1. Martyn, *Journal and Letters*, vol. 2, 3 May 1809, p.240. No comment is made concerning the physical state of the men carrying the palanquin.
2. There seems to be confusion over the date of his arrival. Mrs Sherwood wrote that Henry arrived on 30 May 1809, yet we find Henry writing letters from Cawnpore on 3 May 1809 and conducting his first worship service with the soldiers on 14 May 1809.
3. Martyn, *Journal and Letters*, vol. 2, 3 May 1809, p.240.
4. *Ibid.*, vol. 2, 3 May 1809, p.240.

5. *Ibid.*, vol. 2, 22 May 1809, p.242.

6. *Ibid.*, vol. 2, 15 May 1809, p.241.

7. Sherwood, *Life*, pp.345 ff.

8. Martyn, *Journal and Letters*, vol. 2, 18 September 1809, p.256.

9. *Ibid.*, vol. 2, 19 November 1809, p.273.

10. *Ibid.*, vol. 2, 19 April 1810, pp.294-7.

11. *Ibid.*, vol. 2, 8 July 1810, p.308.

12. *Ibid.*, vol. 2, 14 August 1810, p.310.

13. Grenfell, *Diary*, p.71.

14. Sherwood, *Life*, p.353.

15. *Christian Hymns*, Evangelical Movement of Wales, 1977, no. 460.

## Chapter 18 — A new start

1. Sherwood, *Life*, p.350.

2. *Ibid.*, p.381.

3. *Ibid.*, p.393.

4. *Ibid.*, p.394.

5. Martyn, *Journal and Letters*, vol. 2, 22 October 1809, p.265.

6. *Ibid.*, 3 April 1810, p.292.

7. Sherwood, *Life*, p.354.

8. *Ibid.*, p.355.

9. *Ibid.*, p.395.

10. *Ibid.*, p.357.

11. Martyn, *Journal and Letters*, vol. 2, 11 September 1809, pp.254-5.

12. Sherwood, *Life*, pp.384-6.

13. *Ibid.*, p.386.

14. Martyn, *Journal and Letters*, vol. 2, 1 January 1810, p.280.

15. The remainder of the quote is found in Sargent, *Life and Letters of Henry Martyn*, p.268.

16. Martyn, *Journal and Letters*, vol. 2, 1 January 1810, p.280.

## Chapter 19 — Time to leave Cawnpore

1. Martyn, *Journal and Letters*, vol. 2, 3 July 1809, p.245.

2. *Ibid.*, vol. 2, 4 November 1809, pp.267-8.

3. *Ibid.*, vol. 2, 14 November 1809, p.271.

4. *Ibid.*, vol. 2, 3 April 1810, p.291.

5. *Ibid.*, vol. 2, November 1809, p.272.

6. *Ibid.*, vol. 2, 19 November 1809, p.273.

7. *Ibid.*, vol. 2, 16 April 1810, pp.293-4.

8. *Ibid.*, vol. 2, 18 April 1810, p.294.

9. *Ibid.*, vol. 2, 17 August 1810, p.312.

10. Sherwood, *Life*, p.399.

11. *Ibid.*, p.398.

12. Sargent, *Life and Letters of Henry Martyn*, p.275.

13. *Ibid.*
14. Sherwood, *Life,* p.398.
15. Smith, *Henry Martyn, Saint and Scholar,* p.288.
16. Sherwood, *Life,* p.399.

## Chapter 20 — Moving on

1. Smith, *Henry Martyn, Saint and Scholar,* footnote, pp.311-12.
2. *Ibid.,* p.315.
3. Martyn, *Journal and Letters,* vol. 2, 3 October 1810, p.319.
4. *Ibid.,* vol. 2, 6 October 1810, p.320.
5. Sargent, *Life and Letters of Henry Martyn,* p.276.
6. *Ibid.,* pp.276-7.
7. Martyn, *Journal and Letters,* vol. 2, 31 October 1810, p.323.
8. *Ibid.,* vol. 2, 20-22 November 1810, pp.324-5.
9. Padwick, *Henry Martyn, Confessor of the Faith,* p.240.
10. Quoted in Padwick, *Henry Martyn, Confessor of the Faith,* p.240.
11. Padwick, *Henry Martyn, Confessor of the Faith,* p.238.
12. *Ibid.*
13. *Ibid.,* p.239.
14. Martyn, *Journal and Letters,* vol. 2, 20-22 November, 1810, p.324.
15. *Ibid.,* vol. 2, p.326.
16. This address was published under the title of, 'Christian India; or, an Appeal on behalf of Nine hundred thousand Christians in India who want the Bible'.
17. Page, *Henry Martyn, His life and labours,* p.121.
18. Martyn, *Journal and Letters,* vol. 2, 4 February 1811, p.332 (The letter is quoted in full on pp.332-7).
19. Padwick, *Henry Martyn, Confessor of the Faith,* p.244.
20. *Ibid.*
21. Martyn, *Journal and Letters,* vol. 2, 4 February 1811, pp.333-4.
22. Sargent, *Life and Letters of Henry Martyn,* 27-31 January 1811, p.283.
23. Martyn, *Journal and Letters,* vol. 2, 17 February, pp.339-40.
24. Sargent, *Life and Letters of Henry Martyn,* p.284.

## Chapter 21 — From India to Persia

1. Martyn, *Journal and Letters,* vol. 2, 20 February 1811, p.340.
2. Smith, *Henry Martyn, Saint and Scholar,* p.329.
3. Padwick, *Henry Martyn, Confessor of the Faith,* p.247.
4. Martyn, *Journal and Letters,* vol. 2, 1 March 1811, p.343.
5. *Ibid.,* vol. 2, 26 February 1811, pp.341-2.
6. *Ibid.,* p.342.
7. Padwick, *Henry Martyn, Confessor of the Faith,* p.247.
8. *Ibid.,* pp.248-9.
9. Martyn, *Journal and Letters,* vol. 2, 26 March 1811, pp.346-7.

10. *Ibid.*, vol. 2, 22 April 1811, p.349.
11. *Ibid.*
12. *Ibid.*, vol. 2, 22 April 1811, p.350.
13. *Ibid.*, vol. 2, 23 April 1811, p.352.
14. *Ibid.*, vol. 2, 21 May 1811, p.355.
15. Martyn, *Journal and Letters*, vol. 2, 26 May 1811, pp.356-7.
16. *Ibid.*, vol. 2, 27 May 1811, p.357.
17. *Ibid.*, vol. 2, 28 May 1811, p.357.

Chapter 22 — The journey to Shiraz
1. Sargent, *Life and Letters of Henry Martyn*, p.291.
2. *Ibid.*, p.292.
3. *Ibid.*, p.293.
4. *Ibid.*
5. *Ibid.*, p.294.
6. *Ibid.*, p.297.

Chapter 23 — Life and work at Shiraz
1. Quoted by Smith, *Henry Martyn, Saint and Scholar,* pp.447-8. The poem was written by Alford when he was Dean of Canterbury.
2. Martyn, *Journal and Letters*, vol. 2, 12 June 1811, p.361.
3. *Ibid.*, vol. 2, 24 June 1811, p.367.
4. Sargent, *Life and Letters of Henry Martyn*, p.310-11.
5. Martyn, *Journal and Letters*, vol. 2, 12 September 1811, pp.377-8.
6. *Ibid.*, vol. 2, 12 December 1811, p.383.
7. *Ibid.*, vol. 2, 23 June 1811, p.299.
8. Sargent, *Life and Letters of Henry Martyn*, p.309.
9. Martyn, *Journal and Letters*, vol. 2, 8 June 1811, p.394.
10. *Ibid.*, vol. 2, 24 June 1811, p.366.
11. *Ibid.*, vol. 2, 12 September 1811, pp.375-8.
12. *Ibid.*, vol. 2, 12 December 1811, pp.381-2.
13. Sargent, *Life and Letters of Henry Martyn*, p.303.
14. Martyn, *Journal and Letters*, vol. 2, 1-8 January 1812, p.384.
15. Sargent, *Life and Letters of Henry Martyn*, p.353.
16. Martyn, *Journal and Letters*, vol. 2, 23 June 1811, pp.363-6.
17. Grenfell, *Diary*, 5 March 1810, p.71.
18. *Ibid.*, 28 March 1811, p.75.
19. This would have been Henry's letter of 22 April 1811, or that of 23 June 1811. Lydia's reply reached Henry on 12 July 1812.

Chapter 24 — Standing firm
1. In 1824, Samuel Lee, D.D., Professor of Arabic, and afterwards Regius Professor of Hebrew in the University of Cambridge, translated into English and edited the controversial tracts on Christianity and Islam by Henry Martyn,

which contained the substance of his public disputations at Shiraz with the learned Muslims.

2. Mohammed (also known as Muhammad or, in older writings, Mahomet) was the founder of Islam. His teachings encompassed the whole of life. He was born in Mecca around A. D. 570. His father died before he was born, and his mother passed away when he was just six years old. He was a quiet, sensitive person who lived a very moral life. In Syria he met and spoke with Christians and married a rich widow, Khadija, when he was twenty-five.

He spent time meditating in a cave near Mecca, and it was there that he claimed to have met the archangel Gabriel, who is said to have declared him to be the final prophet of God. Mohammed began preaching what had been revealed to him and commenced writing the Koran, which he was convinced was God's final revelation to mankind. The Koran is believed by Muslims to be infallible.

He suffered opposition and finally was forced to escape with his followers from Mecca in A.D. 622. He arrived at Medina eight days later. This *Hegira* ('emigration') marked the start of the Islamic calendar. He accepted Jews and Christians as 'peoples of the Book' and urged his followers to live at peace with other religions. His followers taught that he was able to intercede with God on behalf of sinners.

His wife died in A.D. 619, after which he married nine women.

He died in Medina on 8 June 632.

3. Sargent, *Life and Letters of Henry Martyn,* pp.303-11, contains the record of discussions that took place over several days.

4. *Ibid.,* pp.317-18. See also Smith, *Henry Martyn, Saint and Scholar,* pp.399, 400-401.

5. Sargent, *Life and Letters of Henry Martyn,* p.317.

6. Smith, *Henry Martyn, Saint and Scholar,* p.403.

7. Sargent, *Life and Letters of Henry Martyn,* pp.318-19.

8. Smith, *Henry Martyn, Saint and Scholar,* p.404.

9. Sargent, *Life and Letters of Henry Martyn,* pp.322-3.

10. *Ibid.,* p.323.

11. *Ibid.,* pp.310-11.

12. *Ibid.,* pp.312-16.

13. *Ibid.,* p.320.

14. *Ibid.*

15. *Ibid.,* p.321.

16. *Ibid.*

17. *Ibid.*

18. *Ibid.,* 16 January 1812, p.343.

19. Padwick, *Henry Martyn, Confessor of the Faith,* p.274.

20. Smith, *Henry Martyn, Saint and Scholar,* p.359. The references to the 'founder of the empire' are to Cyrus (see 2 Chronicles 36:22-23; Ezra 1:1-4; Isaiah 45:1-7).

## Chapter 25 — Off to Tabriz

1. Sargent, *Life and Letters of Henry Martyn*, p.361.
2. *Ibid.*, p.363.
3. *Ibid.*
4. *Ibid.*, pp.364-8.
5. *Ibid.*, p.367.
6. *Ibid.*
7. *Ibid.*, p.368
8. *Ibid.*
9. *Ibid.*
10. *Ibid.*, p.371.
11. *Ibid.*
12. *Ibid.*, pp.372-3.
13. *Ibid.*, p.373.
14. *Ibid.*, pp.373-4.
15. *Ibid.*, p.376.
16. *Ibid.*

## Chapter 26 — The road to paradise

1. Martyn, *Journal and Letters*, vol. 2, 12 July 1812, pp.394-5.
2. *Ibid.*, vol. 2, 12 July 1812, p.396.
3. Smith, *Henry Martyn, Saint and Scholar*, p.482.
4. According to Smith, the actual figure is 1,542 miles (see *Henry Martyn, Saint and Scholar*, p.536).
5. Martyn, *Journal and Letters*, vol. 2, 28 August 1812, pp.398-400.
6. Sargent, *Life and Letters of Henry Martyn*, p.382.
7. *Ibid.*, p.384.
8. *Ibid.*, p.386.
9. *Ibid.*, p.388.
10. *Ibid.*
11. *Ibid.*, p.393.
12. *Ibid.*, p.394.
13. *Ibid.*, p.395.
14. *Ibid.*, p.401 (the reference is to Hebrews 6:19).
15. *Ibid.*
16. *Ibid.*, p.403.
17. *Ibid.*
18. *Ibid.*
19. *Ibid.*, p.404.
20. *Ibid.*

## Chapter 27 — Home at last!

1. Padwick, *Henry Martyn, Confessor of the Faith*, pp.295-6.
2. Martyn, *Journal and Letters*, vol. 2, 5 October 1812, pp.406-7.

3. Joseph Masters, *The Nestorians and their Rituals*, London, 1852, quoted by Smith, *Henry Martyn, Saint and Scholar*, p.527.

4. Smith, *Henry Martyn, Saint and Scholar*, p.528. In a footnote Smith claims that the slab had been placed there by the British Resident of Baghdad, Mr Rich. He also comments that it is apparent from the inscription that Mr Rich did not know Henry Martyn's Christian name.

5. *Ibid.*, p.527.

6. *Ibid.*, p.530.

7. *Ibid.*, p.516, footnote. It is interesting to read Smith's comment that this poem was written by Thomas Babington Macaulay when he was not yet thirteen years old.

## Chapter 28 — News of a death

1. Sherwood, *Life*, p.424.

2. *Ibid.*, p.428.

3. Grenfell, *Diary*, 12 December 1812, p.80.

4. *Ibid.*, 26 December 1812, p.81.

5. *Ibid.*, 4 January 1813, p.83.

6. *Ibid.*, 1 February 1813, p.85.

7. *Ibid.*, 20 February 1813, pp.86-7.

8. Martyn, *Journal and Letters*, vol. 2, 28 August 1812, pp.399-400.

9. Smith, *Henry Martyn, Saint and Scholar*, p.550, footnote.

10. Grenfell, *Diary*, 13 February 1814, p.99.

11. *Ibid.*, 2 April 1826, p.140.

12. Sargent, *Life and Letters of Henry Martyn*, p.411.

13. Smith, *Henry Martyn, Saint and Scholar*, p.543.

14. *Ibid.*

15. *Ibid.*, pp.311-12, footnote.

16. *Ibid.*, p.312.

17. *Ibid.*

18. *Ibid.*, pp.536-7.

19. Sargent, *Life and Letters of Henry Martyn*, p.406.

20. Henry's journal was not fully published by either Wilberforce or Sargent. Wilberforce omits sections and refers the reader to John Sargent's biography. However, the page numbers only match Sargent's earliest editions, making it difficult to harmonize the two accounts now.

21. C. Bell, *Henry Martyn*, Hodder and Stoughton, London, 1880, p.149.

22. Smith, *Henry Martyn, Saint and Scholar*, p.491.

## Chapter 29 — Brilliance and sadness

1. Smith, *Henry Martyn, Saint and Scholar*, p.227.

2. J. Sargent, *Memoir of the Rev Thomas Thomason, M.A.*, 2nd edition, London, 1834; quoted by Smith, *Henry Martyn, Saint and Scholar*, pp.227-8.

3. Sargent, *Life and Letters of Henry Martyn*, p.230.

4. Finnie, *Beyond the Minarets,* pp.149-50.

5. *Ibid.,* p.150.

6. Smith, *Henry Martyn, Saint and Scholar,* p.420.

7. Martyn, *Journal and Letters,* vol. 2, 25, 27- 29, 31 August, 1807, pp.101-2.

8. Smith, *Henry Martyn, Saint and Scholar,* pp.484-6.

9. *Ibid.,* pp.486-7.

Chapter 30 — Henry Martyn: the man

1. France, 'Henry Martyn', p.302.

2. Smith, *Henry Martyn, Saint and Scholar,* pp.525-6.

3. Bell, *Henry Martyn,* p.151.

# Bibliography

Please note that Henry Martyn Jeffery's *Diary of Lydia Grenfell* appears in the endnotes under the name of L. Grenfell. Similarly, Wilberforce's *Journals and Letters of the Rev. Henry Martyn, B.D.* appears in the notes under the name of H. Martyn, and S. Kelly's *The Life of Mrs Sherwood* appears under the name of M. Sherwood. In each of these cases the name under which the book is listed below is that of the editor. However, in the endnotes these works are attributed to the people who originally wrote the material — Henry Martyn, Lydia Grenfell and Mary Sherwood.

Bell, Charles D. *Henry Martyn*, Hodder and Stoughton, 1880.

Bentley-Taylor, D. *My love must wait — The story of Henry Martyn*, Inter-Varsity Press, 1978.

Finnie, Kellsye M. *Beyond the minarets — A biography of Henry Martyn*, STL Books, 1988.

France, R. T. *Henry Martyn*, in *Five Pioneer Missionaries*, Banner of Truth Trust, London, 1965.

Hopkins, Hugh E. *Charles Simeon of Cambridge*, William B. Eerdmans Publishing Company, 1977.

Jeffery, Henry Martyn, *Extracts from the Religious Diary of Miss L. Grenfell, of Marazion, Cornwall*, Lake and Company, Market Strand, 1890.

Kelly, S. (ed.). *The Life of Mrs Sherwood*, Darton & Co., London, 1857.

Loane, M. L. *Cambridge and the Evangelical Succession*, Lutterworth Press, London, 1952.

Loane, M. L. *They were pilgrims*, Angus and Robertson, 1970.

Lopez, Amy K. *Henry Martyn — Apostle to the Mohammedans*, The Warner Press, Anderson, Indiana, 1929.

Martyn, H. *Sermons*, Church Mission Press, Calcutta, 1822.

Martyn, John R. C. *Henry Martyn (1781–1812), Scholar and Missionary to India and Persia*, The Edwin Mellen Press, 1999.

Moule, H. C. G. *Charles Simeon*, Methuen & Co., London, 1892.

Padwick, Constance E. *Henry Martyn — Confessor of the Faith*, Church Missionary Society, London, 1925.

Padwick, C. *Henry Martyn — Confessor of the Faith*, Inter-Varsity Fellowship, London, 1953.

Page, Jessie. *Henry Martyn. His Life and Labours. Cambridge — India — Persia*, S. W. Partridge & Co. Ltd (no date of publication given).

Polwhele, R. *The History of Cornwall*, Kohler and Coombes Ltd, Dorking, 1978.

Ryle, J. C. *The Christian Leaders of the Last Century*, T. Nelson and Sons, 1899.

Sargent, J. *The Life and Letters of Henry Martyn*, Banner of Truth Trust, Edinburgh, 1985.

Smith, George. *Henry Martyn. Saint and Scholar — First modern missionary to the Mohammedans, 1781–1812*, The Religious Tract Society, London, 1892.

Urwick, W. *Indian Pictures Drawn with Pen and Pencil*, The Religious Tract Society, London, 1891.

Wilberforce, S. (ed.), *Journals and Letters of the Rev. Henry Martyn, B.D.* (2 vols.), Seeley and W. Burnside, 1837.

# Index